Debating Sex and Gende
Eighteenth-Century Spai

Eighteenth-century debates continue to set the terms of modern day discussions on how 'nature and nurture' shape sex and gender. Current dialogues – from the tension between 'real' and 'ideal' bodies, to how nature and society shape sexual difference – date back to the early modern period. *Debating Sex and Gender* is an innovative study of the creation of a two-sex model of human sexuality based on different genitalia within Spain, reflecting the enlightened quest to promote social reproduction and stability. Drawing on primary sources such as medical treatises and legal literature, Vicente traces the lives of individuals whose ambiguous sex and gender made them examples for physicians, legislators and educators for how nature, family upbringing, education, and the social environment shaped an individual's sex. This book brings together insights from the histories of sexuality, medicine and the law to shed new light on this timely and important field of study.

Marta V. Vicente is Associate Professor at the Departments of History and Women, Gender and Sexuality Studies at the University of Kansas. She has published widely on the history of gender and sexuality and is author of *Clothing the Spanish Empire: Families and the Calico Trade in the Early Modern Atlantic World* (2006).

Debating Sex and Gender in Eighteenth-Century Spain

Marta V. Vicente

*Associate Professor, History and Women,
Gender and Sexuality Studies Departments,
University of Kansas*

 CAMBRIDGE
UNIVERSITY PRESS

CAMBRIDGE
UNIVERSITY PRESS

University Printing House, Cambridge CB2 8BS, United Kingdom

One Liberty Plaza, 20th Floor, New York, NY 10006, USA

477 Williamstown Road, Port Melbourne, VIC 3207, Australia

314-321, 3rd Floor, Plot 3, Splendor Forum, Jasola District Centre, New Delhi - 110025, India

79 Anson Road, #06-04/06, Singapore 079906

Cambridge University Press is part of the University of Cambridge.

It furthers the University's mission by disseminating knowledge in the pursuit of
education, learning and research at the highest international levels of excellence.

www.cambridge.org
Information on this title: www.cambridge.org/9781108814218
DOI: 10.1017/9781316671689

First published 2017
First paperback edition 2020

A catalogue record for this publication is available from the British Library

Library of Congress Cataloging in Publication data
Names: Vicente, Marta V., author.
Title: Debating sex and gender in eighteenth-century Spain / Marta V. Vicente.
Description: Cambridge, United Kingdom; New York, NY:
Cambridge University Press, 2017. |
Includes bibliographical references and index.
Identifiers: LCCN 2017022410 | ISBN 9781107159556 (hardback)
Subjects: LCSH: Sex – Spain–History – 18th century. | Gender identity –
History – 18th century. | MESH: Sexuality – history | Transsexualism –
history | Gender Identity | History, 18th Century | Spain
Classification: LCC HQ1075.5.S7 V53 2017 | DDC 305.3–dc23
LC record available at https://lccn.loc.gov/2017022410

ISBN   978-1-107-15955-6   Hardback
ISBN   978-1-108-81421-8   Paperback

Contents

Illustrations

Map

Preface

Weeks ago a friend of mine revealed to me why she had developed such an interest in astrology. She said, "You know, I wanted to understand my family." After years of study, she finally knew why her sister was domineering, obsessive, and moody. She sympathized with her brother who had been struggling with problems of addiction. She even could finally get to accept her own tendencies towards repressing feelings and always trying to bring peace in family situations where resolution was hopeless. I was a little bit disconcerted. How could astrology offer her the answer to such complex human behaviors and relations? She explained to me:

In astrology there are houses, which are supposed to be the most important part of anyone's chart. Then you have the planets. Where they are positioned when one is born and the planets' own relation to each other allow different aspects of one's personality to manifest. Aspects mean tension, which is created between the planets. Then the signs are also important, along with many other things.

Not to get her wrong, she emphasized that the study of astrology was complex and that in spite of the limitations of the horoscope chart, one "could grow into one's sign," meaning that one's habits can help changing some innate predispositions marked by one's astrological chart. Yet, when my friend finally was able to put it all together she found out why her sister, a Virgo with an Aquarius rising sign, wanted to be in control of absolutely everything in her life. When her sister was born the moon was on Gemini, which made her display an extremely temperamental behavior, swinging to extremes. My friend said all this very convincingly. I did believe that her astrology research had brought her peace of mind although I was skeptical how much truth was behind her discoveries. Regardless, it is important for me to retell this episode here to illustrate how while we all acknowledge and understand that human behavior and lives are the complex result of many different components, from physical and emotional to social and environmental, at the same time many of us need to find a one-step solution that explains it all. This is what my friend found in astrology. It allowed her to find order in her life and her family relations. The three siblings had been born out of the same parents and received the same education, yet they all displayed different, almost opposite personalities. Apparently, she did not have to worry so much about the rest and ever since my friend seemed to have been able to accept her family and move on.

The stories I am going to tell in this book happened more than two centuries before my conversation with my friend about astrology, but they share a striking similarity. Both, past and present, focus on finding order, certainty, and clarity, where there is none. The center of my narrative happens around the anatomical discoveries at the turn of the eighteenth century in Europe, which ignited an unprecedented interest in physical and anatomical explanations of the division of the sexes. Anatomical discoveries provided an opportunity to organize society in an orderly and predictable way. The body, just like a machine, was made of distinctive separate organs fulfilling a specific function, and so was society as well organized in ways one could name and recognize. Bodies that represented the ideal – and natural – order of the world had to be clearly separated in their sexual mapping and needed to behave in certain ways. Ultimately the basis for this order lay in the division of the sexes and the control of reproduction. The problem came with bodies that because of their ambiguous anatomy or behavior did not fit within this natural order. The conflict that arose between the desire for order grounded on anatomical differences of the sexes and the presence of individuals that could not be included in this order (individuals that jeopardize sexual reproduction) characterized not only the eighteenth century but also modern understandings of sex and gender in the Western world.

Key to achieving order and stability was in finding ways to make those uneasy exceptions to the rule fit universal explanations. This was not a clear path, even for those who wanted to find that order. Things and ideas move back and forward and even the representatives of the institutions, physicians and lawyers, hesitated themselves when trying to find the solution to the problem at hand. Order seemed difficult to come by. In Spain, the challenges of giving order to one's world were clearly expressed in the political life of the country in the eighteenth century. Political unrest in Spain started with the Spanish War of Succession (1701–14), while the intermittent warfare with England and France colored the rest of the century. Throughout these decades, stability was at the very best a product of people's hopes and fantasies; the tangible reality was constant struggle and change. A parallel needs to be drawn to the human body and its ability to change before challenges. As Rebecca Jordan-Young so well expressed it in her *Brain Storm: The Flaws in the Science of Sex Differences* and her analysis of the contradictions within the twentieth and twenty-first centuries' scientific arguments on sexual difference, differences among men and women are a matter of degree. This author, who combines her interest in science with social theory, invites us to rethink gender and sexual formation and evolution in terms of "development" rather than "essences," and in terms of "processes" rather than "states." Equally, Oliver Sacks' extensive work on the malleability of the brain to constantly adapt to even trauma shows us how life as it happens daily and hourly remains something that is indeed changing constantly, sometimes in unexpected ways.

The processes that Jordan-Young talks about or the malleability and adaptability of Sacks' cases all should lead us towards viewing the subject as multifaceted, constantly changing and adapting, and the mere definition of man and woman as an illusion human beings have themselves created. Think of the growing public visibility of transgender individuals in the past two decades, which makes us all face the reality of the changing and unfixed aspects of sex and gender, both culturally and socially constructed and lived. Why, if all around us is pointing at impermanence, temporality, change, and mutability, do most of us fall into categorizing and dividing: women versus men, nature versus culture, young versus old, life versus death? This book does not pretend to offer an answer to all these questions, which have puzzled many writers and will continue to do so. Instead, I want to look at the history of this struggle: between the human need to find order through division and difference and the reality of a world that, by bearing more sameness than disparity, jeopardizes this project of finding order and universal laws.

The place of my narrative is Spain. Many times Spain has been ignored or neglected in the scholarly debate on the changes and transformations that the eighteenth century brought. I do not want to dwell on the reasons for such lack of works devoted to this important period in Spanish history. Recently, the Voltaire Foundation and its Oxford University Studies in the Enlightenment have published a few titles that address this issue beautifully. Jesús Astigarraga, for instance, takes the bull by the horns, so to speak, and by "revisiting" the Spanish Enlightenment unearths all the dust and the jewels that seem to have been buried with it. He sees the Spanish Enlightenment as much more "pragmatic, utilitarian and applied" than the French or British Enlightenments, which in turn helps us to further explore the Enlightenment as enlightenments in lower letters and certainly in the plural. By focusing on Spain, and looking at how the major European scientific discoveries and changes impacted the theory and practice of anatomy, I do subscribe too to this group of scholars who intend to vindicate the Spanish Enlightenment and analyze its contribution to the general European debate. I also want to bring some light to the debate on the history of science in Spain, arguing that Spaniards were able to share with their European counterparts not only scientific discoveries but the implications of such discoveries in shaping their societies. Yet, despite the singularity of Spain, and because of its distinctive political and cultural framework, this is a European story as writers across nations in eighteenth-century Europe shared similar inquietudes to those of their Spanish counterparts.

I found the seed for this project in the summer of 2005 in a lengthy document housed at the Archivo Histórico Nacional in Madrid. I was then working on a project on notions of sexuality in the eighteenth century. The documents I was consulting were not particularly relevant to the topic at hand. The wrong call number in one of the order slips allowed for a bundle of criminal cases to fall on my lap. Not to waste the time of the archive's worker who had delivered the bundle (*legajo*) to me, I decided to read some of the criminal cases included in the volume. That is how I encountered the case of Sebastián Leirado López, whose criminal trial has become an important case study for this book. Leirado's case is a fascinating example of the struggle characteristic of the eighteenth century and the European Enlightenment: fighting uncertainty and unpredictability by trying – sometimes in vain – to impose order and predictability. The fortuitous finding of this document changed the course of my project. The rest, as they say, is history.

Acknowledgments

I thank the Hall Center for the Humanities and the General Research Fund of the University of Kansas for their generous support for this project. I would also like to thank the organizers of the Gender and Early Modern Seminars at the University of Kansas and the Early Modern Institute at the University of Southern California and its director, Peter Mancall, as well as Lisa Bitel and Sherry Velasco for inviting me on several occasions to present my work. My gratitude also goes to Dan Crews, Ryan Fagan, Rebecca Haidt, Cecelia Klein, Jonathan Lamb, Patricia Manning, William McCarthy, Ann Schofield, Angels Solà Parera, Akiko Takeyama, and Charlene Villaseñor-Black for inviting me to present parts of this book in their seminars and universities. I would like to thank the archivists in Madrid and Barcelona who helped me with my research, and particularly Angels Solà Vidal at the Arxiu Històric de la Ciutat de Barcelona, as well as the digital specialists Pam LeRow and Paula Courtney at the University of Kansas. Darin Grauberger did a super job visualizing in a map of Spain Leirado's journeys and arrests. Elizabeth Friend-Smith and Rebecca Taylor, editors at Cambridge University Press, UK, have been extremely supportive, making each of the steps of the production of this book a smooth one. A number of friends and colleagues read early versions of chapters and parts of this book. I want to thank Thomas Abercrombie, Bob Antonio, Santa Arias, Greg Cushman, Phillip Fox, Megan Greene, Roberta Johnson, the late María Elena Martínez, Mary Elizabeth Perry, Allyson Poska, Elena del Río Parra, Kathleen Sheldon, Bunny Smith, and Sally Utech. Kathy Porsch helped me see the broad implications of my argument and how a Spanish story was also a European one. Sheyda Jahanbani and Roberta Pergher were my research companions throughout the last years of this journey. In the exchange of ideas and drafts of our work, my ideas and arguments grew stronger. Leslie Tuttle generously read the first draft of the entire manuscript and gave me valuable feedback. Barry Reay's work on sexuality has been an inspiration to my own work and his support throughout the years key to the writing of this book. George Klaeren took time out of his precious research in Spain to read chapters of the book. Last, but certainly not the least, I thank Luis Corteguera for his comments and tireless support. This book is dedicated to him and to our young daughter, Isabel Corteguera-Vicente, who loves to see her name in print.

Introduction

A Brave New World

In William Shakespeare's play *The Tempest*, Miranda, daughter of Prospero, marvels at the sight of the men her father has summoned to the island where Prospero's brother had exiled them. She utters: "O, wonder! / How many goodly creatures are there here! / How beauteous mankind is! / O brave new world, / That has such people in't!"[1] Aldous Huxley, borrowing Shakespeare's expression to brand his 1932 novel, "Brave New World," adapted Miranda's promising and naïve brave new world to an imaginary society set in 2540, where science and progress would hold the promise of happiness. Huxley's dystopian novel depicts a world where reproduction is under control of the government with catastrophic consequences. Individuals, conceived in the lab, lose their personal identity before the well-being of the community. As the story opens, the director of the "Central London Hatchery and Conditioning Centre" shows his new students the "Fertilizing Room." There, new embryos are created through the "Bokanovsky's Process," whereby technicians efficiently work in labs to fertilize eggs in vitro, each egg able to divide multiple times into genetic twins. This process will allow, "Ninety-six human beings [to] grow where only one grew before. Progress," the director proudly utters. The students take notes; only one daring young man questions "the advantage" of the process. Scandalized, the director exclaims: "My good boy! ... Can't you see? Can't you see? Bokanovsky's Process is one of the major instruments of social stability!"[2] Human cloning would produce custom-made individuals: Alphas, Betas, Gammas, Deltas and Epsilons, each genetically made-up to happily fulfill a specific role in society without resentment or complaints.

Political and social changes in the early twentieth century fueled Huxley's satirical and critical view of a future society, which centers on the government's control of bodies through science that translates into a loss of individual freedom. A topic also central in other dystopias, famously in George Orwell's *1984*, the advances in technology in

Huxley's novel provoke awe and admiration in John, the single character in the novel born out of a mother and raised in the "Savage Reservation" in New Mexico. John's only knowledge of the outside world comes from his reading of the complete works of William Shakespeare. The son of an outsider, John appears ill-fitted to the community where he was born and raised, and dreams of traveling to London, the ideal place of the World State, where his mother comes from. To him, just like to Miranda, the equally naïve character in *The Tempest*, this has to be a truly brave new world. John, however, becomes a tragic character in Huxley's novel. The World State does not deliver the promise of happiness he envisioned. The novel ends with John's suicide representing the failure of both the London and Reservation societies to provide him with an identity and a place of belonging.

More than 200 years before Huxley and Orwell's time, at the beginning of the eighteenth century, physicians, philosophers and lawyers also felt theirs was becoming a world that science and technology were turning into a promising brave new world. Unlike Huxley's novel, this brave new world was not so much going to be ruled, dominated and dictated by the government but by medicine, and in particular by anatomy. The large number of anatomical works and manuals published from 1650 until the end of the seventeenth century – in England alone from fifty works between 1600 and 1650 to over 200 titles by the end of the century – reflects the interest and curiosity that anatomical observation created not only among physicians but also among educated readers.[3]

At the core of the new scientific euphoria in the eighteenth century was the belief that finally science would provide the tools, through the study of anatomy, to fully comprehend the human body. Their "science" was, to quote the 1726 dictionary of the Spanish Royal Academy, the "knowledge of something by its causes and principles." Anatomists and physicians saw themselves as "scientists," who through observation could discover nature's universal laws. "Physician" was the umbrella term that embraced both the university-trained anatomists and also the surgeons. Some held university degrees while others were trained through the practice of treating patients (think of the barber-surgeon of the medieval period).[4] But it was the anatomist, more than surgeons or other physicians, who became the highest authority on matters of medical science. The anatomists' knowledge of the naked body authorized them as trustworthy guides to translate nature's design onto society and its organization.

From natural philosophers to literary authors, a growing number of intellectuals of the early eighteenth century saw in anatomy and the order of the human body a model of how their new society had to be organized. Institutions would borrow similar bodily organizational principles by which science would dictate the functioning of the rest of society's vital "organs."[5] Medicine, law, natural philosophy, economy, or politics, it all came down to how well they fit within "the organic economy" that nature operated by.[6] In the natural world, everything was connected and had a purpose that could not be understood outside those connections. From this view, humans were the best expression of nature and the body and its functioning had to obey to the utility principle. Thus, anatomy, as the study of the internal workings of human beings, also bore the "organization, size, form and place of all the members that make the human body or of any other animal."[7] Anatomy symbolized such need for order and organization by literally offering a body of knowledge that emphasized observation and systems of relations; a methodology that spread from the human body to other areas of society from law to art and literature.[8] It was knowledge with a purpose, the highest of which was indeed the reproduction of human beings. The observant anatomist only had to point to what was supposedly physically evident, namely, the core differences between men and women, which would lead to the reproduction of humans. Such division of the sexes was certainly "one of the major instruments of social stability," ensuring political continuity and economic wealth.

My book traces the difficult journey that eighteenth-century Spaniards undertook in order to promote social stability, harmony and social reproduction. The achievement of social stability drew on anatomists and physicians' delineation of the differences between men and women based on their genitalia. It also required discarding traditional theories of medicine not based on an anatomical view of the body. The increasing professionalization of medicine fostered the need among these writers and thinkers to purify medical, and thus scientific, notions of sex formation from popular and non-scientific opinions. Other, non-scientific forms of knowledge seemed to jeopardize a desire to organize society into well-structured precepts by which men and women, anatomically and socially defined as such, would guarantee the reproduction of society, physically and culturally. Just as in Huxley's novel, at the center of such new efforts was the control of human bodies and reproduction: nature's ultimate and most noble cause. However, the road towards the establishment of the division of the sexes was long and winding, as the expectation and excitement generated contradictory feelings about where the new century was going to take them. Throughout the century, supporters of what became known as "the new science" had to face the challenges posed by followers of traditional medical theories, and even by followers of the new science themselves, who sometimes fell the need to rely on traditional theories to explain "rare cases" they encountered in their medical practice.

Traditional medicine had provided not only a venue to understand the functioning of the body but also how bodies fit within the larger understanding of the world. The novel view of the body that the new science offered, challenged not only how physicians cured individuals but also the function of bodies in the overall social and divine order. The new science was in fact proclaiming a stricter division of the sexes than the traditional theory and practice of medicine ever had. At the same time, because the new science emphasized the importance of observation and the practice of medicine to reach to conclusions, it was the reality of bodies that did not fit the anatomical division of the sexes that problematized the whole balance. Individuals who displayed an ambiguous sex and gender represented a challenge to those followers of the new science – physicians but also lawyers and philosophers – as they made obvious the limitations of the new theories.

The promise of this brave new world at the turn of the eighteenth century brought fear and anxiety to those who saw it not as a promising utopia, but rather as a dystopia, threatening to destroy the foundations of their world. Anatomy as the bases of social order received criticism from those who still subscribed to the traditional theory and practice of medicine, but also from the Catholic Church, always watchful of heresy among new ideas. The preoccupation of the Church for the new scientific ideas was on their heretical potential, as a mechanical and rational view of the human body might have questioned divine intervention in the formation of the body as well as severing the relation between religion and scientific knowledge. The Church's concerns of the separation between science and religion were well founded. Without ever disregarding the natural world as the product of God's making, seventeenth-century physicians who subscribed to modern medical theories of the body focused their efforts in understanding nature more in connection with society than the divine.[9] This implied a growing need to set aside religious and theological concerns in the production of knowledge about nature.

The practice of separating science from religion turned into a challenge to anyone who subscribed to the new science. Regardless of how much Spanish scientists saw themselves, as true followers of the Catholic dogma, they still wanted to set limits between what was the job of the scientist and that of the theologian. Exemplifying such a challenge were the Spanish geographers of the late seventeenth century, whose work tried to bring together biblical and scientific interpretations of the formation of the earth. Particularly vivid among Spanish geographers, geologists, and natural philosophers was the debate also characteristic of the European scientific community over the biblical "Great Flood," and whether the earth's fossils were its direct results.[10]

Some authors aimed to prove that the Flood was key in shaping the earth's particular relief.[11] Others, such as the geographer and mathematician José Vicente del Olmo (1611–96), secretary of the Tribunal of the Holy Office of the Inquisition in Valencia, while keeping the narrative of the Great Flood argued for a geological explanation of the formation of life on earth.[12] Del Olmo's own life is a reflection of this effort to make religion and science separate while compatible. The geographer was an avid participant of the academies and literary salons in Valencia and key in the introduction of the new science and European ideas into Spain at the end of the seventeenth century.[13] While keeping his role as a main officer in the infamous tribunal of the Inquisition, del Olmo dared to separate religious from non-religious explanations of the earth formation. This led him to argue that the earth and its topography could alter throughout time, so that mountains "will be ruined" just like "the foundations of many ancient buildings."[14] This argument was compatible with the Bible's narrative, as it did not question the continuous presence of God in nature. The quests of men like del Olmo put in evidence the efforts to enter into dialog with religious arguments even when discussing scientific concerns.

The difficulty of separating what was the tangible and scientific from what was not continued into the eighteenth century. Eighteenth-century scientists were asking themselves to rethink the relation between nature and society in terms of "victory over nature." As in Huxley's brave new world, controlling the natural, expressed in the anatomical division of the sexes, would guarantee social stability, progress and ultimately happiness. Moreover, victory over nature translated into social utility or how nature would lead to social stability. This is where the singularity of Spain stands out: linking this emphasis on usefulness characteristic of the European Enlightenment with medicine. We find this applicability of medicine in other European countries such as France.[15] However, it is in Spain where the usefulness of scientific knowledge reaches a political dimension at the end of the eighteenth century as some of the most prominent thinkers of the Spanish Enlightenment held public offices.[16] The first step in such "victory over nature" was in dispelling the well-established traditional views of the body that reigned unchallenged throughout most of the early modern period.

Victory over Nature

Traditional medical theories challenged by the new anatomically-focused medicine were based on Greek natural philosophy and authors such as Aristotle (384–322 BCE), Hippocrates (ca. 460–ca. 375 BCE), and Galen of Pergamum (ca. 129–ca.216 CE), and the theory of balance of humors. Humoral medicine posited that the health of the individual was the result of the balance of four types of humors – blood, phlegm, black bile, and yellow bile – corresponding to the four elements – earth, air, fire, and water. Those four humors had qualities – dry, wet, hot, and cold – the combination of these qualities affected the different human organs and shaped specific characteristic personalities of the individual, depending on the excess or deficiency of a humor and its quality. The humoral theory also explained sex formation in a distinctive way. The balance of the humors allowed the reproductive process to happen, since to be able to conceive, a woman had to be wet and cold while the man was expected to be hot and dry. Variations on such an ideal balance could jeopardize conception. A man who tended to be too cold could become sterile since heat was thought to be indispensable for the growth of the male seed. He could also develop an external behavior that revealed his internal humoral imbalance, which made him closer to the combination of humors characteristic of women.

Following Aristotle's and Hippocrates' teachings, Galen also explained that men's and women's genitals were similar in their composition, the only difference being that women's sexual organs were male organs turned inside. As the French physician André du Laurens (1558-1609) saw it, "the opinion of the Ancients, confirmed by the authority of learned men and the writings of nearly all the anatomists" explained why the female genitalia – that was fundamentally the same as men's but colder and wet – was hidden, while men's – hotter and drier – were "outside and hanging."[17] From this perspective, if men's genitals were thought to be similar in their composition to female genitals and their differences were only in degree of development, it was possible to believe that there were stages in between the full development of male and female sexes. Depending on the humoral balance, a person's sex could change from one to the other. External changes could influence and alter the balance of humors in the body, even having an impact on the sex formation of the individual. From the perspective of the humoral theory, an effeminate man could reveal "a lack of heat" and in some cases a "mixture of sexes," or the existence of female genitals along with the male ones. An external influence or the mother's own diet or habits had the unintended consequence of changing the sex of the fetus from male to female, thus giving birth to a child who while appearing to be a boy bore in himself some of the physical characteristics of females.[18]

The humoral theory persisted throughout the early modern period and informed the new anatomical discoveries in the seventeenth century, partly because of its ability to explain the many changes that the body went through in a lifetime, making it sick or healthy. It was not only a way to understand the body but also a truthful knowledge taught at the university level and in the surgeons' daily practice of medicine. Although the humoral theory was still pervasive in the seventeenth century, it was then when anatomical discoveries brought the physical evidence of the division of the sexes that could no longer be explained on terms of humoral balances alone.[19] This was only the beginning of a process whereby the new medicine, that took the observation of the anatomical body as the measure for all things related to health, sickness and sex, would debunk more traditional theories on medicine and the body. As the French physician Francis Clifton told his readers in 1742, the good physician would be well aware of "the utility of observation in medicine and the inutility of systems and theories."[20] To Clifton the experience of observation overcast reaching at any larger explanation. This fact, the tangible knowledge as the measure of all things, was crucial in the medical theory and practice of physicians of the new medicine. It was the naming and classifying, but also the "seeing and knowing," where true physicians found the answer to all their questions.

Experience and observation in relation to social utility also brought changing notions of sex and sexuality in the eighteenth century. In fact, Thomas Laqueur has argued that "sometime in the eighteenth century, sex as we know it was invented."[21] Not totally abandoning the Galenic principles of medicine, eighteenth-century European physicians transitioned into bearing a more mechanical, anatomically-based view of the body. Under this modern view, the two sexes were separated, each holding a distinctive set of reproductive organs. As some critics of Laqueur have argued, this division of the sexes partly happened before and it simply persisted in the eighteenth century coexisting with humoral views of the human body.[22] However, Laqueur is right to argue that while in the practice of medicine the lines were blurred and Galenic influences were found throughout the century, in the eighteenth century anatomists and physicians were intending a break. This break was accentuated by those who described the medical practices of previous centuries as prone to error and superstition. There was a change in the reality of anatomical discoveries and how much physicians knew of the human body, but there was also very much a change in perception. It was the collective euphoria at being at the verge of a brave new world. This is characteristic in the writings of eighteenth-century physicians bent on an unwavering battle against superstition in general. Likewise, the anatomists of the eighteenth century saw it as their mission to eradicate what they deemed to be an irrational belief in medicine to do with things that before were perhaps accepted to happen, such as spontaneous changes of sex or the existence of hermaphrodites. As we will see, the quest in proving hermaphrodites to be non-existent entities, a creation of the populace's imagination, manifests the need to cast away any physical formation that was not intended to fulfill reproduction.

The work and practice of followers of the new science was part of the Enlightenment project in Europe that looked with increased criticism at "the opinion of the Ancients." The list of anatomists who in their publications and participation in scientific salons were transforming the medical science in Spain is long and mostly exemplified by the new group of scientists and thinkers, known as the *novatores*, the innovators, also translated as "the moderns," a term used by their detractors.[23] Some novatores came out of the training of physicians at university level while others were experienced in the practice of medicine. The innovators progressively detached themselves from the teachings of traditional medicine, embracing the new medicine and its reliance on the physical evidence provided by anatomy. They were also great promoters of the applicability of medicine, thus uniting theory and practice, another component of the emphasis on the "utility" of sciences that would characterize the new century. The innovators were scientists, from natural philosophers to anatomists, coming from different areas of the Iberian Peninsula: mainly Madrid and Seville, but also Valencia, Saragossa, and Cadiz. They shared the desire to first make available to others the innovative theories on the body, but also the application to the practice of medicine. The transition to the new medicine was slow, but soon there were an increased number of physicians committed to eradicating the old medicine to give way to a new understanding of the human body.[24] This was part of an epistemological transformation in European thought: wanting to acquire knowledge through observation and the use of reason, rather than rely on authority. Previous anatomists, such as Andrea Vesalius (1514–64), had emphasized the use of observation and reason in the study of the human body.[25] And even in the eighteenth century, the ability to discard authorities was difficult to put into practice. Yet, the new physicians felt the struggle was about recognizing the only authority which scientists had to respond to, the one resulting from the application of reason to what the senses told a vigilant observer.[26]

The quest of eighteenth-century anatomists in Spain to advance a new science that would expel all superstitions from medical knowledge and practice was not an isolated effort. The networks that these anatomists created revealed their interest in connecting with the anatomical discoveries and novelties in Europe, but also the transmission of knowledge within Spanish anatomists themselves. It responded to a web of scientific relations that transmitted and exchanged knowledge all over Europe. An effort that, as the Royal Society of Medicine and Other Sciences of Seville pointed out in 1736, had started "with curiosity, because satisfied with the recent inventions, shook off the heavy yoke of captivity and proclaimed their freedom."[27] In this transformation of the medical world in Spain, the exchange of knowledge with European experts was crucial. In 1699 the Italian physicians and anatomists Luca Tozzi, Lucantonio Porzio, and Tommaso Donzelli arrived in Madrid to attend Charles II of Spain in his final illness.[28] The king's successor, Philip V, the new Spanish monarch after the war of succession for the Spanish throne (1701–14), furthered the policy of openness to Europe his grand-uncle had started.[29] Anatomists coming from France, such as Florencio Kelli, who arrived in Spain in 1701 with the court of the new monarch, joined a number of French anatomists, such as Blas Beaumont and Guillermo Jacobe. The marriage of the monarch to the Italian princess Isabel de Farnesio in 1714 also facilitated the arrival of foreign experts from Italy, such as the influential anatomist José Cervi (1663–1748).[30] Many of these foreign anatomists settled in Spain to produce their most notable works, becoming key in spreading the knowledge of the new anatomical discoveries.[31]

The involvement of the monarchy in bringing in foreign experts onto Spanish soil blended with a growing interest among Spanish physicians to learn more of the new medical theories and practices. Spanish anatomists thus relied on information from European sources: either physicians transplanted into Spain, manuals arriving from Europe, or the information anatomists themselves could gather by traveling abroad. These three venues represented sources of authority, a "useful and reliable knowledge" to employ the term used by historians of economy and science of eighteenth-century Europe.[32] Used oftentimes in the context of technological advances in pre-industrial Europe to highlight the close connections between science and technology, scientists "used knowledge to create more knowledge." Knowledge of "what and how," what to look for and how to do it, applies to the bold aspiration among Spanish anatomists: to marry theory and practice – the theory of medicine represented by the anatomists, and its application in the hands of the surgeons.

European networks of useful knowledge express the continuous fight for understanding the place of the individual, now more disconnected with the divine, in the natural world. In this book, I examine precisely those controversies that highlight the involvement of the medical community and its emphasis on the division of the two sexes in establishing the main parameters of relations between nature and society. For instance, how did the existence of individuals with ambiguous sex compromise the expected relation between society and nature and the clear division between men and women? Could nature cause people to acquire traits of the opposite sex? Although they did not express it in terms of nature versus nurture until the nineteenth century, philosophers, political thinkers and even writers of fictional works throughout the early modern period asked essentially the same question that nineteenth-century scientists posed: Were natural predispositions powerful enough to overcome the influence of rearing and education? Or, conversely, could a bad education ruin good natural tendencies? In other words, if the division of the two sexes was so important, what did it account for? What made someone a woman or a man? In the eighteenth century, surgeons and anatomists, as well as educators and jurists tried to answer these questions in order to understand the rightful place of men and women in their new society.

The implications of these changing views of the relationship between nature and society go beyond understanding the human body as part of the natural world and instead focus more on the body in its place in the natural and social worlds. It proclaimed man's victory over nature, but this implied that the natural functions of the human body could not be detached from the social ones. Explaining the division of the sexes became all the more important since the parameters that formed that division helped anatomists shape discussions on what the human was in relation to nature, the place of individuals within the natural and divine cosmos and their place in reproduction. Findings about the division of the sexes would have an impact in the legal, philosophical, and educational arenas, in university wards and the practice of medicine, but also in the courthouse. Characteristic of these efforts were their applicability, the practice that must shape the theory and universal laws. Ironically, as we will see, this credo created its own trap as the practice sometimes discredited the theory.

The practice of medicine revealed any overarching theory to be flawed. An example lays in the crime and sin of sodomy. Sodomy tested one of the basic tenets of the Enlightenment, and in particular the Spanish Enlightenment: everything under the sun had to obey the principle of social utility. Sodomy was unproductive sex, sex sans utility; but, unlike masturbation, sodomy trespassed the laws of society and nature to threaten divine laws.[33] We find sodomy at the difficult crossroad[s] where law, religion, and medicine met in the eighteenth century. The union of a man and woman for the procreation of the species was something that still in the eighteenth century theologians, lawyers, physicians, and philosophers agreed upon. As Immanuel Kant stated in his *Anthropology from a Pragmatic Point of View* (1785) the goal of nature's economy was "nothing less than the maintenance of the species."[34] The practice of sodomy was not only a sin judged and punished by the Church but also a crime that attempted against the fundamental premise of the Enlightenment that Kant so well represented. Sex without utility was in fact a social sin as well as a moral one. It severed humans' precious bond with God, but it also permanently altered their place in the social chain. It expelled the sodomite from both gardens of Eden to become doubly ostracized.

The concept of utility that the sodomite attempted against appeared as an invisible thread that united the purpose of nature and the social obligation to comply. A seemingly economic concept, utility, was in fact the point of reference for most of the explanation of things for the men and women of the Enlightenment. Not coincidentally, Kant himself saw the Enlightenment required one thing only: "freedom to make public use of one's reason in all matters."[35] The essence of things lay in their utility. The word utility will appear many times throughout the pages of this book as a way to signify how present it was in the writings of eighteenth-century authors. Notions of utility permeated in all aspects of the European Enlightenment and its multiple ramifications. From the simplest cactus to the precious life of a human being, all forms of life had to obey the natural laws that were heavily grounded on the concept of utility. If Huxley's brave new world showed how victory over nature could become sour and destructive to humans, eighteenth-century anatomists believed all evil was redeemed if such victory came to render both nature and society useful to each other.

With their emphasis on addressing social needs in the name of "utility," eighteenth-century scientists were proclaiming the famous "domination of nature" that Huxley was wary about.[36] They were perhaps referring to a utopia familiar to them, Daniel Defoe's *Robinson Crusoe* (1719), a castaway cast ashore on an uninhabited tropical island, where he spends the next twenty-eight years until his rescue. Crusoe's isolated, solitary and "uncivilized" island becomes his ally when he understands its workings and is able to adapt to his surroundings. He learns how to employ the right tools provided by nature to make his time on the island profitable.[37] The island, a symbol of Crusoe's personal quest for growth and maturity also symbolizes Defoe's society, the England of the early eighteenth century. Robinson Crusoe, in fact, becomes the model for humanity's "domination of nature," or "victory over nature," as expressed in the eighteenth century. It shows the reliance on rationality and the belief that nature could be understood by reason. This, of course, did not come without contradictions. A fruitful literature on the Enlightenment has shown how, in fact, such emphasis on reason grew out of these thinkers' inability to comprehend emotions and sentiments.[38] It was in the particular context of the literary utopia where those conflicts surfaced.[39]

Like Defoe, Spanish physicians also constructed their own utopia, trying to resolve the relationship between nature and society by using the principle of social utility expressed in the division of the sexes. Thrown out of the inhospitable waters of traditional medical knowledge, followers of the new science found themselves on this island, where everything had to be relearned anew according to the laws of nature. Nature in capital letters was a symbolic force, a "moral authority" in itself, in the models that physicians, philosophers, and writers in general created. Physicians in particular appeared as lawful translators of nature and its moral laws. As Michel Foucault saw it, moral authority was connected to reason thus leaving outside the system of natural laws those who appeared as unreasonable, making them immoral. Moral outcasts threatened nature's order expressed in terms of social utility. It was a "moral system of power" that brought "the new division" between the mad and the sane.[40] Normality only became a reality when this division was maintained and the mad, the irrational, was confined and secluded. This regularity also applied to other areas of such divided, an important one being those who in their anatomy and behavior clearly followed the social and natural mandates of the division of the sexes and those who did not. For eighteenth-century thinkers, the division of the sexes became the light that would lift the veil from the knowledge of truth. Based on notions of reproduction and utility these writers shaped notions of sex and gender that modern society inherited. In the making and negotiation of what seemed absolute truths, thinkers of the eighteenth century were creating the basis for the fundamental understanding of nature, society and sexual difference in the twentieth and twenty-first centuries.

How the division of sexes and its gendered expression became regulated was also a process of ordering knowledge. The eighteenth century was the century of classifying, ordering things from which natural history cannot be disassociated. After all, it was by 1699 that the mere concept of "systems" connected to such effort of classifying and organizing took a meaning of its own.[41] This classification and order was done through "a fundamental rearrangement of language," in which the human body was key.[42] In fact, as the next chapter will illustrate, an important part of the anatomists' division of the sexes was in the distinctive denomination of the male and female reproductive organs and parts, which gave them their exact place in the social, natural and moral systems they operated under. First, anatomists constructed an ideal and ordered "systems of differentiation and discrimination;" after that, they found and named the body parts to match.[43] This seemingly simple step was crucial in creating and perpetuating unrealistic divisions between the sexes. The medical discourse produced knowledge and a particular use of gender reflecting the truth about the individual. This truth had to be grounded in a sexual mapping that ultimately had to revert to the supposed "natural" origins of social constructions. Eighteenth-century anatomists did not discover sexual difference in the bodies they examined. Instead, they approached those bodies with a set of assumptions that presupposed such differences already existed.

The series of medical, legal and philosophical discourses in the eighteenth century created their own limits and barriers. And thus, the cases of individuals who appeared to contradict or who questioned expected gender behavior and relations seemed to attempt to alter, not only those same gender relations, but also the institutions that they signified. They also threatened to alter the relation between sex and gender at its core. That is how eighteenth-century writers constructed the argument that society must be divided into men and women to guarantee human reproduction and that this was a non-negotiable condition. In the eighteenth century, everyone from physicians to lawmakers, as well as ordinary individuals, often had to confront the reality of individuals who with their ambiguous sex and gender seemed to threaten "the best founded of collective illusions" that the division of the sexes represented.[44]

Although my focus is Spain one of the points I make is that Spanish physicians and intellectuals were sharing common assumptions with their European peers. It was a way of looking at the world whereby sex, gender, and sexuality remained central. This argument does not go against my previous point of Spain's uniqueness but acknowledges that, while approaching the problem from its distinctive political and cultural context, Spaniards shared in fact the same preoccupation as their European counterparts. As we will see throughout the book, and particularly in the last chapter (which deals with the connection between eighteenth-century problems in twenty-first-century societies), issues such as the impossibility of marrying theory and practice, nature and nurture, and medical knowledge with other kinds of knowledge appear as pre-eminent in the society of the Enlightenment as in modern western societies.

Debating Sex and Gender: A Story in Five Chapters

The eighteenth-century debates about the division of the sexes reflected general anxieties and contradictions that the new modern society would inherit in its quest to conquer nature. The brave new world that the Enlightenment proclaimed had as its basic understanding how nature had divided the sexes into female and male to guarantee reproduction. At the very center of both nature and society lay the relationship between men and women in procreation. The separation of the two sexes was crucial, since it guaranteed not only the survival of the species but of society itself. The contradictions that this basic tenet created appear as a thread that unites the chapters of the book. Each chapter presents a different aspect of how such anxieties and contradictions developed in the medical, educational, and legal contexts, showing the promise and the limits of the new science in order to give birth to a brand and brave new world.

Together, the following chapters will take the reader on a journey of understanding, of the ways in which eighteenth-century anatomists constructed a world neatly separated between men and women, and nothing in between. Three concepts are key to understanding this effort: nature, utility, and social order, since the division of the sexes responded to the symbiotic relationship between natural laws and social needs. Paralleling what Aldous Huxley saw as a dangerously naïve enthusiasm before technology's potential to bring human happiness, Spanish anatomists held the belief that the new science, observation, and departure from traditional ways of understanding the body would indeed bring in a brave new world. However, the outcomes were highly dubious. The gray areas that painted such efforts could not be erased. A number of individuals with ambiguous sex and gender stubbornly felt outside the orderly system of knowledge that anatomists – and later lawmakers, judges, and philosophers – constructed. Those who subscribed to the new science sometimes had to go back to humoral theories to explain these cases. The stories of the clashes between those individuals and the men who examined them tell a different narrative of the Spanish and European Enlightenments.

Besides the difficulties of merging the interests and goals of the new medicine with religious concerns another set of tensions arose, the most glaring being that produced by the clash between theory and practice. Such tensions tell us how the Enlightenment was formed, not so much by light but instead by chiaroscuros, or the contrast that light falling unevenly upon matter creates as it produces light and shadow. The chiaroscuro, an important concept in European art during the Renaissance and the Baroque, created an illusion of depth on a two-dimensional surface. The overarching light that the new anatomic findings were meant to create fell unevenly upon the reality of the lives of people in eighteenth-century Europe. No matter how bright the light of order was, inevitably it would create this combination of lights and shadows adding depth and complexity to the Enlightenment project. The stories I am going to tell construct a narrative that allows for shadows as well as lights, for recognition of the need for order while also an acceptance of those who made such order at the very least problematic.

The majority of the cases I analyze in this book come from criminal and inquisitorial archives. Most of the cases deal with individuals accused of sexual crimes, while a few appeared in medical reports and journalistic accounts of possible hermaphrodites, or people with ambiguous gender. Altogether, they reveal the different aspects of the wide spectrum of sexual mapping in eighteenth-century Spain. In those trials, their protagonists reflected, whether directly or indirectly, upon how nature, family upbringing, education, and the social environment shaped an individual's sex. The men and women who cross-dressed or displayed improper gender traits, such as masculine women or effeminate men, raised moral and social concerns, and could have been charged with a legal misdemeanor, but not a crime. The real concern came when the gender-bending was the sign of a deeper and more troubling problem: the wrong use of their sex, which posed a direct threat to the social stability that the division of sexes was meant to ensure. In the eighteenth century, individuals' gender, or the social and cultural expression of their sexed bodies, fit into a more general aim that ultimately had to do with the basic relations of society and nature, and in particular how sex interrelated with both.

The next chapter, "The Anatomy of Sex," analyzes how, by the eighteenth century, surgeons and anatomists sought to replace earlier popular and learned explanations of sexual difference by establishing direct links between genital formation and gender traits. Basing their theories on the new anatomical discoveries, followers of the new science discredited traditional theories of medicine by linking them to "popular fables," superstitious beliefs characteristic among the populace who believed in miraculous sex changes and the existence of hermaphrodites. The anatomical discoveries and the enthusiastic efforts of anatomists like Martín Martínez, the central figure of this chapter, marked the transition of a before and after, in the understanding of the human body. The new anatomists worked hard on dispelling the myths of a malleable body that the traditional medicine had created. Using the concept of fables, they depicted traditional perspectives on the human body as inadequate to understand the functioning of bodies, which had to be mechanical and predictable. However, what this chapter illustrates is how this certainty created its own problems, an issue that next chapter explores further.

The study of Sebastián Leirado López, the twenty-four-year-old tavern-inn-keeper and part-time actress from Madrid is the main case analyzed in Chapter 2. Specific examples such as Leirado's allow us to see how the anatomists' practice of medicine had to confront the ambiguity of those whose gender was not well defined and may have revealed an ambiguous sex. Their existence compromised the clear-cut division between the sexes and revealed the anatomists' own doubts and ambiguities in their theories. The stories of men passing for women and women pretending to be men had spilled large amounts of ink in European courts, criminal, inquisitorial, and were also the center of many *causes célèbres*. However, the particular interest of Leirado's case is that, as we will see, the sexual mapping of Leirado's body and behavior conflicted with a medical understanding of the sexed human body in the eighteenth century. Such medical understanding intended to match sexual organs, male and female, with its correspondent behavior, man and woman, into distinctive categories. The recurrent gender confusion by observers but also physicians who examined Leirado defied that.

Chapter 3, "Nature, Nurture, and Early Modern Sexuality" examines how philosophers and educators debated the implications of the new anatomical discoveries regarding how a particular social and cultural environment could alter natural tendencies in molding an individual's sexuality. Spaniards' brave new world could certainly not be completed without a new perspective on education. Education had to reaffirm the division of the sexes by educating bodies to guarantee reproduction. In this respect, John Locke appears as an authority in this transitional period regarding education, body, and sex by offering education the powerful upper hand in the relation between nature and nurture. The euphoria on the power of education to guide individuals to a proper sexual behavior that led to reproduction reached its peak at the end of the eighteenth century with the case of the "milk man" Antonio Lozano. Physicians conclude that the capacity of this peasant from Cumaná (Venezuela) to breastfeed his son was a form of social utility, a proof that habit could redirect nature. No longer needing to reproduce, Lozano was able to help out by producing milk to feed his child. The discussion of the impact of education on sexual formation ultimately reveals the influence of the medical discourse on the division of the sexes, an issue further discussed in Chapter 4, "The Body of Law: Legislating Sex in Eighteenth-Century Spain."

This penultimate chapter studies how sexual difference was discussed in the practice of judging sexual crimes and in particular in the crime of sodomy. The judging of sodomy cases reveals the challenges lawmakers had to face in creating a body of law that would consistently judge all crimes for the way they disrupted the social order, regardless of their religious or moral components. It also revealed the impact of the division of the sexes on the law and the changing attitude towards sodomy in the eighteenth century, when the hermaphrodite disappeared from medical discussions. The removal of the hermaphrodite from the medical scene translated into the elimination of ambiguous bodies from the

legal context. Before, the condition of the body could exonerate a hermaphrodite from the crime committed; now those individuals, anatomically and thus legally defined as either men or women, held full
responsibility for their acts and for their failure to contribute to the social
well-being. With the disappearance of sexually ambiguous individuals,
the new view of the body made exoneration from crime increasingly difficult. By reinforcing the ideas of anatomists on the practice of the law,
legislators and lawyers consolidated the brave new world by focusing
punishment on sex that was not reproductive.

In Chapter 4 the reader reviews Leirado's trial and its implications for
the theory and practice of law. Several medical experts were required to
confirm Leirado's sex, while both physicians and lawmakers relied on
changing notions of sexuality in the eighteenth century. A person was soul
and body, but it was the body that made the connection between the natural and social selves. A body gave human identity to a person, but it was
their sex that made the connection between the natural and the social.
Thus, sex and gender were separate but had to match with each other.
Leirado's rather short-lived trial, which lasted barely four months from
November 1769 through March 1770, summarizes the struggle of a century trying to find an ideal model for the two sexes, to build what became
more and more a brave new world; not a dystopia but, on the contrary, a
realized utopia. Leirado's male genitalia defined him as a man and thus
her social and sexual life as a woman confirmed a criminal practice that
society had to condemn. It does not mean that in previous centuries people who practiced sodomy were not condemned; in fact, they suffered
even more as some were executed.[45] This case reveals the struggle to separate the social from the natural at the end of the eighteenth century: a
confirmed separation of the sexes, which was supposed to bring "social
stability;" and also, the importance of the interwoven relationships among
medicine, law, and philosophy in creating this ideal stability.

The last chapter of the book, "Sex and Gender: Reconsidering the
Legacy of the Enlightenment," discusses how eighteenth-century debates
have shaped current feminist discussions of sexual formation and the
difficulties of establishing notions of sex and gender by relying solely
on medical definitions. In *The Second Sex* (1949), Simone de Beauvoir
famously challenged the notion, which grew out of eighteenth-century
anatomical discoveries, that sexual difference could be reduced to its biological basis, excluding cultural and social definitions of male and female.
During the 1980s, increasing concerns about how to categorize transgender individuals, people whose gender identity does not correspond
to their sex assigned at birth, made feminists question such a unilateral
relation between sex and gender, by which sex served as the basis for

assigning gender roles.[46] Scholarly as well as popular discussions of sex and gender increasingly focused on questions similar to those expressed in the medical, legal, and philosophical debates of eighteenth-century Spain: for example, who was entitled to define what constituted a man or a woman? Someone may appear to be a man culturally, while legally she may be a woman. In spite of reliance on scientific evidence to define "man" and "woman," we cannot separate the understanding of sex and gender from what it means to be a human. As Judith Butler pointed out, through different "ways of knowing and modes of truth... the human is recognized."[47] The historical construction of the individual shapes the limits and possibilities of sex and gender.

The parameters that the eighteenth century established offer an important point of departure for contemporary feminists who, in trying to understand sex and gender, are bypassing some of the main ideas of the Enlightenment. Recently, feminist theorists have pointed out that for John, the character of Huxley's novel, our World State did not deliver its promise of happiness. Feminists have realized that the promise of the Enlightenment was never fulfilled: the division of the sexes never brought modern society social stability, harmony, and happiness. Those who did not fall within the expected division between men and women threatened the heteronormative project that was at the bases for social reproduction. Yet, rather than crying over the illusion of an ordered and perfect society, for the scholar the future path is to analyze where and why the Enlightenment failed. Why were the euphoria, optimism, and energy of the eighteenth-century followers of the new science thwarted? In this book, I explore the causes of these shortcomings while acknowledging that, as humans, the makers of the Spanish Enlightenment were entitled to successes and failures that nonetheless shaped notions of gender and sex in Western Europe.

1   The Anatomy of Sex

At the turn of the century, in the midst of political turmoil and economic uncertainty, the Spanish scientific community was witnessing a period of optimism, even contained euphoria.[1] In their jubilation, scientists expressed what would be characteristic of the new science in the early 1700s: observation and experimentation had to tell the parts of the body and by extension allow them to understand the natural and social worlds.[2] In particular, anatomy, the light "and true north of the great pilots of medicine," would alone allow physicians not to risk "their ships in the immense ocean" that the practice of medicine was.[3] The truthful light of anatomy would let its watchful pilot replace a "feminine and litigious medicine," taught at the universities, with a "useful, experimental and masculine medicine."[4] The new "masculine" view of the human body, mechanical, predictable and rational, was the only way to unveil the mysteries of its functioning.

The energy of this new group of scientists and learned scholars, who subscribed to the new medicine, burgeoned in informal gatherings and *tertulias* or literary gatherings rather than at universities.[5] In these weekly meetings physicians and anatomists, as well as intellectuals and natural philosophers interested in promoting the new science, avidly read the new medical literature about the latest anatomical discoveries coming from Europe.[6] Participants discussed the theories of René Descartes (1596–1650) and Emmanuel Maignan (1601–76), lectured on anatomy and ran experiments in physics, chemistry and botany.[7] The new societies also lobbied to bring renowned European anatomists to Spain to preside over dissections and teach Spanish surgeons and anatomists the latest medical advances. At the turn of the century, Spaniards working under the protection of the monarchy were traveling to neighboring countries to learn of the latest developments in medicine and science.

The Spanish Crown sponsored many of the European journeys by anatomists, who immersed themselves in the new discoveries and medical advances. In 1680, the engraver and anatomist Crisóstomo Martínez

(1638–94) traveled from Valencia to Paris to work with some of the major authorities on anatomy in the French capital, where "the printing presses, the inks and water make prints shine with perfection."[8] His aim was to complete one of the first atlases of anatomy in Spain (Figure 1.1). In Paris, he worked with the French anatomist Guichard Joseph Duverney and the Danish-born artist professor of anatomy in Paris, Jacobe-Benigne Winslow. Nine years after his arrival, in May 1689, Martínez revealed to his mentor – the anatomy professor at the University of Valencia, Juan Bautista Gil de Castelldases – his excitement and anxiety at the constant novelty of publications in the French capital. He could not help it, but each time he saw a new edition of an anatomy book he felt "obligated in some ways to alter the economy of my drawings because its prints are so finely produced I have to do the same with mine, because my work does not deserve less than that." This meant that the now fifty-one-year old had to "to study again and rethink all things, because lately all this material has tripled, not only in France and specially in Paris, but also in Sweden, Holland, England and other places."[9] A year later, the engraver-anatomist, initiator of microscopic research in Spain, had to abandon the French capital after accusations of spying for the Spanish monarchy. He died in Flanders in 1694, four years later, leaving his major work on anatomy unpublished.[10]

The exchange of anatomical knowledge that Crisóstomo Martínez fostered worked both ways: foreign experts also moved to Spain to practice their skills. Juan Bautista Juanini (1636–91), a physician-surgeon from Milan, settled in Madrid, becoming court physician to Charles II. In Spain, Juanini produced one of the first medical manuals that departed from traditional medicine. In his *Political and Physical Discourse* (1679), Juanini claimed his method was based on observation and "mechanical experiences, with which we can reduce any evidence no matter how difficult the matter is."[11] More than two decades later, in 1701 the French anatomist Florencio Kelli, known for his emphasis on proving anatomical theories from the evidence of anatomical dissection, arrived at the court of the new Spanish monarch, Philip V of Spain. Kelli, teacher and mentor to some of the key figures of the new medical world, such as Manuel de Porras and Martín Martínez, gained his reputation in the "anatomical theater of the court" in Madrid, where he performed about twelve annual public dissections.[12]

By the early 1700s, all this scientific activity and exchange gave the new societies and their members international visibility. The *Journal de Trévoux*, the French Jesuit journal running articles on "Who is Who" in the European literary and scientific scene, listed the Royal Society of Medicine and Other Sciences of Seville in one of his monthly issues.[13]

Figure 1.1 Engraving "Skeletons and Bones" (ca. 1680–94) by Crisóstomo Martínez.
Biblioteca Nacional de España, Madrid

The appearance of the Seville Society in this widely read academic journal could only escalate the society's visibility, as well as the exchange of ideas with other academies.[14] In fact, Diego Mateo Zapata's *The Medical Crisis about the Antimony and Response Letter to the Royal Society of Medicine of Seville*, a short pamphlet on the new medical ideas requested by the Royal Society itself, appeared in the listed bibliographic index of the *Journal de Trévoux* in 1704, three years after Zapata's publication. It was translated into French shortly after.[15] This exchange of information between the Spanish scientific scene and its French counterpart reflected a contagious excitement over what was new and a growing skepticism of what the old theories had to offer.

One of the first presidencies of Seville's newly established Royal Society of Medicine and Other Sciences fell on the person of Martín Martínez Pérez (1684–1734) – unrelated to the engraver-anatomist Crisóstomo Martínez.[16] Martín Martínez was the main representative of this group of scientists and philosophers aware of Spain's need to connect with the scientific changes across the Pyrenees (Figure 1.2).[17] Born in Madrid in 1684, in 1700 when the Royal Society of Medicine and Other Sciences of Seville was founded, Martínez was already a student of medicine at the University of Alcalá de Henares, north of Madrid. Six years later, in 1706, he gained a position as one of the main physicians in the general hospital of Madrid. In 1717 he became the president of the Seville society, and was physician to Philip V of Spain.[18] With one major publication already under his belt in 1717, before his death Martínez published four other major works that made him one of the leading and more controversial anatomists in eighteenth-century Spain.[19] The controversial aspect of this anatomist's work lay in his relentless attempts to discard old theories of the study of the human body, which were based on the traditional humoral model. Instead, modern physicians like Martínez wanted to replace humoral with anatomically based theories, which relied on observation and physical evidence as the only way to the establish truth about the workings of the human body. While Martínez did not seem to have traveled to neighboring France or Italy, his work reflected a radical change in the theory and practice of medicine characteristic of the medical world in Europe: a distinctive view of the body that precluded a different understanding of the sexes.

For Martínez, observation had to be based on the experience of practising medicine and treating patients. What Martínez called *experiencia*, which can be translated in English into experience but also experiment or trial, was at the core of any of the anatomist's scientific bases. Experience had been a crucial component in natural philosophy for centuries but it was the central component of observation and experience in the new medical practice that became unprecedented. Any conclusion had to come out of the observation of the naked body and it was the experience and practice of Martínez that would allow him to reach to such conclusions. As the entry for *experiencia* in the Spanish Royal Dictionary (1732) reveals, experience referred to the "knowledge

Figure 1.2 Portrait of Martín Martínez; etching from a drawing by Valero Iriarte, engraved by Juan Bernabé Palomino.
Biblioteca Nacional de España, Madrid

of things, acquired by usage and practice." To Martínez experience was at the core of any knowledge of the natural world, becoming his scientific method. Moreover, to the "usage and practice" Martínez would add "utility" or *uso*. One had to find out through experience the utility of things in the natural world.[20] Martínez was a true Baconian, and mentioned his admiration for Francis Bacon's experimental method in some of his most important work.[21] The Spanish anatomist was attracted to Bacon's emphasis on individual experience and observation as key to grasp as much as human beings can perceive and understand of nature.[22] Martínez's work, in fact, reveals knowledge of Bacon's main philosophies contrasting with those of Descartes, whom the Spanish physician was critical of, albeit acknowledging the usefulness of the doubts raised by Descartes' ideas. To Martínez, Descartes' "cogito ergo sum" could not be proven and tested by experience. Reasoning in itself could not identify the body and its parts; it was the experiment on the body that would tell the observer the name of the different body parts: "We believe we think and therefore we are, but we doubt about our thoughts and even about our own physical selves."[23] Martínez, as the heir of the new epistemological turn at the end of the seventeenth century, saw observation, experimentation and the use of the senses to be connected. Knowledge came through reason, but it all had to rely on experience.[24]

Martín Martínez's production started with his first manual, *Anatomical Evenings or Compendium of Anatomy*, published in 1717.[25] Like other natural philosophers of his time, Martínez wrote the text as a dialog between a surgeon and an anatomist (a self-portrait of Martínez). Written early in his career, *Anatomical Evenings* already expressed the sense of novelty and "modernity" that would characterize Martínez's entire opus.[26] This manual contained Martínez's first statement about how anatomists like him preferred to call the female "testicles" ovaries, a "modern" view not only of the female body but of its nomenclature. Written in Spanish, rather than Latin, *Anatomical Evenings* was also Martínez's first effort to connect the new anatomical discoveries, in Spain and elsewhere in Europe, with the practice of medicine. It also reveals Martínez's long-standing aim to make the findings in his works available not only to Spanish-speaking surgeons, who perhaps would not know Latin, but also to a wider educated public across the Spanish empire, including the Spanish American colonies, where his works were particularly well received.[27]

Martín Martínez's influential work reveals two important aspects of the Spanish medical world in the eighteenth century.[28] First, it confirms an interest, characteristic of the Enlightenment, to connect the natural and social worlds. Second, it also reveals the frustration of many physicians like him in understanding the workings of the human body without having to resort to what they labeled "superstitious" popular beliefs. Martínez himself, along with men like Benito Jerónimo Feijóo (1676–1764), tried to rid Spain of what they thought was the practice of superstitious medicine, influenced by popular tales rather than serious study of the human body.[29] Martínez criticized the popular interpretation of the Galenic system of humors that allowed for the explanation of spontaneous sex change.[30] In particular, his work *Anatomical Evenings* reveals the physician's frustration that the scientific method of studying the human body was still unable to "find the name."[31] He complained in his work about the lack of contact between the practice and theory of medicine, which would allow him to understand how the different parts of the body worked together. The practical application of Martínez's theory was part of the fame that the anatomist achieved. Anatomists in the Spanish empire, as elsewhere in Europe, did not work in a vacuum; their observations were only relevant because surgeons had to apply them when examining their patients. In the practice of medicine, and in their daily work with patients, surgeons' knowledge of anatomy was crucial to expelling old, superstitious beliefs in miraculous transformations of the body.

Although *Anatomical Evenings* represented novelty and modernity, Martínez expressed elsewhere his deep commitment to promoting the practice of anatomy in Spain. Martínez, student of two major anatomists, Florencio Kelli and José Cervi, soon gained his own place in the Spanish medical world and acquired fame throughout Madrid for his popular public dissections. In 1728, Martínez applied all this knowledge to his best-known work, *Complete Anatomy of Man*, a book that became an immediate success among medical professionals and intellectuals of the early part of the century. The eight subsequent editions over the next seventy years testified to this unprecedented success. Martínez dedicated this book to one his teachers, the Italian anatomist living in Spain José Cervi, who promoted teaching anatomy with the latest European methods of "observing nature in itself."[32]

Complete Anatomy of Man is the work of a modern physician who wants to distance himself from those physicians and natural philosophers who formed their general theories without tangible physical evidence. In particular, Martín Martínez displayed his modernity in the study of the generation of beings and the formation of the sexes during gestation. To him, generation, or "the production of a living being from another living being," was one of the body's most important and obvious "mechanical needs."[33] It was implicit that this need required appropriate organs, rather than the other way around. This view established Martínez's attitude to the relationship between the natural and social orders. In his work, Martínez emphasized the importance of the physical, but it was all subordinated to the mechanical needs of the body; needs that fulfilled a social function. To establish the basis of such mechanical needs, Martínez pointed out the distinct differences between the features of the female and male organs: the female's clitoris, vulva, and uterus were clearly differentiated from the penis, testicles, and prostate glands characteristic of male organs. The reproductive organs of each sex had different shapes and appearances since they had very different functions. Accordingly, sexual classification had to be based solely on the body's anatomical characteristics. Genital malformation aside, different organs made individuals male or female.

It is important to highlight the connection Martínez drew between the division of the sexes and the functional and mechanical component of difference. Without explicitly saying so, by establishing that the male and female organs, and their function in the reproductive system, are very different, anatomists like Martínez were rethinking very basic notions of the place of the individual in the relation between nature and society. Using physical and tangible evidence, these anatomists were recasting things that are in principle natural, such as sexual difference, and explaining them in terms of social utility. In order words, they tried to understand nature by observing its mechanisms, but these mechanisms had to obey society's notion of functionality. Thus, the anatomical differences between the sexes forced Martínez to determine how these differences allowed one sex to complement the other in reproduction.

Anatomists, not unlike other physicians of this time, prioritized reproduction in order to understand nature and the functioning of the body. Writing against Aristotelian thought, which argued that a new being was already contained in the "seed" of the male sperm, modern philosophers saw the complementarity of the two sexes as necessary for the formation of the embryo and the new person. In this mechanical process, the key was that the two separate organs of the male and female sexes performed different functions in facilitating conception and nourishing the new being. Martínez believed the function of generation determined the specific physical shape of the male and female sexual organs, so he de-emphasized any possible similarities between the two. The womb's particular shape was meant to help expel the fetus, and the muscles of the clitoris had the "function of closing the orifice of the vulva and of compressing the penis." This, Martínez stated, contradicted what "some argue," that the clitoris contracted in order to ejaculate sperm.

According to Martínez, sex difference in the forming fetus also followed a mechanical function. The entire process of generation depended on the proper nourishment of the embryo from the "nutritive juice" that the mother provided during gestation. The sperm would "communicate its character to the offspring," forming either a male or a female, but that process could be altered. The lack of proper nourishment was one explanation for the formation of individuals with ambiguous sex. These "monstrosities" were not "true hermaphrodites," but rather unfinished products of the natural course.[34] The clear separation of the male and female sexes that the work of Martínez illustrated represented a construction; one could even say an invention. As the practice of medicine revealed, there were many individuals whose sexual ambiguity called this strict separation into question. Yet, delineating the exact difference between the sexes was entirely necessary, not only for the purpose of human reproduction, but also for the organization of society that sexual difference articulated. The imperative division of the sexes responded to principles of social organization, based on a division of work between men and women that paralleled their role in reproduction. Martínez devotes only two chapters of his *Complete Anatomy of Man* to sex and sexuality. Yet, the division of the sexes appears as a central theme in the anatomist's work, as it provides the parameters on how to see and name the body based on its social functions.

It is difficult to tell what came first, but I would like to argue that Martínez felt the need to "find" the sexual distinction based on anatomical observations because of a larger social impulse. The paradox was that this social division was immersed in larger notions of nature and society, and the relationship between the two that defied strict scientific definitions to accommodate moral rules. This represented a problem, since many eighteenth-century writers already displayed a "modern" view of sexuality in which moral truths had to be built upon scientific evidence, which provided a solid basis for all truths, perhaps exchanging one queen of the sciences for another.[35] The paradox results from the struggle to acknowledge the variability and the malleability of a body that constantly adapts to its social environment, while believing the physical body must be grounded in static, predictable and immobile "natural elements." This contradiction of medical ideas spilled into the major areas of society from law to philosophy. In each of these fields, debates arose over whether this division of the sexes was at all sustainable. There was also certain uneasiness before such natural determinism that questioned the role of free will even before the growing interest in education and the social environment in shaping natural tendencies. Ultimately, these were preoccupations that the Spanish world shared with its European counterparts. It was an eighteenth-century problem that, while unresolved, provided the fundamentals for modern definitions of sexual difference.

The Popular Fable of Sex Change

Aware of the stubborn persistence of humoral theory even among new anatomists, Martínez consistently worked towards dispelling all contradictions and nuances in his observation of the human body. Even the "rare cases" (*casos raros*) listed in his works – such as the boy born with his testicles and scrotum on the back of the head (*occipucio*) – could only reaffirm for the anatomist that the testicles and scrotum did not belong there.[36] Identifying the exception confirmed that the rule was incomplete, but it also allowed anatomists like Martínez to see those rare cases as useful components of his broader knowledge of the workings of the human body.[37] In other words, although never expressed in such ways Martínez could regard anatomical exceptions from Aristotle's principle that nature aims at perfection but nature's imperfections, such as the production of females, are in fact necessary to maintain the harmonic functioning of the whole.[38]

Dispelling the appeal of the humoral theory was key to reaffirming the authority of the new medicine. Martínez did it by constructing a clear before and after whereby the dividing line was the rational view of the world based on experimentation and observation. Previous explanations, not based on anatomical observation, were "fables" that only the populace, or those driven by the fantasy of fables, could believe. The traditional medicine was far from being a "fable." Throughout the early modern period prestigious physicians, trained in universities across Europe, had subscribed to the humoral theory, having received support from Crown and Church. This established medicine was difficult to eradicate; Martínez knew that. His best bet was to rely on his readers' "rational" and "masculine" understanding of the human body and to construct the theory of the humors as irrational, effeminate, fantastic inventions of the untrained mind. What started as an anatomical project was in fact an epistemological revolution. It anticipated the modern way of thinking and its gendered component: a brave new world that was going to be masculine and rational, leaving behind the illusory world of tales and fables, the feminine realm, to explain the meaning of things. Humans' different genital mapping was proclaiming not only the division between the sexes but a view of society divided into opposite genders.

Martínez discredited the "feminine and litigious medicine" and saw it as the product of "popular fables," the most important of them being the "fable of sex change," which maintained that sexual characteristics were unstable; consequently, a sex change was possible in adulthood.[39] "The popular fable of sex change," a term Martínez himself coined, derived from a humoral view of the body. A person's sex depended on a balance of bodily humors that, if upset, could produce a "mixture of sexes," which under rare conditions might even provoke a spontaneous sex change. Following an Aristotelian view of the generation of humans, by which nature would always aim at producing males, women were thought to be more likely than men to experience a sex change.[40] When a woman

changed sex and became a man, she was confirming the natural order –
always aiming at perfection – since males were, unlike females, complete
and perfect beings. The transformation from female to male usually happened when the woman's hidden penis emerged. This was the case of
thirty-four-year-old Magdalena Muñoz, a nun from Úbeda in southern
Spain, who in 1617 experienced a sudden sex change. The transformation occurred after a strenuous effort heated up the nun's humors, thus
changing from cold to hot, heat being a characteristic of men in contrast
to women. In the case of Sister Magdalena, the appearance of the male
genitals ended the nun's life as a secret hermaphrodite and turned her,
physically and legally, into a man named Gaspar Muñoz.[41] After the new
sex revealed itself, Magdalena was allowed to leave the convent, to live
as a man and inherit his father's estate. The sources for Muñoz's case
are not of the same anatomical and experimental kind as Martínez's.
They are descriptions of accounts of religious origin, yet they prolifer-
ated much more abundantly in the sixteenth and seventeenth centuries
and reflect the fundamental medical practices and theories of humoral
medicine.

In 1617 chroniclers of "rare cases" had considered the story of
Magdalena Muñoz as one of "nature's miracles." This was also the
term the Spanish painter settled in Italy, Jusepe de Ribera, or José de
Ribera "Il Espagnoletto," chose in his 1631 painting of fifty-two-year-
old Magdalena Ventura. Ribera depicts, "the bearded lady from Abruzzi
[Italy]," along with her husband. The couple are staring at the viewer
while the new mother is breastfeeding her infant child. Next to the couple
is a table bearing a Latin inscription which points to this birth as, "a great
miracle of nature." The symbols on the table, the spindle and the seashell,
reveal the possible hermaphroditic nature of Ventura (Figure 1.3).[42] The
Spanish physician Juan Huarte de San Juan (1529–88) offered a physical explanation for the existence of women like Magdalena Ventura.
According to this author, sex alterations in the process of gestation could
lead to giving birth to girls who later in life could have manly manners
and look, and boys that as men could have "womanly manners," "soft
and luscious voice" and even an inclination for "women's jobs."[43] It was
then plausible that, as in the case of Magdalena Muñoz, after a strenuous physical effort a woman could change her bodily humors from wet
and cold to hot and dry, and with this provoke the appearance of hidden male genitals. These and similar stories were reprinted several times
throughout the seventeenth century and they usually involved women
whose physical efforts had heated up their humors, thus allowing their
hidden penises to emerge. The way an individual behaved, whether too
manly for a woman, or too feminine for a man, could reveal his or her

Figure 1.3 "Magdalena Ventura with her husband," painted by José de Ribera (1631).
Fundación Casa Ducal de Medinaceli, Seville

internal sexual organs. For instance, Sister Magdalena's fellow nuns described her as a "manly woman" having the strength, disposition and condition of a man, which led to doubts about Sister Magdalena's true sex. Facial characteristics could also reveal the hidden sexual organs of an individual. In fact, one of the claims of the study of the face, known as physiognomy, was that by recognizing some characteristic facial features one could find out about the internal aspects of the individual – whether psychological or physical.

Throughout the early modern period medicine and physiognomy had shared interests, since both fields aimed at determining how the external and the physical could afford the observer a glimpse of the internal and the intangible. In 1591 the physiognomist Luis Fernández followed Huarte de San Juan and Hippocrates when linking external physical character-istics, and in particular the face, to humoral imbalances.[44] According to Fernández, physiognomy allowed the viewer "to know the state of the body, the proportion of all its parts and the general and particular tem-perament." Fernández probably found inspiration for his work in one of the most important treatises on physiognomy: Giambattista della Porta's *On Human Physiognomy*, originally published in Latin in 1586; translated into Italian and published in 1598 as *Della fisionomia dell' huomo.*[45] In the sections "Characteristics of the Effeminate" and "How the Effeminate becomes Hardened," the author connected facial traits with improper sexual behavior. One could spot the effeminate man by his facial and physical characteristics, "beardless, wet eyes, small mouth and delicate eyelashes," but one could also recognize the effeminate man in the way he moved his hands, the way he walked, his delicate voice and his skin, too white for a man. Moreover, the physical characteristics usually extended into womanly behavior as "he will want to stay home always wearing a skirt, [and] will tend the kitchen."[46]

Such ideas on the biological and social explanation for effeminacy inform the fascinating case of twenty-four-year-old Francisco Roca, or the "woman married as a man."[47] Francisco Roca, "tall, beardless and with small eyes," was born in 1624 in Perpignan, in Southern France, before the city formally became part of France. Around 1642, when Perpignan was besieged and taken by the army of Louis XIII of France, Roca had to flee the city. It was then that Roca entered the service of Philip IV of Spain "in secret affairs that concern that province coming and going from some parts to others." Those trips took Roca to several parts of the empire, including Madrid and Naples. In 1646 he married his first cousin, María Fuster, in Valencia.[48] Three years later, in 1649, Roca's wife and two other women, a slave in their household and Roca's cousin, denounced him before the tribunal of the Inquisition in Valencia for his sexual encounters with men. The wife denounced her husband to the Inquisition after she had secretly seen him, on "fourteen or fifteen" occasions, sleep with other men. She testified that during the sexual act, Roca and his male lovers behaved "as if man and woman were together." Her husband, she declared, was no hermaphrodite but "had no use as a man" either. Moreover, during the sexual act, Roca played the part of the submissive female.[49]

As the inquisitors gathered the testimony of several witnesses, they agreed that Francisco Roca had "feminine ways." He also had beautiful blond hair. His skin was fair and hairless, and he had "small eyes."[50] One of Roca's household servants was even under the impression that his master was a woman dressed as a man. Another witness declared that he had seen Roca in Madrid and he "had it for certain [she] was a woman," although she was "dressing as a man pretending to be a man." Another testimony reaffirmed this and added that there were also rumors in the kingdom of Naples that Roca was a woman. The testimonies also pointed out that Roca dined and slept with several men, and some were convinced she had sexual relationships with them. One of Roca's alleged lovers declared he also thought of Roca as a woman, since she seemed to have big breasts underneath her shirt. Others declared that they had heard rumors to the effect that Roca was a hermaphrodite who "used no other sex than that of a woman," meaning that he did not use his penis for sexual intercourse, and some had heard "he had the same nature as a woman, and a very big one." Roca's servant was not surprised when he saw his master kissing and embracing other men. Moreover, Roca's wife testified her husband had stopped sleeping with her.

The inquisitors ordered two examinations of Roca's genitals, which dismissed such claims. However, the physicians who examined Roca acknowledged that he had unusual physical characteristics. His anus "was as wide as a finger and it was located further up [closer to the genitals] than was natural and normal" in a man. Roca and his lovers may have concluded that the unusually wide and oddly positioned anus was an underdeveloped vagina. Physicians in this case dismissed any claims of hermaphroditism and concluded that although Roca's anus had an unusual position, nevertheless he was a male. Aristotle already pointed out in his *Generation of Animals* that the sexually ambiguous formation in children was not uncommon as some boys had the base of the penis united to the conduit from which urine is expelled. They had to squat like girls to urinate, and from afar they seemed to have both female and male sexual organs.[51] But Aristotle did not attribute the category of hermaphrodite to these boys. Similarly, the particular shape and location of Roca's anus confused physicians who examined him. However, this particular oddity did not make him a woman, or even a hermaphrodite. The case concluded in 1651 when the tribunal, based on the evidence provided by the physicians and the testimony regarding Roca's relations with other men, condemned Francisco as a "passive sodomite."

He was punished according to the "style and laws of the kingdom" and was incarcerated and his goods seized.

The case of Francisco Roca is an example of how already in the mid-seventeenth century physicians were reticent to acknowledge the possibility of sex change and instead grounded individuals' sex on the physical evidence of their genitals. Medical perspectives on hermaphrodites throughout early modern Europe had already been interested in naming the distinctive genitalia of the hermaphrodite.[52] There was then already a different sentiment in the medical community versus literary and popular accounts of the hermaphrodite. What eighteenth-century physicians aimed at was to keep the myth and the palpable reality of the medical observation of the human body separate.[53] Yet, popular perceptions of sex change were not based on the medical examination of individuals like Roca, but instead they were fed by extraordinary stories like that of Sister Magdalena. The story of this and other individuals were part of a more popular perception of sex change than real medical cases could in fact reveal. Physicians never examined Sister Magdalena; instead two priests saw and touched the male genitals to make sure they were not a fraud.

At the end of the seventeenth century, the popular belief of sex change, for which humoral ideas about the sexed body provided an educated basis, became progressively detached from the theory of medicine, represented by the world of surgeons and anatomists. The new view of the human body, as made up of a set of independent organs that acted together following mechanical laws (the field of iatromechanics), paralleled a similar understanding of how the "social body" of a nation worked. Distinctive institutions (from church to government) run nations, each having a specific role for the proper functioning of society. The jobs that men and women were expected to perform in society were a continuation of their expected roles in reproduction. In society, as well as in the physical human body, each organ had its specific place and function. Under this principle there was no room for a transition from one sex to the other in adulthood. This intimate connection between social and natural laws was the basis of most of the medical works in eighteenth-century Spain, as physicians tried to detach themselves from "the popular fable of sex change."

By the early 1700s when Martín Martínez, the anatomist "worth of immortal praise," published his works, the spectacle of "nature's miracles" had progressively moved from discussing cases of hermaphrodites in medical literature, gazettes and chronicles to observing nature itself, as expressed in the human body, in anatomy theaters.[54] The removal of the hermaphrodite from the medical discourse did not mean its disappearance from popular imagination. It was precisely this linkage between hermaphrodites and popular beliefs that further reinforced Martínez's project to discredit the traditional humoral medicine as unable to provide answers that the new rational medicine could instead deliver. In fact, the didactic interests of medical professionals contrast with the surprising fact that cases of hermaphrodites, such as Magdalena/Gaspar Muñoz, were almost always absent in the extensive number of proceedings of the royal colleges of surgeons, as well as in the practice of public dissections in the popular anatomy theaters.[55]

The removal of the hermaphrodite from the practice of medicine and anatomy theaters was meant to guarantee the consolidation of a sexual difference that could only include men and women.[56] The hermaphrodite, also a central figure in the study of alchemy that was being discredited in the eighteenth century, became either a non-entity, as some physicians denied their existence, or a monstrous spectacle, like the "Famous African" hermaphrodite displayed in London in 1741.[57] Men and women bought their tickets for just two shillings and sixpence and gathered at the Golden Cross to see this "strange twist of nature."[58] The popularity of the twenty-five-year-old Angolan seemed to confirm Martín Martínez's statement that hermaphrodites appealed to the fantasies of the credulous populace, what the English labeled "the Crowd," or "the vulgar," *le peuple* in French, or *el vulgo* in Spanish.[59] No longer an object of wonder or ridicule, the existence of individuals who claimed to be hermaphrodites, or of those who in spite of their genital formation acted and looked like the opposite sex, became uneasy exceptions that compromised the perfect functioning of the machine-body and the perfection of nature itself. Ironically, it was the emphasis of the new medicine on experimentation and the day-to-day medical practice that put these very same theories into question.

The popular fascination with hermaphrodites like Sister Magdalena had a long tradition that went back to classical antiquity and Pliny the Elder's explanation of the formation of hermaphrodites in his *Natural History* (ca. 77 CE). Pliny's view of the hermaphrodite as an entertainment more than a "portent," well summarizes later medieval and early modern understandings of the hermaphrodite: from the Greek mythological account of Hermaphroditos as the offspring of Hermes and Aphrodite to the hermaphrodite as a mythical display of nature's uncanny potential.[60] The telling of the myth and its power for "entertainment" colored views of hermaphrodites and their medical and legal perspective throughout the early modern period.[61] Yet, in spite of physicians' scientific approach to hermaphrodites and the possibility of sex change, it was precisely anatomists and surgeons' medical curiosity that remained at the core of what historians have labeled "medical journalism."[62] A trend initiated in 1665 by the *Philosophical Transactions of the Royal Society of London* and the *Journal des Savants* of Denis de Sallo in France, medical journals were gazettes in the spirit of the later "Reader's Digest;" highlights of recent medical discoveries that were meant to arouse the curiosity and amazement of the general public.[63] It is no surprise, then, that by the 1700s, and in spite of efforts by physicians to "debunk" the myth, the sometimes-distorted figure of the hermaphrodite reigned magnificently in the imagination of many during the age of the Enlightenment.[64]

Towards a New Medicine

Martín Martínez presented his ideas on the human body as an unprecedented change in the medical world, a daring move to replace a "feminine and litigious medicine," with a "useful, experimental and masculine" one. Others shared Martínez's excitement, people with the authority of the Benedictine friar Benito Jerónimo Feijóo, or the reputable physician Juan de Cabriada (1665–1714). It was a revolution in knowledge and as in all revolutions it faced challenges from outside and within its ranks. The division of human sexuality into "perfect" men and women was bound to follow the fate of all universal precepts: it became "a site of contest, a theme and an object of democratic debate."[65] Not everyone agreed with the clear-cut division of the sexes. There was disagreement among professionals themselves, as some surgeons and anatomists questioned the validity of an absolute and definite separation between the sexes. The challenges represented by this new medical approach derived, not only from the rejection by the feminine and litigious practitioners but also from hesitance regarding the new approach that some of the modern physicians displayed. Physicians like Diego Mateo Zapata were at first devoted supporters of the traditional medicine, then switched to the new medicine, and sometimes went back and forth between the two. Equally, Martín Martínez's flirtation with the humoral theory in his works and some of the old medical explanations seemed to flare up in his sections on "rare cases."[66] The anatomist placed in this category the examples of medical rarities that the new mechanical and anatomically-based medicine found difficult to explain.

The blend of the old and the new characterized the theory and practice of a group of anatomists at the turn of the century, who we could label transitional figures of the new science. They acknowledged their legacy and reliance on humoral medicine yet moved forward towards a more mechanical view of the body. These physicians prepared the ground for anatomists like Martín Martínez to flourish and revolutionize the medical thought of the eighteenth century. Physicians such as Juan de Cabriada, Juan Muñoz y Peralta, Manuel de Porras, and Diego Mateo Zapata, made up a fruitful group of young physicians ready to change the course of scientific thought in their native land. In particular, Juan de Cabriada, author at twenty-two of *Philosophical, Medical-Chemical Letter* (1687), a criticism of some of the practices of Galenic traditional medicine, revealed the dualist character of some of the new physicians at the end of the seventeenth century.[67] To Cabriada, modern physicians, among whom he counted himself, were like youngsters, "on the shoulders of a giant, although young, they can see all what the giant sees and further more." Cabriada acknowledged the achievements of traditional medicine while criticizing the blind faith on the teaching of medical authorities of the past, to which some physicians had become "slaves." An admirer of William Harvey (1578–1657) and his discovery on the circulation of blood, Cabriada also followed the work of Thomas Willis (1621–75) and his work on iatrochemical theories. Cabriada's focus on experimentation and observation in medical theory and practice received the attack and criticism of those who consider traditional medicine as untouchable truths.[68] Cabriada's focus on experimentation connects him with the new medicine and its faith on "the new anatomical inventions," from the circulation of blood to the discovery of the human cell, which married with the increased interest and practice of dissections of the human body at the end of the seventeenth century.[69]

The importance of the observation of the body was also fundamental in the theories of these transitional physicians, connecting their theories and practice with the new medicine. Dissections of bodies at different stages of the life cycle, from the incipient fetus to old age, were to aid the anatomist in the discovery of "a completely different human body" at the onset of the eighteenth century.[70] The study of human anatomy promised precise tools for observing and demonstrating the physical distinctions that determined sex, particularly during medical lectures in anatomy theaters.[71] In these spaces, which interestingly were shaped like theaters, professors of the medical faculty performed public dissections and taught anatomy to a diverse audience that included medical students and professors as well as nobles, clerics, and even ordinary people. As the Catalan anatomist established in Madrid, Antoni de Gimbernat (1734–1816) advised, the ideal anatomic theater had to have

ample ventilation, with capacity for up to four hundred people, semicircular in lay out, interior gallery with three or four tiers for the comfort of professors and audience, and space at the ground level, just like any other anatomic theater as seen in Spain, France, England, Scotland and Holland. Close to the

Figure 1.4 *Amphitheatrum matritense*, or anatomy lesson in the dissection room of the Hospital General of Madrid. Frontispiece of Martín Martínez's *Anatomía completa del hombre*; engraved by Matías de Irala. Biblioteca Nacional de España, Madrid

amphitheater needs to be the ward for anatomical dissections for the students of anatomy[72] (Figure 1.4).

The quote points at Spain's place in the European anatomic theatre: Gimbernat comparing his teaching to that in neighboring France, but also in England, Scotland and the Netherlands, where most of the anatomical discoveries were coming from. It also points at the importance of anatomical theaters as sites for the teaching of anatomy, where theory and practice correlated.

Public dissections had been part of medical practice since Galen, in the second century CE, and became popular in anatomy theaters all over Europe from the second half of the sixteenth century. But it was at the end of the early modern period that the nature of anatomy theaters as true public spectacle reached Spain. In the eighteenth century, the first of these anatomy theaters opened in Madrid in 1703, in Cádiz in 1748 and Barcelona in 1761.[73] The basis of anatomy was the observation of the human body, a process that required time and precision. Thus, the anatomy theaters became spaces of knowledge, offering anatomists and their students the opportunity to observe for hours at a time the motionless body, upon which one could "work without fear, examine with care and reflect on what was performed."[74] To prove their expertise, anatomists applying for admission into the prestigious Royal College of Surgery in Madrid, Barcelona, and Seville used "rare cases" of sexual difference.

At the forefront of such dissection-based movement we find Manuel de Porras (fl. 1691–1716), student of Diego Mateo Zapata and Florencio Kelli. De Porras had summarized his emphasis on observation and the importance of dissection in his *Bone of Surgery and Exam of Surgeons* (1691), a manual meant to give physicians clues regarding how parts of the human bodies and organs were making individuals not only natural but social beings.[75] Author of the first anatomical treatise published in Spain, *Modern-Galenic Anatomy* (1716), to illustrate his treatise de Porras commissioned the well-known illustrator, artist, and Franciscan friar, Matías de Irala (1680–1753), who produced the engravings that accompanied de Porras's work.[76] The nineteen images included in *Modern-Galenic Anatomy* are precursors to what we will see in the twenty engravings of Martín Martínez's *Complete Anatomy of Man*, also Irala's authorship.[77] Yet, the images of men and women – even the male and female skeletons – have a more anthropomorphic layout in de Porras' work than what Irala would compose a decade later (Figure 1.5). They remind us, in fact, of the spectacular engravings the anatomist-engraver Crisóstomo Martínez produced a few decades earlier (see Figure 1.1). In de Porras' text, the illustrations representing the female and male organs, albeit kept in separate pages and sections of the book, bear Galenic influences: the uterus is represented as an inversion of the male organs. In fact, Porras' Galenic view of the human body was something Martín Martínez criticized in his *Anatomical Evenings*. Yet, and in

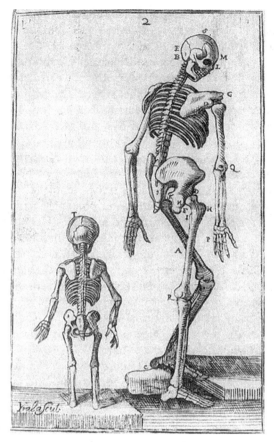

Figure 1.5 Engraving by Matías de Irala for Manuel de Porras'
Anatomía galénico-moderna.
Biblioteca Nacional de España, Madrid

spite of its reliance on Galenic medicine, by giving a central emphasis to
the observation of the body de Porras put "traditional medicine," as he
called it, in a secondary position before an emphasis on guiding oneself
on the observation of the parts of the body to understand its functioning.
Manuel de Porras's emphasis on the importance of the observation of the
human body in dissections, as well as day-to-day examination of patients,
shaped the way other anatomists viewed the human body in the eighteenth century. It was the physical and tangible evidence of the human
organs, arteries, and tissues, and the ability to give a specific name to
each of them, that characterized their approach to health and illness.

The transition to a new model for understanding the human body was not complete until, in 1728, Martínez published his *Complete Anatomy of Man*. We can visually trace the change again with the work of Matías de Irala, the illustrator of both de Porras and Martínez's anatomical manuals. The change in the illustrations from one to the other work reveals the way anatomy evolved in the twelve years that separate Manuel de Porras' *Modern-Galenic Anatomy* and Martín Martínez's *Complete Anatomy of Man*. In Martínez's work de Irala's engravings, and their location in the text, speak of a radically new way of understanding the human body. In *Complete Anatomy of Man* de Irala, who probably copied the drawings from other anatomical European works, highlights the detail in each of the engravings, responding to Martínez's emphasis on "naming the parts." Moreover, each engraving is accompanied with a list of references for all the parts Martínez wants to highlight. The engravings, interestingly, come before the narrative, emphasizing the importance of the visual for the anatomist. Moreover, unlike most anatomical texts, which showed the illustrations of female and male genitalia side by side, *Complete Anatomy of Man* displayed them separately and with the form of each organ's differences shown. The vagina was no longer represented as a penis; the latter was shaped as cylindrical while the uterus had a tubular shape (see Figures 1.6 and 1.7).[78] Needless to say, the "lesson" on the male anatomical parts comes before the female's.

Ambiguity still remained even in Martínez's own vocabulary as he stated, "the clitoris [is] a sort of glandular body, round and large, very similar to the virile member." Martínez reaffirmation in his anatomical division of the sexes while showing here and there "slips of the tongue" is characteristic of the new anatomists of the early 1700s, still very much formed by Galenic traditional medicine. Still, Martínez departs from previous physicians by re-establishing whenever possible the anatomical divisions. Writing about the clitoris he observes, "it grows and becomes hard like the virile member; and sometimes it has grown to the point that [some women] have been able to abuse Venus with other women, and give occasion to the populace to believe fables of women turned into men."[79] Thus, to Martínez, the emerging penis of the nun Magdalena Muñoz discussed before may have been in fact an enlarged clitoris. Muñoz's enlarged clitoris does not contradict the separation of the sexes. A clitoris is still a clitoris, and although some women have used it "to abuse Venus with other women," it does not allow them to take the role of a man in reproduction. Still, Martínez may have wondered why nature allowed such an aberration. An aberration that to the enlightened anatomist did not really qualify as "nature's miracle." This leads us to the importance of Martínez including sections in his *Complete Anatomy of Man* for rare

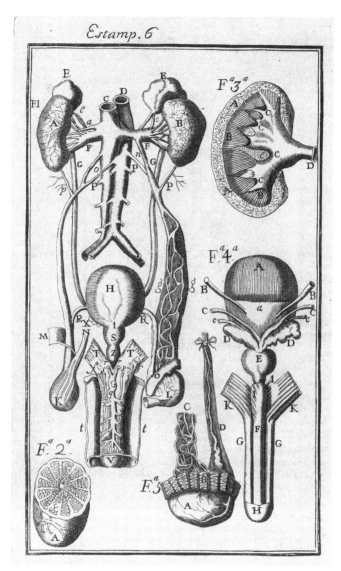

Figure 1.6 Engraving by Matías de Irala, "where the urinary tracks and parts of the generation of man are shown," for Martín Martínez's *Anatomía completa del hombre*.
Biblioteca Nacional de España, Madrid

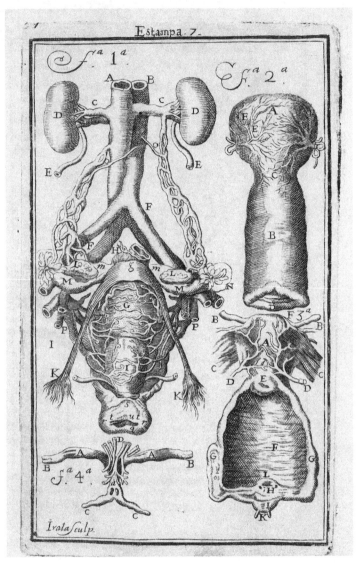

Figure 1.7 Engraving by Matías de Irala, "where the parts of the generation of woman are shown," for Martín Martínez's *Anatomía completa del hombre*.
Biblioteca Nacional de España, Madrid

and unusual cases, which he does on multiple occasions. It reinforces this sense of paradox, not having everything so neat-and-tidy, as he would like. It may seem that ultimately Martínez accepted that sometimes not all pieces of the puzzle were neatly fitting, or as suggested before, that the anatomists saw these rare cases as the exceptions that confirmed the rule.

The division of the sexes is also part of Martínez's effort in creating an order and classification and of his interest in understanding how to conquer the natural world, the "victory over nature" that the Enlightenment precluded. While acknowledging the importance of seventeenth-century natural philosophers and their emphasis on observation, nevertheless eighteenth-century anatomists like Martínez devoted a special emphasis to how nature could not only be understood through observation but also organized and classified. It was part of the emergence of a truly self-organizing mind in the eighteenth century that questioned how reliable information could be. A general anxiety about authenticity and its uncertainty permeated among medical professionals, philosophers, lawyers, and all the intellectuals, observers, and thinkers who shared similar goals we could call enlightened.[80] The "order and organization of life" gave meaning to life itself.

In the effort to organize, understanding nature and its changes was paramount. While there was hardly any attention devoted to the term nature in previous centuries the eighteenth century scrutinized the term itself as well as its expression. If Sebastián de Covarrubias Orozco briefly mentions "nature" (*natura, naturaleza*) in his *Dictionary Treasure of the Castilian or Spanish Language* (1611), defining it as simply "condition and being," the eighteenth century displays a renewed interest in defining, classifying, and grasping the sense of the word.[81] In 1734, the Spanish Royal Dictionary elaborated its entry for *naturaleza* ("nature"), no longer the Latin term *natura* or "the essence and being of each thing." Twenty-six years later, in 1780, the same dictionary offered fourteen different definitions of "nature" adding to "the essence and being of each thing" there was a broad spectrum of interest, from "the compiled (*agregado*) order and disposition of all entities that made up the universe," that which is "independent from artifice," or "the virtue, quality or property of things." There was also in this end-of-the-century definition an effort to connect nature with its innate utility: nature was also "the instinct, tendency and inclination of things aiming at their conservation and increase (*conservación y aumento*)." Nature, which can also equal to sex "specially the female sex," is not only limited to the natural world, since "habit can also be another nature." As John Locke (1632–1704) had well established in his *An Essay Concerning Human Understanding* (1690) habit could in fact be "a second nature." The complexity of the term itself revealed the changes that had been taking place in the eighteenth century. Nature had become part of the realm of "science," progressively separated from natural philosophy. It was also part of a concept of science as something that provided an absolute truth. But it was still in the observation of the human body that nature would be found, dissected and understood.

New concepts of nature applied to the understanding of the body and the emphasis on body parts in determining human sexuality. This new emphasis, however, threatened to impose material determinism for human behavior. As Baruch Spinoza (1632–77) had pointed out, "the human mind is united to the body," but the mind cannot be reduced to the body.[82] In Catholic Spain, Spinoza appears to have had a more profound impact on the thought of some eighteenth-century Spanish thinkers, than other more famous rationalists, such as Descartes. Spinoza's works were prohibited in Spain, yet the erudite Benedictine Fray Benito Jerónimo Feijóo agreed with this conclusion (Figure 1.8). Feijóo, who admired the anatomical findings of men like Martín Martínez, read the Dutch philosopher through Pierre Bayle's interpretation in his *Historical and Critical Dictionary*.[83] Feijóo condemned Spinoza's "atheism," but he may have agreed with the Dutch philosopher that the body was much more than its distinctive anatomical parts.[84] Feijóo may not have had the malleability of genders in mind, but instead the idea of the soul/mind/will forming the body. Although Spinoza's thought itself reveals Descartes' influence, when it came to explaining the relation between body and mind and in particular among how emotions and the body interacted intellectuals like Feijóo may have found Spinoza's acknowledgment of nature's uncertainty more attractive.

Spinoza's conception of matter allowed a more inclusive and all-embracing presence of God. To Descartes, God was the force that ultimately moved things, while for Spinoza God was both the force but also the essence of the body itself.[85] As stated in his Ethics I (proposition 25) Spinoza believed, "God is the efficient cause not only of the existence of things, but also of their essence."[86] In the thought of the Dutch philosopher, divine force was able to permeate deep into a world that was becoming more and more rational. The essence of things can be explained rationally while still acknowledging the presence of God. This is key for understanding ideas regarding the body of the Spanish enlightenment that never saw a reductive atheism a la Voltaire or d'Holbach. The body had a mind and a soul, and Catholics believed they could influence the body and human behavior.

In particular, for Catholic Spaniards the concept of free will posed a challenge to the discoveries of the anatomists. Free will, *libre albedrío* in Spanish, meant that individuals had the ability to make choices

Figure 1.8 Portrait of Benito Jerónimo Feijóo (1781) by Juan Bernabé
Palomino.
Biblioteca Nacional de España, Madrid

that were morally compatible with their religion.[87] It enabled individuals to overcome particular social influences, education and upbringing to act according to the dictates of the Catholic faith. Likewise, the
notion of free will challenged natural determinism since it gave individuals agency to choose their actions regardless of natural inclinations. In
this sense, where anatomists could not explain why physically perfect

men and women behaved in ways contrary to their nature, the concept of free will could offer an explanation: those individuals had chosen to act against nature out of vice or, on the contrary, they had fought their nature to remain virtuous. The latter was the case of the thirty-six-year-old capuchin Mother Fernanda Hernández, from Granada in southern Spain, who at twenty-seven began to recognize in herself the signs of the male sex. After Hernández left the convent and began living as a man, the archbishop of Granada asked him how it was possible that in his "convent garden, with so many flowers, none was wielded." Hernández responded, "with grace and simplicity: 'Your Grace must thank the modesty of the gardener'."[88] Thus, despite a transformation from female to male, the capuchin used extraordinary will to respect the virtue of the nuns in the convent.

Although the concept of free will gave a plausible explanation to individuals who overcame their nature to lead a rightful and virtuous life, most medical professionals still believed religious explanations had to be separated from the practices of observation and experimentation characteristic of the scientific method. Yet, positions did not easily break down into a religious versus a scientific camp. This was particularly true for writers in the first half of the eighteenth century. For example, Fray Benito Jerónimo Feijóo was torn between his open and enthusiastic support for the new medical theories and his conviction that medical explanations could not provide the answers to all the mysteries of the human body. For Feijóo "all in medicine is disputed and therefore all is doubtful."[89] Feijóo's view was part of the movement of Spanish "skeptics" (escépticos), who dominated the medical and scientific scene during the first part of the eighteenth century.[90] These physicians and intellectuals, among whom we find Martín Martínez, battled the need to understand the object of their experiments, the human body, with the awareness that knowledge of the body was ultimately uncertain. Moreover, exactly how one could classify and organize the parts of the human body in order to understand its functioning remained a mystery. Feijóo concluded that it was futile to attempt to fully understand nature and thus the workings of the human body. To the Benedictine erudite, as well as other key figures of the early Enlightenment in Spain, it was God who remained a vital force for a full understanding of human beings.

The skeptics' discussion of religion's role in shaping scientific knowledge impacted the thought of professionals, intellectuals and erudite writers after them. Key issues such as free will, divine and natural design, and the possibility or not of studying the human body outside of Church dictates led some of the discussions regarding the division of the sexes at the end of the eighteenth century. Yet, although writers of the second half of the eighteenth century in Spain and elsewhere in Europe were aware of the difficulties of reaching an agreement on exactly how the human body functioned, they were much less comfortable with uncertainty than Feijóo seemed to have been. In the second half of the century, writers and intellectuals who saw themselves as *ilustrados*, thinkers of the Spanish Enlightenment, were more eager than ever to pin down the exact knowledge of the human body and sexual differences. Still acknowledging the divine intervention in the creation of nature and its laws, these writers understood the knowledge of nature as a human problem, detached from the mysteries of God. Science would lead observers to a true comprehension of natural laws, which ultimately dictated the functioning of society and its institutions.

Despite physicians' and philosophers' efforts to detach science from religion, challenges still arose. Even if religion was set aside from the knowledge of the body, the understanding of the human body in relation to nature and society remained problematic. Was it the physical body that established individuals' behavior in society or did the needs of social organization also have a role in defining how the body adapted to its environment? Many eighteenth-century writers, from physicians to philosophers and educators, inherited this problem from the previous century's controversial contemplation of the influence that the mind had over matter.[91] Could the physical body gain total independence from the social needs that individuals had created? Could the mind, which nonetheless was also part of the natural formation of the body, guide the needs of the human body? These questions ultimately reveal the concerns of a society in formation, which in the attempt to be "modern" found it difficult to live with natural precepts that were not clearly defined. Social divisions had to be clearly ordered, and for that purpose man had to have the tools to find this same and parallel order in nature. Ultimately, the emphasis on the relationship between nature, society and the body overshadowed debates over religion. Moreover, by trying to detach themselves from religious influence, writers gave overriding attention to the study of how the intervention of society shaped the human body. In an effort to "secularize" the body, writers – from physicians to philosophers and lawmakers – created yet another omnipotent force in the shaping of difference, sexual and otherwise: education, and its potential to not only mold but even alter nature. One could say that these writers ended up crafting their own fable.

It was in the practice of medicine that the new theories got proven and at the same time challenged. Those accused in criminal and inquisition trials for witchcraft, sodomy and other "excesses," which included cross-dressing as a way to deceive others, brought dissent to the new medicine. Supposed hermaphrodites turned up in these trials when the accused protested they were not guilty of the crime of which they were accused, claiming that their "mixture of sexes" was the reason for living the life of the other sex. Appearing before the physicians who examined the accused and the lawyers who questioned them, these individuals created their own narrative of what they thought constituted a man or a woman. In fact, it is in the study of these narratives that the conflictive view of what defined sex and its social expression surfaces. Taken together, the stories of the accused, the questioning of the lawyers, the reports of the physicians and the testimony of witnesses reveal a complex picture of what it meant to be a man or a woman in the eighteenth century. As we will see, opinions often went back and forth in establishing whether or not sex was stable. They also raised the possibility that in spite of having male genitals, an individual who skillfully performed a woman's job, had a high-pitched voice and soft skin could indeed be a woman. The social division of work and sex could in fact become so powerful as to threaten to overturn biological givens.

2   Medical Theory versus Practice: The Case of Sebastián/María Leirado

The Limits of Anatomy

Anatomy, that light and "true north" meant to guide eighteenth-century anatomists, surgeons and physicians in the practice of medicine, was not always infallible.[1] The practical application of the anatomical inventions of the previous century revealed precisely this: how incomplete anatomical knowledge was meant to understand the practice of the new ordered human body. In some cases, the ideal body, lying motionless in the anatomic theater, hardly resembled some of the bodies physicians had to confront in their medical practice. In particular, the apparent clear division between the sexes and their differences did not apply to some individuals whose social behavior and external physical appearance made people question the sex they had been assigned at birth.

The conflict between the theory and practice of medicine is generally absent in medical manuals of the eighteenth century. Instead, it is in the context of the courtroom, in the criminal cases of men and women who had to be examined by the physician to certify whether a particular physical trait exempted them from their alleged crimes, that abstract theories of anatomy and medicine were put into practice. It is this world that I want to examine next in order to understand the challenges that an anatomy-based theory of the two separate sexes posed. To anatomists and surgeons, the establishment of a clear anatomic difference of men and women's reproductive functions could not work in a vacuum. The female and male sexual organs looked different from each other because they responded to a series of social needs that also separated men's and women's activities. For most eighteenth-century anatomists, this main premise presented a conflict that was difficult to resolve. If the natural and social bodies had to match, what happened when this was not the case? Anatomists ultimately established someone's sex based specifically on the physical body, but the constant nagging of a social body that did not correspond to such physical specificity called any definite answer into question.

The scientific emphasis of the anatomists and their need to match their observations with the social functions of men and women proved to be an interesting paradox. Although medicine had to separate the investigation of the human body from its social component, the fact was that the medical community found it difficult to set apart the physical body from the way men and women were expected to act in society. Social behavior was a reflection of natural mandates and the body was, after all, an expression of the natural world. However, this meant that many factors could distract anatomists from achieving their goal. Sexual organs could not be detached from the perception of sex, or from the series of norms and practices that allowed people to identify someone as a human.[2] In the process of defining and delimiting the sexed body, the anatomists were confronted with notions of what the human was that defied such strict division. They had to face the fact that such norms and practices did not separate the natural from the social. It is precisely in this context and its series of new questions and interests that we need to understand the challenges surgeons and anatomists faced and the results of this conflict. In this chapter, I examine two specific elements that helped to define the human and its sexual intelligibility from its social expression. First of all, regardless of the anatomical definition of individuals, it was their appearance and the trades they performed that allowed people to discern someone's sex. A second factor also carried an extraordinary weight in determining an individual's sex: people's self-fashioning and narrative, or how they presented themselves when confronted and asked to identify themselves either as a man or a woman. Sometimes this narrative could in fact alter the perception of physical reality itself.

The pages that follow will explore the different aspects of the construction of the self, and how such multiple layers and angles made it difficult for anatomists and surgeons to draw definite conclusions regarding the sex of an individual.[3] In particular, the trial of Sebastián Leirado López, an innkeeper, singer, and actress in late eighteenth-century Madrid, sets the stage for a discussion of medical and popular views of sexuality in Spain. Leirado's case expresses the interest of physicians to follow their principles on anatomical evidence for the division of the sexes. At the same time, it also shows physicians' hesitance in accepting a clear separation when other non-physical and tangible factors indicated that such separation might not be entirely possible. This also applied to other areas such as miracles, exorcisms, and the supernatural. They became "dreams of pure evidence," that vanished in the waking hours, when physicians encounter the ambiguity of individuals like Leirado.[4] As we will see, the multiple physical examinations of Leirado reflect the ambivalence of medical professionals trained in the new medical theories to fully dismiss a more fluid view of the sexed body.

The Medical Exams of Sebastián Leirado

On the early afternoon of November 20, 1769, three Madrid officials accompanied one of the city's royal court judges (*alcaldes de casa y corte*), Domingo Argandoña, to the Leirados' inn on *calle* San Ildefonso at the heart of Madrid (Arrests of Leirado, Map 2.1). Accompanying them was the twenty-year-old tailor Antonio Fernández, who had denounced to authorities an alleged woman, "dressed in man's clothes."[5] She lived with her parents in that inn, and Antonio Fernández claimed she had given him a venereal disease. When the five men entered the inn, they found a man "who by his clothing we give faith he was since he was wearing black leather shoes, black cloth boots, breeches and a jacket made of red cloth, covering his head he had a white and red checked scarf and a three-corned hat on." The officers asked Antonio Fernández to confirm that this individual was "the same who, as said in Antonio's deposition, had illicit relations with him and the same who gave him syphilis." Antonio Fernández confirmed that this was the individual. Next, the alcalde asked the accused standing there about his "age, nature, job and place of origin." He answered: "as you see me dressed as a man then I am." His name was Sebastián Leirado López, an unmarried tavern and innkeeper, who had previously worked as an assistant to the count of Peñalba in Valencia. He declared to be from Madrid. He was the son of José Leirado and Rosa López, both from Lugo in northwestern Spain. Shortly after his brief declaration, the officials took Antonio Fernández and his alleged lover to Madrid's royal prison near the Plaza Mayor. Once there, they handed over the prisoners to the alcalde de casa y corte Benito Antonio de Barreda, former judge of Guipúzcoa in northern Spain, who from then on would be in charge of this puzzling case.

The same afternoon of the arrest, Barreda ordered the surgeons of the prison to examine "the one who claims to be Sebastián Leirado," and if found not to be a woman, "as it is said of him," but a "perfect man" then to examine his "rear part," and declare "if it could have been used in a way not normal." The first to examine Leirado was forty-year-old Manuel González y Toro, surgeon of the royal prisons. He had already examined Leirado in January 1769, when the young innkeeper had been arrested at the Plaza Mayor. The officers who arrested Leirado at the time thought she was the famous actress María Teresa Garrido, who had been banned from Madrid in 1761 and who had come back to the city disguised as an innkeeper. In January, surgeon González had found

Leirado to be "a perfect man with proportion and shape to his height and able for generation." Ten months later the results of the exam of Leirado's sex were inconclusive. Although the surgeon claimed to have "inspected with great care the parts of generation and anus of Sebastián Leirado," and found them "in perfect state without injury, being a perfect man," this time the surgeon became aware of new details of Leirado's body. González found his sphincter, the muscle that allows the anus to open and close, to be very loose. This could have been the result of hemorrhoids, which produced a flux that the surgeon had interpreted to be the cause of Leirado's supposed menstrual bleeding during the first examination. But another explanation could have been the introduction of an "extraneous instrument, or a fall or blow," which may have caused the irritation. Moreover, Leirado had in the neck of the penis (*pescuezo*) "venereal scrofula that has been opened from some time and with matter." The surgeon pointed out, moreover, that the lower part of Leirado's shirt was stained with dried blood coming from this particular wound.

While ten months before González had certified with great certainty that Leirado "had no trace of the female sex," this time he wondered whether perhaps the unusual size of Leirado's anus might have been the sign of a "mixture of sexes." Or perhaps the surgeon suspected that the recurrent practice of sodomy was the cause of the shape of Leirado's anus. Either way, González felt unqualified to offer a final verdict and declared this to be "a most peculiar case." He recommended that other surgeons "concur and declare with most certainty" on Leirado's sex. Three days later, on November 23, 1769, the alcalde Benito Antonio de Barreda asked forty-two-year-old surgeon José San Martín to come to the royal prison to examine Leirado. San Martín reached the exact same conclusion as his colleague that this was "a most peculiar case," and thus required the help of yet a third expert. Finally, on November 30, the alcalde resorted to calling on the greatest authority on human sexuality in Madrid at the time, the fifty-eight-year-old Juan de Dios López, surgeon of the royal hospital of Buensuceso, to perform an examination of Leirado "front and rear." Manuel Fernández, surgeon of the royal hospitals of Madrid, assisted him.

Unlike the two previous surgeons, López and Fernández began their testimony by describing Leirado's overall physical appearance, observing he was a "young subject, of beardless and effeminate face." Asking Leirado to take his clothes off and examining his genitals, both surgeons concluded they were "proportioned to his condition and male sex, without mixture of the other sex." They found Leirado had "his penis with prepuce, the scrotum with the testicles, the groin glands with some swelling and two large venereal tumors." The two surgeons asked Leirado to turn around, and while standing up, to bend forward. They next examined Leirado's anus, which had: "several small and large venereal warts ... and in short the anus is able to easily receive any foreign body of lesser resistance than the index finger." This time the surgeons requested an explanation from Leirado.

In the same room where Leirado's anus and genitals had been examined, the young tavernkeeper told the two surgeons how eight years before, an Italian master, for whom Sebastián worked as an apprentice had forced the sixteen-year-old to engage "in the unmentionable act (*acto nefando*)," meaning the master forced him to have anal sex. Here, it is interesting to note that Leirado did not label the practice "the unmentionable sin," which was the way criminal authorities would usually refer to it, but described it instead as an "act." Leirado explained that, at the time, a surgeon had removed the venereal warts resulting from the act, but was still left with other symptoms. Leirado also assured the surgeons he had never had sexual relations of any kind with women, and concluded: "In the act I had with Antonio Fernández, the said Fernández was convinced that I was a woman." As Leirado pretended to be the woman Fernández thought she was, they "performed the act face to face," as a man and a woman would. This declaration prompted the surgeons to examine Antonio Fernández, in whom they only found "scrofula at the sides of the neck of the penis and the groin." Although Fernández stated, "in the act I had with Leirado I felt he grasped my penis and introduced it (somewhere) moving it back and forth from which I was left with gonorrhea and other venereal symptoms," the surgeons suspected that Fernández was not telling the truth, and that anal intercourse in fact took place. They also found Sebastián Leirado to be "a true man without mixture of the female sex and he has a venereal vice," by which they meant that Leirado had venereal symptoms in his groin. And so, both surgeons concluded, "we are left without a doubt that he has frequented the crime of sodomy." Thus, the physicians' testimony revealed a new element in Leirado's life that the previous surgeons did not record. Juan de Dios López not only established Leirado's sex as male but undoubtedly labeled him a sodomite. The two previous surgeons must have suspected this not only because of Leirado's wide anus but also because of the venereal warts.

The two surgeons could only determine Leirado's sex and sexual practices; the criminal authorities would judge the gravity of the act. For that purpose, on December 13, thirteen days after Leirado's final medical examination, Barreda finally called Sebastián Leirado to testify. The testimony, transcribed by Pedro de los Martínez, spanned throughout the next three days. Leirado's narrative reminds us of the picaresque genre famously characterized in *The Life of Lazarillo de Tormes and of His Fortunes* and *Adversities* (1554).[6] In this work, "Lazarillo achieves importance precisely by telling his story."[7] Unlike the charismatic literary character, who moves from master to master, traveling all over Spain and using his wits to overcome all sorts of unexpected situations, Sebastián Leirado instead appeared as the unwilling victim of the circumstances. Leirado also traveled throughout Spain and frequently changed masters, but was never the maker of his own story. Instead, those who interacted with Leirado seemed to tell the story of Sebastián/María. Without ever explicitly declaring she was a woman, Leirado narrated a story intended to make people doubt his sex as a male. In this narrative, Leirado, just like the Lazarillo, was the antihero, traveling across Spain to earn a decent living while her appearance as a woman gets him into all sorts of troubles. Leirado's story per se is not remarkable; instead the listener is expected to find the "moral" of the story in its telling and the narrative of the constant, and recurrent doubts about Leirado's sex. Leirado's fashioning of a sexual self was based on this continuous doubt. The sexual organs may have said one thing to the physicians who examined Leirado, but the way others saw the young tavern-keeper could tell a very different story.

Leirado started by telling Barreda how at age fourteen he had become the servant of the actress María Teresa Garrido, and stayed with her until Garrido was banished from the city.[8] After that, Leirado moved to work with another actress, María Ladvenant (1741–65), with whom he stayed for only a month (see Figure 2.1). Ladvenant was one of the best-known actresses of late eighteenth-century Spain, a theater diva also known as "The Divine." In fact, Ladvenant, who was the epitome of femininity in eighteenth-century Spain, probably was the woman Leirado wanted to become.[9] It is not clear why Leirado left The Divine. Sebastián's departure around 1761 might have coincided with the actress's acquisition of a female servant as well as the birth of Ladvenant's daughter, Silveria María Pascasia.[10] After Leirado left Ladvenant, he became the apprentice of an engraver from Naples named Mosu Laporta. He was the engraver's apprentice for a year, but he also left this master "for reasons that I will later explain." In fact, he had already told the physicians who had just examined him the engraver had forced him to have anal sex. Leirado's next master was the actor Manuel Espejo, with whom he stayed for eight months. Espejo was his last employer in Madrid. After leaving him, Leirado traveled throughout Spain serving several masters, the first of whom was D. Juan, a captain of a regiment whose last name Leirado could not remember.[11] With him, he went to Saragossa (in north-eastern Spain) and stayed for about thirteen months. He left the captain after they arrested Leirado for "having quarreled with other soldiers." Next, he worked for the count of Peñalba,

Figure 2.1 Theater costume in the old Spanish style (portrait of María Ladvenant) by Juan de la Cruz Cano y Olmedilla.
Museo de Historia de Madrid

with whom he moved to Valencia, where he stayed for three years. After that time Leirado came back to Madrid to visit his parents for a couple of weeks. Soon after, he moved to Málaga (in southern Spain) to work with D. Manuel Pineda, lieutenant colonel of the Soria regiment. After some time in Málaga, Leirado and the colonel traveled back to Madrid (see Map 2.1).

The itinerary   The arrests

1763–1767 { Madrid / Saragossa { 1764 / Valencia { July 1766 / Valdemoro { July 1766 / Madrid

1767 { Madrid / Malaga / Madrid

1767–1768 { Madrid / Arguedas / Vilafranca { 1768 / Madrid

Madrid { Jan. 1769: Plaza Mayor / March 1769: Plaza Mayor / Nov. 1769: Leirado's tavern-inn on calle San Ildefonso

1770 { Madrid / Pamplona

Map 2.1 Map of Spain. Leirado's arrests and travels.
Prepared by Darin Grauberger, from the cartographic services at the
University of Kansas

At this point, we need to interrupt Leirado's narrative to add information from the documentation included in the case but external to the process – in particular, the documents leading to Leirado's arrest in Valencia in 1766 for "wandering as a vagrant," and "for wearing women's clothes." Leirado, who in fact had left his employment with the count of Peñalba before arriving in Valencia, found a job in the city as a stonecutter. Expelled from the city to return to his parents, Leirado was arrested again in Valdemoro, a town a few miles outside Madrid. In this arrest, Leirado also offered a declaration, which was also a narrative of his life up to that point. He included specific details this time that he would omit in his arrest three years later in Madrid. That was not all: In his declaration in 1766, Leirado told authorities a very different story. In this version, Leirado arrived in Valencia with a merchant named Juan Gómez, with whom he had traveled from Saragossa. Soon afterward, he left this employer to serve and cook for the war commissioner D. Juan Suárez. According to Leirado, this employer did not pay him enough and that is why he changed masters again. After he left the war commissioner Leirado worked for the count of Peñalba until Leirado fell ill and had to leave his service. Once he recovered his health, Leirado became a construction worker of the royal road. There, the engineer in charge of construction denounced him to the local authorities, "because he had a fine voice and his face looked like a woman's, word spread among the workers that he was a hermaphrodite." On July 5, 1766, city officials took Leirado to the *Casa de la Misericordia* (House of Mercy), where the nuns in charge reported to the higher religious authority, the archbishop of Valencia. To clarify Leirado's supposed hermaphrodism, the archbishop ordered a medical examination. The surgeon's declaration of Leirado's sex as a male prompted the archbishop to order Leirado to leave Valencia and return to his parents in Madrid.

The trip from Valencia to Madrid offered Leirado yet another opportunity to describe the confusion that his female appearance caused in those who met him. This narrative comes from his arrest at Valdemoro. Officials, who were escorting Leirado from Valencia back to Madrid, had made a final stop in the town of Valdemoro. It was the last day of July, and officials probably planned to spend the night in an inn while Leirado was left lying asleep in the cart. Soon after, as Leirado explained it, "the wife of the *alcalde* (mayor) and her daughters arrived" and woke him up. The women asked Leirado to dress up as a woman because "they wanted to see him sing and dance a few *seguidillas* like La Ladvenant," for whom Leirado had worked and likely had learned to imitate. Once at the women's house, one of the daughters lent Leirado a skirt that he wore on top of his breeches, a white scarf that he placed around his neck and an apron. When Leirado expressed his fears that he could be arrested, the three women reassured him that he was in the mayor's home and had nothing to fear. They grabbed one of the male servants in the house, and Leirado soon found himself singing and dancing the popular Spanish folks dance, the seguidillas, with his dancing partner (Figure 2.2). Unfortunately, word had spread in the neighboring town that a woman dressed as a man had arrived in Valdemoro and was dancing at the mayor's house. Soon after the performance had begun, two officers from a nearby village broke into the party and arrested Leirado. Back in his man's clothes, the amateur actress was taken to their mayor. Thus, Leirado again found himself in prison, examined by surgeons, and shortly thereafter released to finally go to his parents' home.

Leirado's own narrative, given before Barreda in December 1769, omitted his arrests in Valencia and Valdemoro. Instead, he focused on the highlight of his career: the years following his return to Madrid to visit his parents. According to Leirado, these were the years when the confusion that her appearance as a woman provoked had peaked. Leirado started the story of mistaken identity in the winter of 1768, more than a year and a half after the Valdemoro episode. In this narrative, Sebastián/María had returned to Madrid from Malaga with one of his employers. Once in Madrid, Leirado became the servant of Captain Manuel Uzqueta, with whom he traveled to the town of Vilafranca (Navarra), in northern Spain. There, "rumors spread that I was a woman because of the jobs I carried out of ironing, sewing and cooking. All this reached my master, who ordered a surgeon of this town to find out if I was a man or a woman." In a separate declaration, his employer, Captain Uzqueta, explained it was Leirado who had in fact fueled these rumors. While spending the night at an inn on their way to Navarra and while his Captain Uzqueta was already in his room, other servants in the inn asked him whether he was a woman. Leirado confirmed she was a woman, but asked them to keep silent so the captain would not find out. Once Captain Uzqueta found out about the exchange he asked a surgeon from Vilafranca to examine Leirado. Although the surgeon found Leirado "with all the perfections of a man and not lacking anything," the captain still fired Leirado "because all the whispers" that could bring. Leirado in fact did not leave the town, and four months later Sebastián was arrested again for unknown reasons. Shortly after the arrest, in July 1768, the mayor of Vilafranca allowed this "beardless" individual to go back to his parents in Madrid. Meanwhile, in a series of letters dated June 1768, Leirado's father had written to both his son and the captain to find out about his son's whereabouts, with no response. Sebastián Leirado did not return

EMBOTADAS E LAS SEGUIDILLAS BOLERAS

Figure 2.2 "Steps of the Seguidillas Boleras" by Marcos Téllez Villar. Museo de Historia de Madrid

to Madrid until September 1768, two months after being released from the last arrest.

Leirado's version of the time after Uzqueta's dismissal from service was quite different, declaring that Uzqueta had never fired him; instead Leirado had left his service and gone directly to Madrid after Uzqueta's death. But the captain was, in fact, still alive in 1769 and able to testify before Barreda. According to Leirado's narrative in December 1769, after he had returned to Madrid, he had first worked for an innkeeper and next for an Italian dancer, whom he left to establish his own tavern. One afternoon, in January 1769, when Leirado had gone to the Plaza Mayor to purchase supplies for his tavern, she was suddenly arrested, suspected of being the actress María Teresa Garrido dressed as a tavern keeper. Leirado explained a rumor had spread that she was the actress who had been banned from Madrid and suspected to be wandering around Spain still performing her art. Leirado in fact may have spread these rumors, as some of her love letters revealed she pretended to be the actress herself, cross-dressed as a tavern keeper. She also asked one of her lovers to address her as María Teresa Garrido. In fact, Garrido had died two years before, in June 1767, and I have found no evidence she was ever banned from the city.[12]

In this arrest in January 1769 Leirado declared that "although it is believed I have two natures, I have no other nature than that of a man, although I am in the disposition that the nature of woman to be discovered because I have signs of that. I menstruate every single month and my face is effeminate and because of that many had been persuaded that I am a hermaphrodite." This arrest occurred more than two years after the workers constructing the royal road in Valencia thought Leirado was a hermaphrodite. With this declaration, although Leirado still left the question of his or her sex open to interpretation, the tavern-keeper provided the indispensable link between physical appearance and hidden sex: she menstruated and had the face of a woman. The surgeon Manuel González, the same physician who would examine Leirado just a few months later in the final arrest, examined the arrested in January 1769 and established that Leirado did not "have any sign of the female sex."

A couple of months after the release, officials arrested Leirado again while buying pork in the Plaza Mayor because observers had alerted them "he was a woman dressed as a man." José San Martín, a surgeon who would later examine Leirado in the final arrest in November 1769, examined the accused "front and rear" and declared him to be a male. It was Leirado's sixth medical exam in three years. The same month of Leirado's arrest, Sebastián received an offer from a group of artisans and amateur actors drinking at the tavern to play Octavia, the main female role in the seventeenth-century play *The Devil Preacher and Most Contrary Friend*, by Luis Belmonte Bermúdez.[13] Sebastián must have already gained a reputation in Madrid's underground acting world for specializing in female roles, particularly those who cross-dressed, which were quite abundant in the literature of Golden Age Spain. In *The Devil Preacher*, Octavia cross-dresses as a man to gain Feliciano's love. Sebastián had already played Rosaura, one of the female roles in Pedro Calderón de la Barca's *Life is a Dream*, who cross-dresses as a man to avenge her honor. Both roles must have been Sebastián delight: always thought to be a woman (María) dressed as a man (Sebastián, the tavern-keeper). Octavia was an even better part than Rosaura, since this time it meant Sebastián would play the main female role. *The Devil Preacher* had to be performed first on Easter Sunday, when the theater season officially opened in Madrid after the intermission during the months of Lent.[14] On the second day of the play's performance in April, Leirado, dressed as a woman, returned to her home with Antonio Fernández and the events that led to the final arrest took place.

After Leirado finished the long declaration, Barreda still could not reach a conclusion. After all, this was the seventh (known) arrest for Leirado. Before the arrest in November 1769, authorities had arrested Leirado in 1764 in Saragossa; in 1766 in Valencia and Valdemoro; in 1768 in Vilafranca of Navarra; and in January and March of 1769 in the Plaza Mayor of Madrid (see Map 2.1). In each of these arrests, Leirado had been subjected to separate medical examinations to determine the sex of the accused. The young innkeeper even kept a certificate from the surgeon of the town of Vilafranca as a form of "sex passport" to show to anyone who doubted his sex. As it happened, it is unlikely that Leirado used this certificate, since Sebastián seemed to have reveled in the confusion that sex and gender provoked. But it is precisely in the medical and popular confusion about Leirado's sex as well as the early modern debates on sex formation that we need to understand each of Leirado's medical examinations.

Medical Notions of Sex Formation

When surgeons confronted the case of Sebastián/María, they found themselves at the crossroads of, on the one hand, a long tradition of understanding sex formation as fluctuating and undetermined, and on the other, a renewed interest in the eighteenth century in establishing a clear distinction between the male and female sexes. Although physicians examining Leirado's genitals concluded he was undoubtedly a male, the external elements that characterized this young innkeeper provoked confusion and made people, including physicians, think he might be a woman. Leirado's skin was soft, she could not grow a beard and her voice was high-pitched. Altogether, these were physical characteristics that people identified as feminine. She was also good at mending clothes, ironing, doing women's hair, cooking and performing other domestic tasks that women carried out. In fact, one of Leirado's employers declared that people suspected she was a woman because she could iron, cook and sew. And thus skin, voice and skills became external marks of a possible hidden sexual transformation, which suggested the possibility that Leirado could be a hermaphrodite. Although physicians did not openly acknowledge such connections between external physical characteristics and sex, the surgeons who examined Leirado most likely compared this case to those of past hermaphrodites. To try to understand this "most peculiar case," they had to set aside new medical theories and resort to medical ideas from the past to be able to explain the reality of a sex and gender that were highly ambiguous.

By 1769, when surgeons examined Sebastián Leirado's supposed claims of hermaphrodism, Martín Martínez's manuals had become widely used and popular among surgeons and anatomists trained in the university setting, particularly at the University of Alcalá de Henares where he had been a student.[15] Among the followers of Martínez were Juan de Dios López, the physician who last examined Leirado, also a student at Alcalá.[16] López, royal surgeon and founder of the Royal Academy of Medicine of Madrid, was also part of this renewed interest in cleansing Spanish medical knowledge of popular superstition heavily based on a loose interpretation of the Galenic system of humors. An avid reader of the latest French anatomists, like other surgeons and anatomists of his generation López kept a library of the latest advances in medicine, which included the works of both Manuel de Porras and Benito Jerónimo Feijóo.[17] Juan de Dios López's major work, *Anatomic Compendium Divided in Four Parts*, was published originally in Madrid in two volumes that came out between 1750 and 1752, and re-edited three times in 1767, 1791, and 1818.[18] The *Compendium* became the main anatomic manual for surgeons training at the general hospital in Madrid and in the Academies of Surgery of Madrid and Barcelona, replacing Martín Martínez's *Complete Anatomy of Man*.[19] López's direct influence were the works of the anatomists Frederik Ruysch (1638–1731) and Jacob Winslow (1669–1760), and their emphasis on observation and experimentation with the practice of dissections, as well as the physician César Verdier (1685–1759) and his *Abridged Anatomy of the Human Body* (1734).[20] López's work thus reflects the intimate connections that the Spanish medical knowledge had with its European counterparts at the end of the eighteenth century.

European anatomists, like López, were interested in incorporating the practice of observing the human body in the study of anatomy and sexuality. López's *Compendium*, however, does not reflect his concerns over the ambiguities of the human body. It is, after all, a manual that responds to a mechanical and factual understanding of the human body. As López put it, anatomy would not only tell the anatomist of the "division and separation of the parts that made up for the organized body," but more importantly through dissection he would find out about the "connection, structure and reciprocal correspondence of all its parts and use."[21] The emphasis on use (*uso*), a characteristic of the body of knowledge of the Spanish Enlightenment, appears as the most outstanding characteristic of López's opus: the emphasis on the practical application of the observation of the body.[22] In principle, exact knowledge of the anatomical parts of the human body – and López even studied the skeleton of the fetus in its different stages of gestation – would explain to the physician how the human body worked. However, and in spite of having in his manual "rare cases," López's *Compendium* does not reveal the many challenges that the surgeon must have faced in his medical practice and of which Leirado's case was one example. Surgeons trained in the experience of visiting patients and in the practice of medicine with master surgeons still had to face the problematic of individuals who showed signs of not belonging to the sex they had been born with.

The case of Sebastián/María must have been particularly interesting to López since it posed for him the problem of marrying the theory and practice of medicine, influenced by popular beliefs. In particular, Leirado's difficult-to-determine sex illustrated the difficulties of matching anatomical evidence with an individual's behavior and activities, which complicated a definitive answer to the question of what society deemed to be a man and a woman. Following his own *Compendium*, López clearly concluded that Leirado was a man because of his male genitals. But Leirado's external characteristics, and in particular the jobs he carried out, complicated the case. Most of all, if women and men were distinctive and separate, then were the jobs men and women carried out the product of their different sexualities? Why did Leirado know how to perform women's jobs? Why did Sebastián give up his rightful role in reproduction by having anal sex with men? Medicine alone could not answer these questions, and we may think that López resorted to some less scientific aspects of his medical training that would help him further understand a case like Leirado's.

Juan de Dios López had been trained in the theory of medicine at the University of Alcalá. The interest in physiognomy had decreased in the eighteenth century from the previous century. Yet, a field such as physiognomy, which promised to reveal the intimate connection between individuals' external appearance and their inner characteristics, still ignited the curiosity of the medical community throughout the 1700s. In fact, it was precisely during the eighteenth century when Jerónimo Cortés's *Physiognomy and the Several Secrets of Nature*, first published in 1598, witnessed a growing popularity, with nine reprints throughout the eighteenth century.[23] Moreover, it was perhaps Cortés' belief that "education, social and physical circumstances greatly contribute to alter the features of the face," which made him a popular author in the age of the Enlightenment, and his treatise may have influenced the judgment of those surgeons who analyzed Leirado's case. This reflects the fact that, even in the eighteenth century physicians and anatomists probably thought physiognomy was important to their understanding of physical as well as psychological ailments. Physiognomy, like anatomy, relied on the power of the visual in knowing the body. It allowed a number of medical professionals in France, England and in the newly established United States to "think visually" in order to connect "the book of nature with its author."[24] Still at the turn of the century physiognomy held the promised to offer the observer the clues to the bridge that connected mind and body.

Leirado's physiognomy was clearly an important factor in the recurrent confusion over determining sex. And thus, López had to face similar problems to those of the physicians who had examined Francisco Roca's body (studied in Chapter 1) more than a century before. In fact, in his report the first thing López noted was Leirado's external attributes, the same attributes that had caused people to believe she was a woman disguised as a man. What Juan de Dios López noticed in Leirado's face was the lack of beard, and he may have recalled what the seventeenth-century physiognomist Esteban Pujasol wrote in his 1637 *Treaty of Physiognomy*, a work reprinted several times in the eighteenth century. According to Pujasol, beardless men lacked the heat indispensable to growing a beard. These men were cold – just like women – instead of hot and had given up "their virile constitution."[25] Besides having a feminine face, Leirado performed women's jobs.[26] Huarte de San Juan would have concluded that Leirado was the victim of an indecisive womb. Initially programed to be a female, the capricious uterus changed its sex to that of a male. And, while this explanation was not acceptable to someone like López, he still had to confront the problem of determining the sex in an individual whose gender characteristics were at the least highly ambiguous.

López's reaction to Leirado's case illustrates one of the many challenges physicians often had to confront: how the formation of gender and sex encompassed much more than what medicine alone could empirically establish. One had to listen to other discourses to name the anatomical part. Medicine could not explain it all. The example of the treatment of the hermaphrodite in eighteenth-century France reflects this. In the French Enlightenment the hermaphrodite no longer seemed to have a place within the cosmic order, and instead it was relegated to the realm of "fiction." The hermaphrodite was relegated to the category of "legend," or "childish fables," as the Chevalier Louis de Jaucourt's entry for "hermaphrodite" in the *Encyclopédie* reveals. The French philosopher and naturalist Georges Louis Leclerc, Comte de Buffon (1707–88) while acknowledging the existence of hermaphrodites in the natural world denied there were human hermaphrodites.[27] Even in the production of the most representative work of the thought of the Enlightenment, the French *Encyclopédie*, undertaken by Denis Diderot, the treatment of the hermaphrodite appears as ambivalent. On the one hand, Louis de Jaucourt's entry for "hermaphrodite" reveals an absolute rationale according to which no individual could bear two perfect sexes, responding to the belief that everything that nature produced science could rationally explain.[28] To Jaucourt it was "unnatural" for two sexes to be found in the body of one individual. Nature was clear, straight and organized. It could not be open to "confusion" and chaos. The sex of a child was established at birth, and hermaphrodites or tales of sex change, he would have agreed with Martín Martínez, were fables of the credulous populace. Since the essence of being a male or a female was their distinctive role in reproduction, a hermaphrodite had to be an individual with two perfect sexes, and to Jaucourt that was impossible. Yet, when we look at the plates on hermaphrodites in the supplement of the *Encyclopédie* (1776–77) – created by Charles-Joseph Panckoucke and without Denis Diderot's approval – we see a "plurality of discourses." In an effort to "clarify" the human body, the figure of the hermaphrodite in the plates meets the literary and historical: resulting from the inseparability of body and cosmos in order to understand a medical phenomenon.[29]

This ambiguity in the midst of an effort of rationalization and precision that starts in the knowing of the anatomical body also appears in the view of the hermaphrodite in the work of well-known eighteenth-century scientists like the Swiss Albrecht von Haller, also an author for the *Encyclopédie*. Haller acknowledged that, in spite of its exceptional character, the rare cases of hermaphrodites were in fact a display of nature's amazing ability to create new "forms."[30] Just as his Spanish counterparts Martín Martínez and Benito Jerónimo Feijóo did years before, in his *Dissertation Hermaphroditis* (1752) Haller admitted "nothing can be defined as true or false, unless a detailed anatomical description" is run. Yet, if after such "detailed anatomical description" the anatomist still cannot offer a certain verdict, one needed to accept the limits of science before the ambiguity of certain bodies. Anatomists like Haller had to ultimately confront the fact that the body was a physical entity, but it was also the moral and social components that made the definition of body parts all the more difficult to obtain. If anatomists, albeit acknowledging science's limitations, would not attempt to integrate other discourses to understand sex, people in other areas were playing with the altered aspects of sex and gender.

Becoming María: Sex and Gender in Eighteenth-Century Spain

The eighteenth-century medical perspective on sex change reflects the belief that the structures of nature and society were intrinsically connected. The mechanisms of one could help unveil the functioning of the other. For instance, the division of work according to sex in society could help entomologists explain how and why bees distributed tasks the way they did.[31] From this point of view we can understand that, although physicians wanted to refute Galenic influences that led people to believe in the "fable of sex change," these same physicians were hesitant to establish that someone like Sebastián Leirado was a man, even after examining his genitals. Leirado acted, looked and behaved like a woman. Centuries before, physicians examining Leirado would have agreed, as Huarte de San Juan did, that an alteration of humors in the womb could have changed a person's intended sex from female to male. However, for eighteenth-century physicians like Juan de Dios López, this explanation was no longer possible. Yet, although López did not see humoral changes as an explanation for Leirado's potential hermaphrodism, her female gender traits were confusing, partly because Leirado's social body did not correspond to his physical body. Such problematic interpretation of the body of Sebastián Leirado takes us to the complexity of how people understood sex and gender in early modern Spain.

Generally, scholars who have studied sex and gender during the age of the Enlightenment have taken current notions of sex and gender and analyzed them in the context of the eighteenth century. The problem is that what eighteenth-century writers understood by "gender" was never spelled out in any of their texts. Thus, for early modern Spaniards gender was sometimes understood as a manifestation of sex, and therefore it could have biological as much as environmental and educational components. Gender in the context of the eighteenth century was established in a set of changing relations with nature, culture and even religion. In the specific context of the debates over sex formation, gender appears more as a social expression of sex, rather than a cultural construction of a sexed body. Life was successful only when the organisms were able to adapt to the constant physical, environmental and social changes that an individual had to face. In the thought of the Enlightenment "life was a notion of synthesis, system and fusion," and as such physicians like Juan de Dios López saw sex as the product of the whole organism, not just of the reproductive organs.[32]

For someone like Juan de Dios López, "femininity" was acquired not only by birth but also by custom and habit, two important terms in the period that tell us about the social construction of an individual. In fact, it is interesting to note that in the Spanish Royal Dictionary the word used to identify "femininity" and "female" was the same. Feminine (*femenino*) meant what was "proper of women" as well as referring to "woman or female of an animal species."[33] In this context, it makes sense then that women could only be seen as fully women if they were doing "womanly things." Such womanly things included mainly those revolving around motherhood, but not exclusively; other skills that defined a woman were sewing, ironing, and cooking – the skills that Leirado seemed to have mastered. The French eighteenth-century philosopher and physician Pierre Jean George Cabanis (1757–1808) expressed it in this way: "Nature has not simply distinguished the sexes on the organs alone... between men and women exist other differences of structure which relate more to the role assigned to them."[34] Physicians like Cabanis embraced an understanding of human nature that was physical, mental and social. As such, gender was part of a process of relations that had biological roots and could not be disconnected from them.

In these series of relations between what was physical, mental and social, there were bridges that allowed people to make the connection between nature and culture. One of those "bridges" was the clothing that the individual wore. In fact, people and even physicians attempted to identify Leirado's sex by his appearance (*apariencia*), or what the dictionary described as "the external semblance of something." In this "appearance" the clothing of an individual was paramount. The clothing confused the gender and sex of an individual, since clothing was part of an individual's fundamental "social body." Clothes provided the sign of the hidden sex, particularly when they were consistent with other external signs of one's sex: skin, hair, body frame and the pitch of the voice. Yet, a troubling aspect of clothing was their potential for change, something expressed in the concept of "fashion," or *moda* in Spanish, or as the Spanish Royal Dictionary expressed it in 1780, "what is newly introduced in matters of outfits and ways of wearing."

Fashion's main characteristic was its volatility, its constant change. The lack of reliability and stability of fashion was dangerous because it fostered people's imagination out of desire rather than by appealing to the higher intellectual aspect of imagination.[35] Fashion appealed to the irrational, emotional and sensual imagination characteristic of women.

Therefore, the fashionable man was, just like women, falling for a sensual practice that threatened to remove his manhood. The fashionable man who followed the French fashion, known as *petimetre*, Spanish for *petite-maitre*, was also inclined toward an ambiguous sexuality since his clothes effeminized him.[36] The petimetre provoked a great degree of anxiety in those who observed him. By yielding to the forces of the senses in the form of fashionable clothes, perfumes and all kinds of adornments, all that was excessive and feminine, the petimetre was giving up what made him a man. The type of individual who was socially accepted as a man was one who displayed virtues of economic moderation and restraint.[37] The only discharge of the modern productive man was for useful purposes, the investment in business and the emission of semen into its proper vessel.[38]

By engaging in the excesses characteristic of the feeble nature of the other sex the petimetre became partly man/partly woman, or "man when naked and woman when dressed."[39] The idle petimetres who dressed following the dictates of French fashion were "half men ... who corrupting the nobility and gravity of their sex boasted of looking like, if not females, at least like hermaphrodites."[40] The hermaphrodite signified this ambiguous sexual threshold between one sex and the other, expressed in the gestures and clothing of an individual such as the petimetre. In his introduction in 1763 to the translation from the French of Mirabeau's *A Woman's Friend*, Francisco Mariano Nipho (1719–1803), the well-known journalist, translator and critical observer of Spanish society, also saw the fashionable petimetre as a hermaphrodite. Nipho believed the hermaphrodite-petimetres earned their habits by imitating the actresses who became their role models as they "imitate their actions and even habits, borrowing from the indecency in the ease, immodesty in their manners, the exuberance of their clothes, and what is worse, the fickleness and veniality of their affections."[41] The hermaphrodite, initially a medical category, became a social one in the hands of Nipho. This ideal hermaphrodite-petimetre would be someone like Leirado, who, fascinated by the excess in clothing and demeanor of the actresses for whom Sebastián worked, tried to become one himself.

Nipho feared that someone as vulnerable as the petimetre, easily attracted to feminine excess, could worsen his effeminate ways by frequenting the theater scene. In the theater, all actors were potential hermaphrodites. Such anxiety over the transformative aspect of the theater world was expressed especially well in the performance of the famous actor Manuel Garrido (not related to María Teresa Garrido, Leirado's first employer and the actress she later try to impersonate). In 1786 Garrido represented a satirical short-song, a *tonadilla*, called "Garrido's caprice about the thrills of cross-dressing," a favorite of the audience and which he acted on numerous occasions at the *Coliseo del Príncipe* in Madrid.[42] In his performance, Garrido dressed up as a female singer (*tonadillera*) to please the audience. In the song, Garrido claimed there were no women who could entertain the audience that day and he himself had to sing the tonadilla. He recited as a prelude:

> I am already a woman
> Although I don't promise
> To find good patronage
> I would like to be a swan but I can't
> Because nature made me a rook,
> But just to please you in any way I can
> I am determined to sing you my song.

> Then he sang his tonadilla:
> So into female
> I was transformed.
> Astrology I got to learn
> How much is
> Nowadays to be a woman?
> And so you see this is not fiction
> My Almanac [is] ready
> Here I go
> Chi, chi, attention.

Perhaps sung at the end of the year, Garrido's tonadilla referred in a humorous tone to the predictions of what was to come. Garrido finished his tonadilla with the dancing of seguidillas and singing:

> Ever since I have been dressing
> In such feminine clothes
> I have felt
> A vehement apprehension.
> I imagine to suffer
> Those aches
> That this sex suffers.
> I have headaches
> I have a stitch (*tener flato*)
> And I become hysterical.
> What if now
> The Devil would do it
> And what has been a put on
> Would become true?
> A strong tremor
> I begin to feel,
> My voice seems to

Become thinner,
And my beard
Is falling off.
Let's get rid of the little hat,
And the outfit as well,
And let it all
Be just a joke.[43]

In his performance, Garrido played with the confusion over sex that clothes provoked and the power that they have in altering physical traits, something earlier educators feared could happen in childhood: external influences could alter biological givens. The actor, however, used these ideas to amuse and entertain. After the seed of doubt was planted, he dressed again in his men's clothes, like the literary heroines of the seventeenth-century Spanish writer María de Zayas, who had many of her female protagonists cross-dress to avenge their honor.[44] At the very moment when, by the Devil's doing, the joke threatened to become reality and Garrido might turn into a woman, he escaped his fate by shedding the feminine attire. Everyone in the audience knew that Garrido was not a hermaphrodite, but the actor played with an idea that had been part of the popular fascination for centuries.

Unlike Shakespearean England, where male cross-dressing of "playboys" compensated for the lack of women on stage,[45] in Spain where female actresses were allowed, cross-dressing of male and female actors had a strong playful and sometimes subversive component. Works such as Tirso de Molina's *The Bashful Man* (1624), or *Don Gil of the Green Breeches* (1635), both with cross-dressed characters represented in the theater scene, fueled the popular fascination with a malleable sexuality.[46] Some actors, like the much-celebrated Juan Rana, made an entire career by performing such cross-dressed roles on stage that created "an ambiguous and evocative stage representation of identity."[47] Rana, an actor with great longevity in the Spanish theater scene (1617–72), successfully fostered fascination and awe among his audience for his personae; an accomplishment partly due to the actor's ability to combine his personal life with his stage characters. Juan Rana (John Frog), stage name for Cosme Pérez, was arrested in 1636 accused of sodomy. Released shortly after, in the next decades the actor increasingly entertained roles that could play out his now public "unmanliness" dressed in many occasions on female garments. Juan Rana was an exceptional actor. Male cross-dressing on stage was rare since the practice did not have the moral telling opportunity of women dressed as men to avenge their honor. Yet, just like his seventeenth-century counterpart, Manuel Garrido's performance at the end of the eighteenth century must have fit within certain expectations among his audience of the uncertainty of sex and gender. At the turn of the century, the hermaphrodite continued to confuse sex and gender like no other.

When looking at the medical debates on human sexuality in the eighteenth century we see that the opposition between the old and the new medicine did not always work. While anatomists and surgeons following the new medical theories insisted on linking the genital mapping of individuals with their expected sexual and social behavior, the reality was that gender traits many times appeared as highly ambiguous, a fact which seemed to reveal a fluctuant and unstable sex. The debates among medical professional themselves reflect, in part, the difficulties in trying to neatly fit these two types of bodies – the social and natural body – into one. The anatomists' hope was for the social expression of sex (womanhood or manhood) to be established by observing an individual's anatomy, established at birth. It was then essential to discard previous interpretations of sex formation and the possibility of sex change in adulthood as popular fables. This was necessary, not only because humoral interpretations of the body had no place in a more mechanical view of the human body, but also because the new medical theorists gained relevance, importance, and authority by opposing the less scientific view of sex formation.[48]

The paradoxes created by the new medical theories extended to other fields that were in themselves changing in the eighteenth century. Changing systems of knowledge were inserting meaning to the body. Professionals in areas such as education and its philosophy, and the theory and practice of law found themselves having to discuss and deal with the same dilemmas anatomists faced. In the next chapter, I will examine how philosophers and educators debated the implications and limitations of the new anatomical discoveries regarding how a particular social and cultural environment could alter natural tendencies in molding a person's sexuality. Their resolution, not unlike the anatomists', was inconclusive. The Spanish philosophers and educators of the eighteenth century, reacting partly to inquietudes also shared by their French and British counterparts, began to discuss the role of education in the formation of the individual. They believed in the power of education to shape an individual in every possible way; in particular, education had to reaffirm the clear division between the sexes that responded to the needs of reproduction.

3 Nature, Nurture, and Early Modern Sexuality

The new anatomical discoveries of the seventeenth century impacted the world outside medicine to alter ideas about the relationship between nature and nurture and the power that education had to mold natural tendencies. In the eighteenth century, philosophers, educators, and even some physicians whose interest in understanding human behavior led them to consider the implications of the new anatomical findings on the body, discussed how education could, and should, reinforce the division of the sexes to guarantee social harmony. The transformation had to start in early childhood. The goal of education was to teach children to rightfully guarantee that their actions adapted to their sex. It was not so much that nurture had to overcome nature but education instead would guide nature to fulfill its ultimate objective: to allow human reproduction. Education – from social habits, to family rearing or even the proper molding of fantasy and imagination – would be the powerful tool to redirect natural givens that were wrongfully expressed. The change would always be towards productive, rightful social utility.

The promise of education in shaping sex and sexuality was first tested in the practice of raising children. The topic of children's sexuality had been at the center of many early modern treatises on education and the family. From Erasmus of Rotterdam (1466–1536) to Jean-Jacques Rousseau (1712–78), philosophers and educators focused on the importance of the role of the family, tutors, and masters in disciplining the child's natural tendencies toward sensual pleasures and sexual experimentation. Children's sexuality was also the concern of physicians writing on women's health.[1] Both women's and children's health were linked to the family since, in many ways, what happened in the family had a direct impact on the physical well-being of the individual. For educators and physicians, what remained an attractive point of discussion were the factors that shaped children's rearing and education, and the impact those factors had on their bodies and social interactions. Good education was crucial since improper rearing might even induce social practices characteristic of the other sex. Wrong gender practices could even lead to a mistaken role in the sexual act, altering an individual's place in procreation and thus blurring the differences between the sexes.

The debate over whether education was powerful enough to counteract natural inclinations was not new in the eighteenth century. Throughout the early modern period, discussion had centered on whether social habits could shape biology and if this was only possible in childhood or among grown-ups as well. According to Galenic medical theory, arduous physical exercise could, in fact, reveal the hidden male nature of a woman. Such was the case, related in previous chapters, of the cloistered nuns who unexpectedly developed the dry and hot nature of a male as well as a penis after their humors had been heated up. In the eighteenth century, however, the debate over how and why a woman – more rarely a man – could see their sex altered in adulthood shifted toward answering the question by detaching actions and behavior from biology. Anatomy defined and separated men from women, but it was difficult to determine why certain individuals displayed an improper use of their sex. If sex was now believed to be immutable and not subject to miraculous transformation, then wrongful sexual behavior could only be the result of the incorrect social influences and improper education in childhood.[2]

Discussions over wrongful sexual behavior tended to focus on the effeminate man, which allowed writers to study the impact of education on people's habits. The effeminate man, more than the masculine woman, was a puzzle to writers, doctors, and observers. While writers paid little attention to the rearing of masculine young girls, the focus of criticism was against those parents who instilled inappropriate social practices in their children and, with this, provoked effeminate behavior in boys and wrongful habits. The effeminate man who, unable to control his passions, engaged in the practice of sodomy was changing his rightful place in procreation. From the religious perspective, he was a moral monster. However, by rejecting his role in the well-being of the community, he also became a social monster that jeopardized the harmony of the nation. Sexual difference guaranteed procreation. Not only by being effeminate but also by performing the role expected of a woman, the sodomite made reproduction impossible, thus offending both religion and society. The question was whether the effeminate man was the product of external elements – education, climate, even the food he ate – or whether there were natural tendencies that made the process inevitable.

Nature, Nurture, and the Making of an Effeminate

Early modern writers discussing the relationship between nature and nurture in shaping the individual bore the implicit argument that proper education stored the power to direct passions, and their influences on body and mind, into their proper channels. Through good habits and, most importantly, the repetition of adequate practices, the young body could learn how to control passions and desires. As John Locke saw it, this repetition imprinted in children a sense of second nature, since they would not have to resort to memory to remember what to do that was socially acceptable. The body would perform without a script.[3] Centuries later, sociologist Pierre Bourdieu pointed at how "the opposition between male and female" was realized in such physical repetition of practices.[4] To Bourdieu, "what is 'learned by body' is not something that one has, like knowledge that can be brandished, but something that one is."[5] What the body learns the body becomes. And thus, the fear among many early modern writers was precisely that the male body could equally learn the wrongful repetitive habits characteristic of girls and with this, become in theory and practice an effeminate – and female – body.

Typically, early modern texts blamed effeminacy on nature, nurture or a combination of both. "Nurture" (*crianza* in Spanish or "the work of raising, nurturing and feeding"[6]) encompassed three areas of utmost importance in children's sexual development: maternal rearing, education outside the family, and the child's social environment could instill either proper or improper behavior that affected his or her sexual development. The first, and most delicate, part of nurture was maternal rearing. Nearly everyone agreed that mothers should not allow sons to become too attached to them. Such attachment could make boys as weak and effeminate as their mothers. In order to avoid making boys effeminate, the ancient Greek physician Hippocrates had advised mothers to wean them by age two or when the first teeth came out. Maternal attachment after the age of two could have disastrous consequences, since women were unable to judge what was best for their sons in order to raise them as men.[7]

The 1730 anonymous English pamphlet *Plain Reasons for the Growth of Sodomy in England* is an example of this concern, characteristic among authors in Europe, that blamed the growth of effeminate men on poor education during childhood.[8] The pamphlet claimed the manly education that had produced the "fine gentleman of former days … dutiful and humble to his parents" was long gone. Nowadays, the author wrote, parents raise boys to become "little masters," the same fashionable petimetres of Spanish literature, both in turn versions of the French "petit-maître." This little master was a mama's boy. He was "brought up in all respects like a girl." The English Little Master remained too long under the care of his mother. She kept him in the nursery until the age of five. She dressed him in effeminate clothes. He wore a colored silk coat and his hair was "stroked over in front and cocked up behind."[9] This maternal attachment ended up transforming Little Master into an effeminate boy, with possible disastrous consequences.

The second aspect of nurture that had an important impact on children's sexual formation was formal education. Educators urged parents to put their young sons in the care of male tutors or send them to boys' school. Instead, the English Little Master went to a girl's school. There his schoolmistress taught him "dancing and reading, and generally speaking, [to] get his minuet before his letters." He also learned to play with dolls and to drink tea instead of coffee. Little Master was never allowed to play with "rude boys," which deprived him of hardy physical exercise. The third aspect of nurture consisted of the social environment parents and tutors created for a boy. Once again, instead of manly activities, Little Master attended theater and Italian opera with his mother. Later, he would imitate the effeminate gestures and attire of actors and actresses. Little Master even fancied the fashion of kissing and holding hands with other boys. The power of education in turning a boy into an effeminate man could be such that it shaped his sexual behavior. Such harmful practices would make him grow up incapable of procreating and fall into the unspeakable sin of sodomy.

One last element that shaped Little Master's behavior was his inadequate diet. According to the author of the pamphlet, sodomy was "most predominant in those to whom Nature has been so sparing of her blessings that they find not a call equivalent to other men." In other words, nature could endow certain boys with traits that made them more prone to sodomy. Yet, an inadequate diet could worsen their natural inclination for sodomy. Drinking tea, wine, and taking potions from the apothecary spoiled Little Master's "tender constitution" and made him impotent. But perhaps this was not such a bad outcome after all. Had Little Master procreated, he would have engendered "a race as effeminate as himself." In short, the failure to rightfully shape nature by providing appropriate nurture could contribute to turning a boy into an effeminate. By looking and acting like a woman, Little Master was putting himself at risk of becoming a sodomite.

In its criticism of the frivolous practices of the aristocracy, the English pamphlet described how fashion, effeminate and French, would render men incapable of performing their male duties in society and in the home. In particular, this male effeminacy had its more direct consequence in a feared corrupted sexuality, a man that acted like a woman in the sexual act. These texts, pamphlets, plays, and satires about the dandy clearly link sodomy, effeminacy, and bad education. In a society that was progressively connecting the virtuous gentleman with a body that was restrained in its appearance and movement, the body of the aristocratic man, with its excessive adornment and gestures, had turned him into a woman. However, social critics, such as the author of the English pamphlet, could not agree on the degree to which nurture was the cause of effeminacy, and whether there were some natural immobile components that drove a man to become a sodomite.

Education as the main tool to mold the young child into the ideal citizen was not exclusively characteristic of early modern society. In fact, early modern authors drew their theories of education from medieval and classic texts of Rome and ancient Greece. Yet, it was in the early modern period that educators gave renewed emphasis to the importance of the proper education in counteracting unnatural inclinations in a child. This emphasis placed on education by early modern philosophers had a larger aim: to produce adults who would fulfill their role in society. In particular, in the eighteenth century the concept of social utility colored views on children's education and their sexuality. Aware of the physiological characteristics of children, the malleability of their brains and bodies, philosophers sometimes doubted how much nature could remain intact, and if indeed the needs of social utility could alter nature.

The awareness of the social environment in education adhered to a seemingly impossible combination: the growing importance of the general social good and the heightened focus on the individual.[10] In this sense, Locke was a transitional and key figure in understanding child sexuality in seventeenth- and eighteenth-century Europe.[11] Many authors of eighteenth-century Spanish philosophy, and in particular those focusing on children's education, were influenced by John Locke, whose *Some Thoughts Concerning Education* (1693) was translated into French in 1695, and Spanish in 1797.[12] According to Locke, children were not born with preconceived knowledge, they were a "tabula rasa." It was in the course of their young lives, and mainly under the watchful eyes of parents and tutors, that they were able to develop their skills and abilities. While "nine out of ten [men] are what they are, good or evil, useful or not, by their education," the proper education was only possible by bringing out what was natural and innate in men.[13]

Education allowed innate tendencies to develop properly by "laying the first foundations of virtue." This interesting relationship between nature and nurture, where there was this dual and almost symbiotic collaboration, would become attractive to eighteenth-century writers interested in education. In fact, it was with Locke that the relationship between nature and nurture shifted toward the primary role of nurture and the importance of social conditions over natural predisposition. Yet, the philosopher still saw that children had "various tempers, different inclinations and particular defaults," and therefore the system of education had to fit their "natural genius and constitution" to allow the child's potential to properly develop.[14] Thus, Locke would have agreed with the author of the English pamphlet in arguing that there could be a tendency toward effeminacy in a child but it was an improper education that ultimately would lead him toward the wrong sexual behavior.

In his *An Essay Concerning Human Understanding* (1690), with French translation in 1700, Locke posited that humans acquire knowledge of the physical world through their senses.[15] According to Locke, individuals reach general knowledge through the experience and perception of things, which is only deduced by the senses and naming the particular. This knowledge, however, is always incomplete and open to error. Knowledge of God, on the other hand, had to be considered in a different manner because of its different nature: it was a knowledge that could not be perceived through the senses. This knowledge fell into the category of what Locke labeled "substance," where he also placed moral knowledge.[16] Locke's separation of lay from religious concerns, while still accepting the central role of both natural influences and God's intervention, made him an acceptable philosopher to Spanish writers and authorities. Locke's philosophical concern in measuring the impact of education on an individual's social interaction and behavior cannot be detached from the shifts in medicine at the time. These shifts were geared toward offering a more central role to the individual in the well-being of the community. While it could not conquered it all, proper education would guide nature towards its original intend: the clear separation of the sexes to guarantee the reproduction of humans.

In the case of Spain, we can see the impact of Locke's ideas in the work of physicians who were interested in women's reproductive health, and who produced works on children and education that addressed the issue of children's sexuality and its causes. One of these physicians was the Catalan Agustín Ginesta (1756–1815), a longtime member of the Royal Academy of Surgery of San Carlos in Madrid, where he occupied the position of "deliveries, diseases of women and children, and venereal diseases."[17] The combination of these three elements – obstetrics, gynecology and children's health – also became representative of many of the health manuals in Spain at the end of the eighteenth century.

Ginesta's work was part of the growing field of public health that linked health with population – and thus, reduction of mortality, especially infant mortality – and the wealth of the nation. For eighteenth-century Spanish anatomists and surgeons sexuality had turned into a social concern. This meant that studies on health and sex had to go hand-in-hand with studies on education. In the case of the physician Ginesta, his career revealed an interest in combining the studies on human sexuality with women and children's health. In fact, Ginesta's work on women and children, and in particular the study of obstetrics, brought him to examine the complexities of human sexuality.[18] Ginesta's main work, *The Preserver of Children*, published in 1797, focused on the topic of children's mortality and how to palliate the problem by asking mothers to follow a few hygienic and dietetic rules.[19] Among these basic rules, he highlighted avoiding bathing children in cold water or giving them alcoholic drinks – although a little bit of wine was not a practice the physician discouraged. In his work, Ginesta was echoing the royal order issued by Charles III in 1788 to improve the care and monitoring of children in orphanages. Once out of orphanages, children would go to schools to receive better education so they could become "useful subjects."[20] Accordingly, Ginesta placed special emphasis on the individual care by mothers and their role in practicing healthy habits that would guarantee their children became such expected useful subjects. These recommendations, from breastfeeding children instead of sending them to wet-nurses to wearing loose and comfortable clothing, were meant to allow children to conform to their true nature and to perform their expected role in society.

Other authors besides Locke influenced Ginesta, such as the Spaniard José Clavijo y Fajardo (1726–1806), who believed "the first seed of bad education" was the "bad raising" (*mala crianza*) that wet nurses planted on the young child. To Clavijo y Fajardo "almost all disorders come from this first deprivation which alters the moral order and extinguishes what is natural in all hearts." When mothers return to breastfeeding their own children, "Nature would be re-established with all its rights," and extinguish "the dangerous influence of all those French fashions that effeminate."[21] In spite of his criticism of "French fashions" and influences, Clavijo y Fajardo was himself a follower of Rousseau and his views on nature and the individual. In fact, the Spaniard's emphasis on mothers breastfeeding their children as almost a patriotic duty reminds us of Rousseau's famous statement in *Émile* (1762): "When mothers resume nursing their children, morals will be reformed; natural feelings will be revived in every heart; the state will be repopulated; this first step alone will reunite everybody."[22] To Rousseau, as well as Clavijo y Fajardo, in the female breast lay the seed for a new morally renewed society. As with many other works in French, *Émile* was not translated into Spanish, although copies of Rousseau's book made it to the Iberian Peninsula and to the Spanish American colonies.[23] Clavijo y Fajardo likely read Rousseau since he followed this author's belief that individuals had to return to their natural self to be able to fulfill their duties as citizens of the republic.[24] Hence, his emphasis on women breastfeeding their children to restore the proper division of the sexes expressed in each sex's expected social role.[25] As Rousseau envisioned in France, Clavijo y Fajardo also saw breastfeeding as imbued with a patriotic value that would populate Spain with strong and healthy citizens.

Key to Agustín Ginesta's project was to make his work available to the public. Thus, the Catalan physician aimed at positioning himself outside his circle of colleagues and specialists, to offer advice to mothers on how to properly raise children to reach a general public; just like French physicians such as Antoine Petit (1722–94), whose work on childbirth became an important influence in Ginesta's work.[26] Like Petite, Ginesta wrote for the general public in *The Preserver of Children*. Based on the specific cases in his practice and selected lectures to his students of anatomy, Ginesta's text showed a concern regarding what improper education could do to the physical bodies of children. Years earlier, the physician had published a short work on how the illness of the body could alter the spirit; now he was interested in exploring how the spirit could damage the body. For Ginesta the lifelong consequences of poor upbringing were not tied so much to the breastfeeding period, whether or not infants were sent to wet-nurses, but to the onset of the child's socialization. The beginning of socialization exposed the child to improper social interactions that would turn him or her into a social monster, one that corrupted the social laws based on natural laws. Since, after all, as the *ilustrado* statesman Valentín de Foronda (1751–1821) reminded his readers in 1801, "we really are but the product of education;"[27] a sentence that symbolically concluded the century in its efforts to determine the power of education over shaping nature.

From Natural to Social Monsters

In early modern Spain, writers and physicians saw the monster the way Aristotle had conceived it, as something created outside the intention of nature.[28] And thus, the Spanish Royal Dictionary defined the monster as a "sin of nature, which by defect or excess, does not reach the perfection that it was meant to have." The monster altered the order of nature by behaving and acting "outside nature's intention."[29] Effeminate men and masculine women were all altering the order of nature. Yet, the effeminate man more than the masculine woman was able to corrupt nature, since the monstrosity of the effeminate man was worse. As the Spanish Dominican friar Sanedrio Rifer de Brocaldino (1620–80) saw it, following Aristotle, the woman was an "imperfect male" since she was born against the order of nature. Therefore, her wanting to be a man could be understood better than a male wanting to become an imperfect female.[30] Aristotle, moreover, saw the monster as the effeminate, which became a "failure of purpose in nature;" that is, as he claimed in *Physics*, a deformed being within the bounds of reality. The monster's further failure was not to resemble his progenitors.[31] The expected similarity did not only embrace physical resemblance but also the imitation of the progenitor's actions. By carrying out the improper actions, individuals altered their place in the natural order. Thus, by engaging in sodomy, a perfect male became a monstrous female.[32] This would be a wasted individual since, as Aristotle proclaimed, "if everything which Nature does is done either because it is necessary or else because it is better...testes exist for some purpose ... because it is better that they should exist."[33] In the context of the eighteenth century, such concept of "monstrosity" was conferred upon a sex that was unproductive and therefore an economic waste by potentially causing the depopulation and ruin of the nation.[34]

Invariably, although the realm of the monster was usually associated with the fantastic because of its quality as a "sin of nature," the roots of the monster were in the human and natural worlds. In a way, monsters were products of nature itself and its malfunction; hence, people's fascination with them. But beyond their prurient appeal, monsters inspired throughout the early modern world serious reflection about how family upbringing, education and the child's social environment shaped an individual's sex. Precisely because the monster deviated from this natural order, it helped to delineate it more clearly. In his *Confessions*, Saint Agustine of Hippo (354–430 CE) saw this: Monsters need to exist to define and enhance what is normal.[35] The same way the buffoon served to highlight the beauty of the court, the monster was useful to emphasize the order of nature.[36] This reminds us of Martín Martínez's use of "rare cases" in his manuals: just like monstrosities, rare cases seemed to confirm the normality of the rule.

When it came to natural monstrosities, little explanation was necessary. Monstrosities were part of nature. They served to highlight the immense wonder of nature in its correct and proper course, and that is why they became fascinating to the observer. In the eighteenth century, however, natural monstrosities lost their appeal as wonderful expressions of nature's many possibilities and capabilities. This was partly the result of changing notions of nature and its role in shaping society. In medical and philosophical works, nature was giving a rational and predictable component, originally created by God, but running with regularity, order, and predictability. Therefore, natural monsters such as hermaphrodites became the focus of progressively greater skepticism.

The Spanish view on the hermaphrodite shared the perspective of their French counterparts. If in 1780 the Spanish Royal Dictionary had stated that a hermaphrodite was "the person that has the two sexes of woman and man," in 1787 it listed some "credulous belief" that in Africa there were villages where all were hermaphrodites. This belief, as well as some interpretations of the Genesis story, which stated God created Adam and Eve as one, attached by the spine, were all "a fable and a dream."[37] An influential physician like Ginesta also relegated natural monstrosities such as the hermaphrodite to the realm of fables. Accordingly, he issued his report on hermaphrodites to the Academy of Medicine titled *Observation upon the Found Circumstances in a Pretended Hermaphrodite* in 1798, only a year after the publication of his *The Preserver of Children*.[38] In his report, Ginesta concluded that, in fact, the hermaphrodite he observed was only "a pretended hermaphrodite," and that an individual's irregular genitalia was not the same as someone with both complete sexes. Ginesta shared his French counterparts' views. French and Spanish writers agreed then that what was possible was to find incomplete males and females, men and women not capable of reproduction because they had imperfect reproductive organs. Therefore, improper sexual behavior could only be left to natural impulses – perhaps due to mental disposition rather than a "mixture of sexes" – or improper education.

If in the eighteenth century nature was a much more rational and organized entity than it had ever been, and all variations had to have an explanation obeying a functional principle, then the concept of "natural monster" turned out to be less and less useful. The sodomite became a "social or moral monster" because his improper use of sexuality altered in a perverse way the natural order. And thus the behavior of the sodomite revealed his monstrosity more than any physical appearance. Because the monstrosity came from the unnatural behavior, it may also have been the product of human nurture, not nature. Nature could make an individual incapable of reproduction but never turn him into a sodomite. Particularly, once the anatomists had eliminated ambiguous bodies it was bad education that changed the balance and turned a man into an effeminate and, eventually, a sodomite. The sodomite may not have had any physical elements that characterized him or her as a monster but was still a monster. His "vicious" and "sinful" sexual conduct situated him in a realm of monstrosity that went beyond the physical to embrace the moral, as the gestation of a monster bore in itself moral qualities, those of a sin.

The product of human error, social monsters were more disorienting to the observer than natural monsters. Besides being immoral and sinful, as social monsters those who engaged in wrongful sexual acts were guilty of trying to destroy one of the most precious social acts: the one that allowed human beings to reproduce themselves and thus allow the continuation of society. But how did this social monstrosity happen? Did it follow the rule of all other monstrosities – a reversal of the natural order? – or was it the handiwork of man? The Spanish dictionary of Sebastián Covarrubias (1611) defined the monster not only in physical but also in behavioral terms: a seemingly human appearance revealing in its behavior a monstrous origin. A key behavioral element of the monster was its sexual encounters. Of all possible wrongful sexual practices, the worst was the one that altered the essential aim of nature to perpetuate the species. But if monstrosity was more social than natural, then education, company, and society were to be examined.

As in the anonymous pamphlet discussed at the beginning of this chapter, it was the bad company that allowed a child's natural harmful "passions" to grow. The uncontrolled passions that bad education allowed to flare as children grew up could have unintended consequences and turn them into "social monstrosities."[39] As Pierre Boaistuau (1517–66) had pointed out, the effeminate man was an artificial mutation, more monstrous than the monstrosities of Nature.[40] His argument was that natural monstrosities are spontaneous, while there is intention behind the behavior of an effeminate man. Social monstrosities reflected the intervention of human industry in the course of nature. And thus, Boaistuau brought up the concept of monster as a mental state, someone whose behavior goes against human nature. Monstrosities created by nature itself were tolerated, and in many ways useful to the order of things; monstrosities produced by man were condemned as perverse to the natural order, and in no way useful to it.

Unlearning Nature

Humanists had been particularly insistent about the power of a proper education to direct children's sexual development in the right direction. Early modern Spaniards paid special attention to the opinions of two great humanists: Erasmus of Rotterdam and his follower and friend, the Spaniard Juan Luis Vives (1492–1540).[41] Erasmus shared the faith of the ancient Greeks and Romans that the study of history and literature provided boys with ideal models of masculinity. In addition, a rigorous education would foster self-control in children of both sexes and teach boys and girls to avoid sexual misconduct. Teachers should discourage children from engaging in promiscuous behavior, masturbation, and other vices that could lead to wrongful sexual behavior. Vives warned parents and educators to be strict and vigilant of boys' habits, because they teach each other "obscenities and depravities."[42]

Not every child could receive a humanist education. However, from the aristocracy to the peasantry, all parents had a duty to serve as the first model for their children's sexual identity. At the most basic, girls should grow up to become like their mothers and boys to become like their fathers. Resembling one's progenitor was to maintain social order and avoid moral monstrosities. And thus, the physician Jerónimo Gómez de Huerta (1573–1643), in the introduction to his 1602 translation of Pliny's *Natural History of Animals*, followed Aristotle in establishing that whatever did not reach its perfect state "which it is to engender each to its progenitor" became a monster.[43] It was therefore absolutely essential that parents provide adequate models to children so they could resemble their progenitors. From the late Middle Ages to the eighteenth century, Spanish educational treatises repeatedly cited Saint Augustine of Hippo's warnings that children do what their parents do, and say what their parents say.[44] In the fifteenth century, Saint Vincent Ferrer (1350–1419) asserted "children are like a mirror; if you place the image of the Virgin Mary they will act like the Virgin, if a saint, they act like the saint and if you place the image of a devil they will also mimic the devil."[45] Likewise, in the late sixteenth century Juan de la Cerda saw children as soft wax onto which good or bad customs were "as stamps easily imprint."[46] In 1704, the Jesuit Francesc Baucells declared that children could only become virtuous by following the example of their parents' saintly life and customs.[47] Baucells illustrated the dangers of failing to provide a virtuous model to children by repeating one of Aesop's classic tales. In Baucell's version of the story, a father (a mother in the original) repeatedly failed to punish his son for spending too much time in bad company. Not surprisingly, the son grew up to become a criminal and was eventually condemned to death for his many misdeeds. For his final wish, the son asked to kiss his father, but instead bit off the father's nose and then cried at him: "Damned you father! It is your fault I see myself condemned. If you had corrected and punished me, I would have not been sentenced [to death]."

The dangers to children of bad parenting provide the subtext to the real-life criminal trial in 1769 against Sebastián Leirado. Leirado's story is quite different from that of the fictional English Little Master. Whereas the Little Master's mother encouraged her son's excessive dependence on her, Leirado's illiterate mother delegated her nurturing duties to the soft and older tavern-keeper father. Yet, the two narratives, the one by the author of the pamphlet and the other constructed by the lay authorities in Leirado's case, share basic assumptions about the disastrous consequences of poor parental nurturing, an inappropriate education and the wrong social environment.

From the standpoint of Madrid's authorities, Sebastián's father, José Leirado, was too soft on his son and failed to instill in him manly values. José had fathered Sebastián, his only child, at the mature age for early modern standards of thirty-nine. According to the record of baptism Rosa López, Sebastián's mother and José Leirado wife, was only sixteen when her son was born. This wide age gap between the two parents was probably the reason why José took full charge of his son's education and care since the child's teenage mother was perhaps seen as less capable. This older father, however, failed to discipline his young son, and to choose good models to educate him. José Leirado was literate, and he probably taught his son the basics of reading and writing. Sebastián was an adept love-letter writer, and always signed his depositions as Sebastián Leirado. Yet, José's effort to raise a literate son did not compensate for other major lacks. Like the Little Master's mother, who sent her son to a girls' school, in a rather atypical way, José Leirado sent his fourteen-year-old son to serve as a maid to two famous Madrid actresses. First, Sebastián became the maid of the singer and guitar player María Teresa Garrido, for whom he worked for two years. After working for Garrido, he was servant for a month to the famous actress María Ladvenant.

José Leirado's choice of apprenticeship for his son turned out to be a mistake. The common practice in non-elite households of sending children to be apprentices or domestic servants was meant to give them the training to be good workers. The years young men and women spent as apprentices also had to offer them some moral education, in part because they were to be separated from the overly indulgent parental love that would spoil them. The practice of apprenticeship was far from the ideal. High numbers of premarital pregnancies of female domestics make it clear that this was a time of great sexual vulnerability for young women and men.[48] In many instances, apprentices and maids learned an array of tasks far from the ideal set by their parents, who had entrusted their children to masters the children sometimes barely knew. In the case of Sebastián Leirado, instead of manly tasks, the actresses expected this young boy to perform women's jobs; so, he became the seamstress, hair-stylist and maid for his two mistresses. Moreover, his time working for the two Marias made a great impression on the boy, and Sebastián soon began to dress like them and emulate them in other ways. When Sebastián turned sixteen, José Leirado found a new master for his son, the Italian engraver in Madrid, Mosu Laporta. It is not clear whether Sebastián went to Laporta to learn a trade or to work as a servant, or whether José

Leirado realized theater was not a good influence for his son and that is why he chose a more traditional, perhaps manly, trade. But shortly after moving into the Italian's workshop, Laporta raped Sebastián. The incident "broke his father's heart," as José Leirado declared to authorities. Not long after the event, already infected with syphilis, the effeminate Sebastián began to have sodomitic relations with other men in which he played the part of the passive female.

The upper class English Little Master's education differed significantly from that of the working class Leirado, but both boys ended up as theater-lovers. Throughout early modern Europe, moralists regarded theater as a dangerous and corrupting environment. Critics warned that plays did not provide a decent education or encourage good morals. Instead, the unleashing of the senses and passions onstage fostered similar behavior in audiences.[49] And thus, the theater was the kind of place that impressionable children should avoid. As we saw before, the English Little Master ended up imitating the effeminate gestures and dressing in attires similar to those of the actors and actresses he so admired. Moreover, cross-dressing on stage inspired the same off stage. Characteristically, the mothers of the two most famous cross-dressers in eighteenth-century France, Le Chevalier d'Eon (1728–1810) and Pierre Aymond Dumoret (1678–1725), took their children to the theater. Here, the future cross-dressers learned to dress like actresses, make up their faces and adorn themselves with rich jewelry.[50] Leirado learned all about the glamor of celebrity by helping actresses to dress, apply makeup and adorn themselves with elaborate accessories. So, Leirado became a part-time actress known among neighbors for her love of wearing cheap jewelry and costumes. Madrid's authorities may have established the same link between Leirado's exposure to theater as a child and Sebastián's later transvestism, on and off stage.

It is easy to dismiss the idea that a boy who wore feminine attire and learned effeminate gestures would become a sodomite as a mere cliché. But this fear reveals an important concept of childhood sexuality throughout early modern Europe. Still inspired by Galenic notions of medicine, most theorists on childhood education saw sex as not fixed at birth, and instead as fluid and susceptible to a variety of influences, including clothes. Clothing played a key role in the formative years of the future man or woman. Yet, there was no consensus on exactly what kind of clothing the young child should wear. From outfits that mimicked those of their grown-up counterparts to the kind of clothing advised by Rousseau – loose clothing so "the limbs of a growing body should be entirely free" – clothes made the man or woman.[51] Most writers agreed that the power of clothing went beyond mere fabric. Clothes embodied the individual, they made people fit within their proper group or, on the contrary, the clothes people wore could jeopardize their expected place in their group. Throughout medieval and early modern Europe, sumptuary laws restricting expenditure for food, household items and especially clothing testified to that. But besides mere emulation of others' clothing, and with the expected mimicking behavior, clothing also imprinted something of its characteristics onto the one who inhabited it. In his final arrest Sebastián associated his identity of a man to the clothes he wore at the time of his arrest. The officials who arrested Leirado entered the room and found a man. They gave "faith of that because of his outfit." When asked if he was a man Sebastián seemed to confirm the officials' initial appreciation, responding with the succinct "since you see me dressed as a man then I am." Thus, at the moment of his arrest, the clothes he wore removed the tavern-keeper from his identity as María and instead invested Sebastián Leirado with manhood.

Clothing, more than any other object or possession, is closely identified with "the body of the absent wearer."[52] This was all the more important in the early modern period when identity was not expected to precede the powerful social components that shape it, such as clothing.[53] And thus, in their *autos de fe* the Inquisition forced condemned heretics to wear the sambenitos (penitents' garments) to strip from them their previous identity as good Christians. Although admittedly it was not the sambenito that turned the person into a heretic, once they had put it on the garment became forever associated with that person's guilt. In fact, the sambenitos hung for generation after generation from the inside walls of the heretics' local church as a reminder of their deeds.[54]

Clothing could mold an individual's personality, character, and sense of where they belonged in society. This was particularly true in childhood, when the person was susceptible to the external forces that shaped the personality. Clothing in particular seemed to bear the power to physically transform the person. The court physician Pedro García Brioso warned that the use of the fashionable corset compressed women's "most precious parts for the function of their sex," and thus risked provoking miscarriages and even sterility.[55] The Scottish physician William Buchan (1729–1805), translated into Spanish and widely read among physicians, saw the physical impact of the corset transmitted through generations. According to this physician, this popular garment could remove a woman's nipples, something "contrary to nature," a physical characteristic that once acquired was transmitted from mothers to daughters.[56] This medical approach to the effects of fashion on the body was widely shared by different audiences. As we saw in the previous chapter, when the actor Manuel Garrido dressed as a female dancer, he began to experience the transformation of his male body into a female body. The effeminate clothes of the Little Master discussed at the beginning of this chapter could also have the power to change the man into a non-man, as with the Spanish petimetre. Vain, selfish, full of self-contempt, the petimetre challenged everything that was expected of the virtuous gentleman. The gentleman was required to display the moderation that the "economic project" of the Enlightenment demanded; instead, the petimetre indulged in the excess and frills of effeminate fashion. The expected masculinity of the perfect gentleman, in dress and manners, even had the long-lasting impact of guaranteeing population growth, and thus could be turned into patriotism.[57]

In the stories of the fictional Little Master, and of the real Sebastián Leirado, we saw how wearing girls and women's clothes could change a boy's still-malleable sexuality. The Spanish Jesuit Lorenzo Hervas Panduro (1735–1809) summed up the general consensus that parents should dress infants in gowns that reached to the ankles (*hábitos talares*). When clear signs of a determined sex appeared, clothes had to correspond to the child's sex.[58] The Spanish word "afeminar," or to effeminate, reflected such ideas. According to the Spanish Royal Dictionary, to effeminate meant "to weaken, reduce or change someone to the feminine style and condition, making him abandon the virile ways."[59] As mentioned before, Saint Vincent Ferrer's assertion that "children are like a mirror" suggests a mercurial sexuality subject to change. The fluidity or malleability of children's sexuality made it possible for child-rearing and education to stamp boys and girls with the appropriate male and female traits. But that sexual fluidity meant that children might also learn the traits of the opposite sex. In other words, if not properly guided, a boy's natural tendency to imitate might lead him to an unnatural behavior. Bad education would then leave the damaging effect of stopping nature from its intended harmonic functioning of the two sexes to instead create individuals who would upset the union of the sexes for procreation.

Fatherly Love: The Breastfeeding of "Milkman Antonio Lozano"

The figure of the mother as a key influence in the child's first years emerges as a constant reference in the literature on education from the classic period on. The role of the father was not ignored but received less attention; perhaps because of the assumption that fathers needed less guidance and advise than mothers. Yet, the figure of the father was pivotal in the symbolic world of early modern societies. From the father-figure in the political symbolism of the nation-state to the construction of the ideal view of the artisanal family with the master-father at the head of the workshop, fatherly love appeared as an expression of guided devotion, of discipline and wisdom.[60] It was precisely in the eighteenth-century, when writers began to show a renewed attention towards fatherly love, moving from an image of a rather disciplinary figure to a nurturing, caring father; a transition that some historians have connected with the birth of the new, "democratic" society.[61] At the same time, a heavier responsibility fell upon the father of the family who not only represented "the image of the law through whom the [family] sexuality was structured,"[62] but held an extraordinary role in the literary and artistic imagination of the eighteenth century. At the end of the century, in his "domestic simplicity," the father would represent nature and its endless possibilities for order in the new society.[63] The example I will analyze next, the case of Antonio Lozano, is evidence not only of this new role of the father, caring, loving, and above all "domestic," but how the needs of the advent of a new society could also have an impact on the sexed body of the new father figure.

José Leirado's immense love for his son and the wrong choices he made for his education jeopardized his sexuality by turning Sebastián's role in reproduction upside down. The case of another devoted father gives a different perspective on the limits of fatherly love. It shows that, when guided by the rightful purpose of social utility, nature could adapt and even allowed a male body to evolve into a breastfeeding body. In this case, the rightful practice – directed by love – brought in a physical transformation; an alternation not of the son but of the father's own masculine body. The ideal, immutable, sexual difference could in fact be altered if the goal was social utility. This was the case of Antonio Lozano, the fifty-year-old peasant and schoolteacher from Pampliega, close to Burgos (Spain). In 1786, when the event I am going to relate took place, he was a resident of San Fernando, a village close to Cumaná (in Venezuela). "Milkman Antonio Lozano" was known in the town and beyond for having breastfed one of his twin children, the boy Juan Francisco Cosme, for fourteen years, "particularly with his left breast, in the same way as a woman." He did that for years and had as much milk as "the most abundant woman would have."[64] Unintentionally perhaps, Lozano became the poster child for the "Enlightened time of medicine," as this case of fatherly love showed to scientists and the public in general how, in fact, nature was at the service of social needs.[65]

The first document the case produced, housed in the Archivo General de Indias in Seville, is the letter sent on May 20, 1786, by the governor of Cumaná, Juan Sky de Eustace, to the secretary of state, the count of Floridablanca. The governor related to the minister "the rare phenomena: that Antonio Lozano has raised a son with his breast, abundant with milk just like a woman's breast."[66] The second document was the report that one of the main physicians who examined Lozano, José Castellar y Sans, wrote also in 1786, immediately after his observation. Castellar sent his medical narrative to the San Carlos Royal College of Surgery of Madrid. Castellar submitted a slightly changed version of this report, again to the same Royal College, in 1790.

The story of milkman Antonio Lozano begins on February 6, 1786, when governor Sky de Eustace called on his general administrator of the royal treasury – D. Manuel de Navarrete – to order the surgeon of the royal hospital in the town of Cumaná, José Castellar y Sans, to observe and report on the case of Antonio Lozano. The governor felt this extraordinary case was an example that could "adorn our knowledge of nature transfer to where it can be useful." The governor was responding to the concerns among physicians of rumors concerning the case in dispelling the "credulous ignorance of the populace" who believed Lozano was a hermaphrodite. The governor felt one had to be careful since many have believed in stories "that after they had been confirmed by great men who believed to have seen what it was not there, later on they were declared to be little tales."

On February 11, 1786, Lozano, who had traveled the 370 miles from rural San Fernando to the cosmopolitan coastal town of Cumaná, was called upon at 8:30 in the morning to go to the house of the governor so "a board of dignified subjects could witness the examination of Antonio Lozano's breasts." But the milkman had left Cumaná unexpectedly the night before to return to his village "with the pretext" of some family illness. Castellar, who pointed out the fact that Lozano had "gladly agreed" to the public examination of his breasts, suspected Lozano had grown anxious about it. Although the peasant affirmed he would return to Cumaná, all efforts to bring him back were fruitless. Finally, weeks later on March 4, Lozano returned to Cumaná and to the governor's house for the examination in front of a "dignified audience" of fourteen men, who ranged from priests and military officers, to constables and three physicians, José Castellar y Sans, the French surgeon Juan Mercier, a resident of Cumaná since 1764, and the surgeon Andrés Caballero. The three physicians would examine the milkman to certify whether he was a hermaphrodite and, if not, how he could produce enough milk to nourish his baby son.[67]

The examination went as follows: Dr. Castellar asked Lozano to remove his shirt to show his bare breasts, the left one bigger and fuller than the right. From the left breast, the milkman was asked to squeeze milk into a clean silver spoon so everyone could witness the texture and color of the liquid. And, the surgeon pointed out, Lozano had "tender flesh" just like a woman, no hair on his chest or between his breasts. He "does not sweat and is not a friend of copulation; months pass by without him having any sexual desire." Dr. Caballero, added, on Lozano's "soft voice and gaze, skimpy beard, and small size." He observed the peasant's manners and speech resembled that of a woman as he confessed having to overcome his "natural modesty" to please the governor and allowed himself to be examined by the surgeon. Thus, the surgeons who examined Lozano "found no sign of the other sex; on the contrary, he is always a male (*constantemente varón*)." Proof of this was that Lozano had fathered eight children with his wife, María López. When, at thirty-six, Lozano became the father of twins, "he helped raise them, particularly the boy, breastfeeding him day and night on those occasions his wife was busy with other occupations," and so he did the same with some of his other children, for a total of fourteen years. Lozano's case was not unique, and Dr. Caballero mentioned the 1773 case of another milkman, Pedro de Salas, a carpenter from Seville who nevertheless had better-quality milk than Lozano. Salas' milk was "whiter and more dense." Caballero seemed to be more critical of Lozano's extraordinary deed than his colleague, Dr. Castellar. And so, Caballero pointed at the possibility that Lozano's breastfeeding could revealed "an excessive love for his son," excess being a harmful element to a well-ordered society.[68]

Dr. Castellar quashed discussion of Lozano's possible hermaphroditism in 1790, when he composed a summary of the case for the Royal Academy of Surgery of San Carlos of Madrid.[69] Four years after the examination in Cumaná took place, the surgeon regarded the extraordinary case as an example not only for medical students to study but also as a case where one could see how perhaps the need to preserve the family was so intense as to change the natural body. In his 1790 report Castellar also altered the family story in order to shape the narrative as a heroic effort of Lozano, not unlike the woman of valor in the Bible, who overcomes her feeble nature to save her family. In this version of the events, Castellar did not mention the other children Lozano had breastfed and instead focused on the twin boy. This time, the reason for his breastfeeding was not the wife's other occupations but her lack of milk and the couple's extreme poverty. Moreover, Castellar also added two elements not present in the initial report. First, he offered a detailed anatomical and physiological explanation of how breastfeeding was physically possible for a man (adding how it was also possible among other mammals such as the case of the bull who breastfed a calf). Second, he related how Lozano's breastfeeding altered his role in reproduction since, though still being a man, he lost interest in intercourse and had become impotent.

The take-home analysis of the 1790 report, missing in the 1786 version, was that Castellar proposed Lozano's case first as an example of the workings and laws of "human nature and how they can shed light onto people to get rid of the stupid fanaticism in which they sleep satisfied and with which they occupy their sentiments." The case of Lozano also served as an inspiration for physicians and surgeons to have more men emulate "the milkman Lozano" in order to be "useful to humanity." In his almost euphoric report Castellar pointed out that finally "we can say the happy day of the Enlightened time of medicine has arrived," a time in which the "economy of nature" would adapt to the needs of society. Castellar's proposal did not have the expected reaction from the Academy. The physician who evaluated the proposal, José Ribes, succinctly wrote advising against Castellar's plan since "women have better disposition than men" for breastfeeding. Eight years later, in October 1798, Castellar reported the case again to the Royal Academy of Surgery of San Carlos: a report that likely yielded a reaction similar to Ribes'.[70]

The case of "the milkman Lozano" became proof for the enlightened public of how the laws of nature conformed to the principle of social utility. A characteristic of the European Enlightenment, the concept of "useful knowledge" was particularly important for the Spanish *ilustrados*, who believed social utility could guarantee man's ultimate goal of shaping nature to bring individual and collective happiness.[71] Nature, thus, was at the center of the large scheme of the Enlightenment. Nature was not capricious or inconstant but responded to the needs and demands of society. Every part of the natural world had its intended place in the overall functioning of this precious machine. This basic principle translated among humans into social utility. Even the sometimes-uncanny power of nature could be reverted to its proper and domesticated order when it obeyed to the needs of social utility. Both in nature and society, bodies needed to be useful, or *útil*, defined as "profit, convenience; interest of product that is drawn from something physical or moral."[72]

The body's social expression – that is, the individual's actions and social practices – had to be in harmony with the natural system, a principle every human interaction had to obey. Above all, the most basic human interaction, the union of a man and a woman that resulted in the gestation of a new human being, had to follow such principle of utility. The separation of the sexes, necessary for reproduction, allowed society to serve nature in fulfilling its ultimate goal, the survival of the species. Yet, in supporting this definition, these same thinkers forced upon nature notions and concepts that betrayed a political agenda directed to satisfy governmental needs. It was a call to see in nature the reflection of society's own virtues, which included notions of what a man and woman should or should not be: how they should or should not act.

In defining sexual difference and its limits in relation to nature and society, two key concepts, reason and imagination, played an important role. Throughout the eighteenth century, the *ilustrados* debated whether the power of imagination could influence and even alter biological givens. That was not something new of the eighteenth century. The power of imagination to ignite passions of all kinds had been a recurrent topic in early modern literature, from Saint Augustine to Descartes.[73] The range of passions was wide and embraced all kinds of emotions, from pain and fear to pleasure and desire.[74] In his *De l'usage des passions* (1641) (*The Use of Passions*), the French philosopher Jean Francois Senault (1601–72) pointed at how the usage of one's imagination may prove to be useful or harmful to the body. Bishop Edward Reynolds (1599–1676) also saw that "reason and discourse," have their dependence "on the organs and faculties of the body."[75] While these seventeenth-century philosophers had examined the problem of the symbiotic relationship between body and passion, it was in the eighteenth century that the concept of imagination takes an important role in its relation to both reason and reality.[76]

Eighteenth-century concepts of creativity, inspiration, and genius, brought in the question of how exactly the relation between reason and imagination was expected to work. Think of Giambattista Vico's experimental "poetic wisdom," in his magnum opus *Scienza nuova* (The New Science) (1725), or the original form of knowledge by which humans truly comprehend the world. To Vico, reason does not create poetic wisdom; instead, it is the result of human imagination, closer to the soul and the body.[77] Vico, who was particularly influential among the *ilustrados*, offered thus a prominent role to imagination, a characteristic of the thought of the eighteenth century.[78] In his *Encyclopédie* article on "Imagination" (1765) Voltaire (1694–1778), the pen-name of Françoise-Marie Arouet, further explored the problematic relationship between reason and imagination, and found a solution by differentiating passive from active imagination. The passive imagination imprints into the mind things that are external to it. It does not change or alter what is given. In the passive imagination, it was the image that possessed the individual, and not the other way around. The individual possessing a passive imagination, usually a woman, had little control over it. Of all the senses used to feed passive imagination, vision was a particularly vulnerable one, as the individual almost automatically would respond to an image by developing an emotion that had an immediate impact on the physical body. Hence, the theory of maternal imagination, which follows Hippocrates and Aristotle in arguing that the mother's imagination during conception and gestation – what she saw, or even, dreamt – could stamp onto the fetus particular physical characteristics.[79] Despite the claim of eighteenth-century physicians to rational thinking, many still subscribed to the theory of maternal imagination.[80]

In contrast to passive imagination, the bearer of active imagination was in control of his thoughts and creativity. Generally a man, he was able to arrange images in multiple and sophisticated ways. Active imagination was then the source of creativity and productivity. It was behind artistic expression and scientific invention. In his *Regles pour la direction de l'esprit* ("Rules for the Direction of the Mind") and *Les passions de l'âme* ("Passions of the Soul"), Descartes had studied habit and the repetition of actions, such as speech. Descartes agreed with Locke's central point: a child's education could alter the passive imagination, as defined by Voltaire.[81] In an interesting way, Descartes' point on repetition as a way of learning appears as a similar principle to the one applied by feminist Judith Butler in looking at how repeated performance of gender may change the meaning of sex. According to Butler, gender "as an act" is both intentional and performative: "a dramatic and contingent construction of meaning."[82] What is the drive behind habit and such repeated performance? For Descartes, it is the desire to communicate; for Butler, the motor behind "gender performance" is a "corporeal project," the "strategy of survival within compulsory systems."[83] One could say there are drives that are more punishable than others. Thus, the reasons that moved the Bible's Judith to remove her widow's garments and adorn herself with jewels and rich clothing as a means to liberating her people, were far less punishable than the unnamed dancer in the Bible, daughter of Herodias. Therefore, imagination and passion, and their power to impact the body, ultimately are guided by habit and intention.

Despite his interest in spelling out the social impact of one or the other type of imagination, Voltaire did not explain how the need for social utility could alter the nature and value of both types of imaginations. It is in the context of the Spanish Enlightenment, more practical than its French counterpart, that the usefulness of things, imagination included, comes to the foreground to shape the *ilustrados*' understanding of the relation between nature and society.[84] Social utility could direct nature to its proper role, and be so powerful as to make passive imagination into active. After all, imagination, passive or active, could unleash its destructive power if not guided by reason and, most importantly, by social utility. Social utility became the foundation for social and political structures. When guided by the rightful purpose of social utility, imagination could alter nature in the most unexpected and even uncanny ways. As understood by Sigmund Freud the uncanny is this sense of strangeness that one has when something alluring and threatening brings to the mind a sense of familiarity and even hominess.[85] Nature appeared to unleash its most uncanny aspect when it allowed a male body to evolve into a breast-feeding body. The latter, which in principle could threaten the ideal of an absolute sexual difference, could revert to its expected natural and social role when guided by social utility. As in the case of milkman Lozano, social utility could transform the threatening male breastfeeding body into a nurturing body; it could marry natural and human laws with the *ilustrados'* expected "victory over nature."

An interesting aftermath in the line of interpretations of the case of the milkman Lozano is the writing of Alexander von Humboldt (1769–1859), who found the case relevant enough to include it in the first volume of his *Personal Narrative of Travels to the Equinoctial Regions of the New Continent during the years 1799–1824.*[86] Humboldt offered a third possible interpretation, one that moreover gained further retelling of the story into the nineteenth century. Humboldt arrived in Arenas (rather than San Fernando, where the governor's letter had claimed the milkman lived) in 1799, thirteen years after Lozano had appeared before the governor. Humboldt described Lozano's ability to breastfeed as "a physiological phenomena that captures the imagination of those who follow the known laws of nature," an ability that nonetheless did not compromise Lozano's masculinity. The incombustible naturist related how other societies witnessed similar events without risking themselves to fall into a reversal order of nature. For instance, anatomists of St. Petersburg observed how, among the common people in Russia, more than in the "meridional nations," one could find men whose breast produced milk. Humboldt is quick to clarify that "Russians have never been considered either weak or effeminate."[87]

Humboldt's eagerness to provide a compelling narrative of Lozano's case made him fall into some inconsistencies, or overlooked facts. Instead of calling Lozano Antonio, Humboldt refers to the milkman as Lorenzo, a descendant of Spaniards, instead of a Spaniard himself. Humboldt also described a younger man of thirty-two and explained the wife had fallen sick and was unable to breastfeed – which seems to follow Castellar's 1790 version of the story. Humboldt explained that Lozano went to Cumaná to be examined by Humboldt's travel companion, the French physician and anatomist Aimé Bonpland (1773–1858), who found Lozano's breasts large and wrinkled like an old woman's from all the breastfeeding he had endured for almost fourteen years. This examination may in fact had happened but if it did it was nevertheless more than a decade after he appeared before Dr. Castellar and the rest of the committee of "dignified men."

Humboldt's narrative revealed how the case of the milkman Lozano had become part of the popular imagination. It satisfied the curiosity of those who wondered whether in fact nurture could overcome nature. The reasons why, however, were not established and seemed to change in different tellings of the story. It is partly the quality of the myth of the milkman in folklore that persisted well into the nineteenth and twentieth centuries, of "the ambiguity of the symbol, its polysemy and plurality."[88] The myth must, while remaining universal, adapt to each narrator's story and voice. The case of Lozano fits within key worries in the age of the Enlightenment: sexual difference and the division of work, reason and imagination, social utility, and most of all what the historian Joan Scott has called "the frenetic preoccupation with the breast" in the eighteenth century.[89] The Spanish monarchy was not immune to such preoccupation. Breasts identified women as nurturers, a role that men like Lozano took over, thus questioning the division of work and sex. Nature could be changed and reverted. Perhaps the case of the breastfeeding man was not unlike the image of the virile woman in the Bible who, for the sake of her family, could alter her feeble nature and become a man, even if temporarily, to provide for her family.[90]

If the Enlightenment intended to unite the individual and the community, the breast, even if it was the male breast, seemed to bring it all together. Lozano's passion was well guided. The Enlightenment focus on social utility as a way to guarantee social reproduction in fact could have the unintended result of altering biological givens, and in a way jeopardizing that same reproduction. In the case of Lozano, the needs of reproduction and nurture brought all its different narratives to the main moral of the story: social utility can alter nature. A radical change from previous preoccupations with male bodies that performed women's functions: bodies that breastfed or menstruated. Jewish men who were thought to menstruate, or those whose penises vanished, demonstrated an apprehension at how the natural world could be disrupted.[91] In Lozano's case, breastfeeding within the blessing of the family conformed to the enlightened efforts to adapt bodies to social (and natural) needs.[92]

The proposal to encourage men to breastfeed illustrates that social utility was a strong enough ideal to merit altering men's jobs and, with this, jeopardizing their biological differences. Yet, some enlightened observers still feared nature's lack of predictability. One of them was Narciso Esparragosa y Gallardo, the physician who in 1803 examined the supposed hermaphrodite Juana Aguilar, whom he called "Juana la Larga" (Long Juana). The Real Audiencia (Royal Court) prosecuted Aguilar in 1799 in Guatemala City for the crimes of *concubinage* (sexual relations outside marriage) and sodomy. The *Real Protomedicato* (the medical tribunal) in the colonies had commissioned Esparragosa to examine Aguilar and to determine whether she was a hermaphrodite. Esparragosa found she had an unusually enlarged clitoris that allowed her to have sexual relationships both as a man and as a woman.[93] Influenced by Buffon who conceived the existence of individuals who were like some bees who had neutral sex, Esparragosa concluded Aguilar was not a woman or a man but "neutral."[94] The physician saw Aguilar's ambiguous sex as a "prank" (travesura) of nature: "we should not doubt this to be the effect of those pranks with which nature usually seems to disturb its laws." This was a case where imagination and nature in the New World had a different outcome than Lozano's, as the context of the family was missing removing then the altered body from its purposeful role.[95]

There is another element in the case of Aguilar that I have not discussed so far, the issue of race. Interestingly, the race of Aguilar who was a mestiza, the offspring of a Spaniard and a native of the colonies, was an element that Esparragosa did not address directly. Race is also absent in most of the discussions of the physicians and anatomists I examine in this book. The work of many of these professionals influenced the discourse in the American colonies, but their theories and practices of medicine in the Iberian Peninsula did not include race. This is partly because the racial component of the individuals examined by physicians was quite homogenous. However, preliminary research done by María Elena Martínez on the Spanish American colonies reveals that race became part of the overall aim of medical authorities in the Spanish world of the eighteenth century to match the anatomical difference of the sexes with heterosexual goals.[96] Physicians in the colonies engaged in a project that was meant to "naturalize" the body, measuring race formation from the same perspective as they did sex difference. As María Elena Martínez's study of Aguilar's case revealed "what defined a man and a woman, and what constituted being white, black and 'in-between' the sciences of sex and the sciences of race came together in the sciences of reproduction."[97] Race became a tangible expression of a natural source that adapted to reproduction and social utility.

Aguilar's sexual ambiguity blended with her mixed race making her (or him) even more an in-between individual.[98] In contrast with the reality of a racial component in the New World that was far from static and certain, we find that the representation of race dwelled on the fantasy of the predictability of race. Such desire to pin down race just like sex, as predictable was, in fact, expressed in the late eighteenth-century casta paintings, the Mexican pictorial genre that depicted the several racial combinations among Spaniards, Natives of the Americas and Africans. The colorful canvas, reflecting the hierarchical system of "castas," revealed the fascination with an orderly world that showed the many predictable variations of the union of different races.[99] Perhaps Esparragosa's conclusion regarding Aguilar's sex and race was meant to not jeopardize the heterosexual project of the Enlightenment. Aguilar's race and sex both became a prank of nature, the exception to the natural rules and laws. Both in terms of sex and race, Aguilar was an "in-between" individual, difficult to classify, unable to reproduce. As a result, not even social utility could always provide the answer to sexual difference, as sometimes nature seemed all unpredictable and overruling. The same question and quest over what was the exact relationship between nature and society would drive the writings of lawmakers at the end of the eighteenth century.

4   The Body of Law: Legislating Sex
in Eighteenth-Century Spain

The shaping of sex and gender in the legal setting in eighteenth-century Spain needs to be understood in the context of the progressive separation between religious and civil concerns in lay tribunals and how bodies, clearly defined as male and female, allowed this division. The theory and practice of law revealed the difficulty of creating a body of law that would consistently judge all crimes in the way they threatened the social order, not so much on the corruption of morals.[1] This separation of crime from sin responded to a functional and utilitarian view of society, by which the State's "ultimate goal is the security of its citizens."[2] Laws had to work toward securing citizens' well-being, which translated into the establishment of a judicial system that guaranteed social as well as human reproduction. Building on the arguments of anatomists and physicians, eighteenth-century jurists increasingly relied on a legal body that was clearly defined as male or female. Ambiguous bodies threatened social prosperity. As Montesquieu warned, where women's fickle tastes prevail "there will be a single sex, and we will all be women in spirit; and if our appearance changed overnight, no one would notice."[3] In Montesquieu's argument, it was implicit that men who became women would alter the place of each of the sexes in the economy of creation, ultimately ruining society.[4] In particular, effeminate men could fall into the practice of sodomy, a crime difficult to separate from its moral and religious connotations. This fact further threatened the separation of state and church, which was at the very basis of the Enlightenment project.

Lawmakers and judges had to deal with crimes that threatened society and the natural order separately from those that attacked religion. As Benito Jerónimo Feijóo had alerted his readers: "the theologian examines the intrinsic malice of an act, the jurist considers the consequences it has for the public."[5] The law would punish those individuals who threatened nature and society by considering the impact that the crime had upon society's order, rather than measuring the crime's moral implication. It was a new model in the judicial system meant to serve both nature and society, separating them from what was divine. This was a process that represented "the first step towards the secularization of criminal law in Spain," when the concept of crime became progressively detached from sin.[6] It was also the framework for theorists such as Michel Foucault, who saw in the eighteenth century the transition toward a punitive system that removed sin from crime as a separation of church and state.

The practice of secularizing crimes became a difficult task for all those involved. Secular law was based on the submission of divine reason to human reason. Humans' ability to reason was their true nature, their highest power, and the root to human progress. Since God did not intercede in the world, nature's laws were all the more important. There were instances, however, when it was not possible to clearly separate divine from natural and human laws. Some crimes seemed to challenge the division between the natural, social, and religious, equally threatening all three orders. In this respect, of all the crimes under scrutiny, sexual crimes in particular made lawmakers' and legislators' intentions difficult to put into practice. Sexual crimes involved in one way or another the act necessary for the reproduction of humans. This was an act paramount to the continuation and survival of society, but it was also a divine mandate. This double component became a paradox for those writing and practicing law: how could one judge sexual crimes if the scope of their damage went beyond the social well-being to also affect the moral and religious order? Besides the separation of church and state, sexual crimes also called into question the clear division of the sexes. For anatomists, distinctive physical differences separated the two sexes. To legislators, the tasks that men and women performed – divided according to sex – made them what they were and reflected their different natures. If some sexual crimes altered this sexual division of work, expressed in terms of their usefulness to society, was this a reflection of an altered natural division of the sexes? Overall, the judgment of sexual crimes brought to the surface the difficulties of creating a human law guided by reason and nature, but separated from religion.

In this chapter I will analyze how a specific sexual behavior, the sodomitic act, put sexual difference and the separation of sin from crime into question. First of all, the sodomite on trial would reclaim the ambiguous body by declaring she, or most frequently he, had a mixture of sexes, and therefore was not master of his sexual conduct. Second, sodomy troubled legislators, because it was a crime that not only altered the ideal sexual division between men and women but also challenged the growing secularization of the law in the eighteenth century. As the seventeenth-century Spanish theologian Martín de Torrecilla acknowledged, sodomy was a "sin against nature" and "an act of lust against the natural order that is required for procreation."[7] At the end of the century, sodomy was still the one and only sexual crime that stubbornly resisted the death penalty. In fact, laws in France, England, and Italy, as well as in Spain, favored the punishment of this crime with capital punishment.[8] Although many times the death sentence was not applied, most legislators regarded it as a fair punishment. It was a crime that, as the lawyer of the Parlement of Paris Pierre François Muyart de Vouglans (1713–91) stated, "tends to violate the rules prescribed by nature for reproduction."[9] It offended against the basis of natural and social order, as well as a crucial divine mandate: the obligation on men and women to reproduce themselves. It was precisely such a challenge to the natural order that made sodomy a crime that trespassed the division between church and state. It also made sodomy a highly punishable social crime.

Sodomy threatened both nature's intentions and the logic of natural laws. It also attempted against another basic principle: both nature and society were subordinated to divine laws, which dictated their functioning, and organization. It follows that divinity was the inner nature of both the natural and social world. The utility of things had to be ultimately truthful to their inner, divine, essence. Sodomy attacked the very core of public well-being by altering the fundamental sexual division of work, by which men and women produce new offspring to guarantee the wealth of the nation. Thus, sodomy explicitly threatened the essence of nature and society by altering the bases of reproduction itself and the "economy of creation," deeply rooted in religious precepts. Men and women, as Martín Martínez pointed out, had to follow this divine mandate and "act according to the laws imposed by their master and creator."[10] By threatening both divine and natural laws, sodomy was a crime that combined judicial and religious concerns. Natural, divine, and social laws would meld and become indistinguishable. Reason ultimately had to be subordinated to the Divine.

We need to study the legislation of sodomy and its difficulties in separating natural, human, and divine laws in relation to two distinct developments in the eighteenth century. First, in relation to the development of civil law and the growing competition between secular and religious courts, typical of state formation in early modern Europe. Second, we need to analyze it in the context of enlightened ideas, the origins of law in nature, and the necessity for laws to match nature's intentions.[11] Utility, how bodies needed to become useful to society, was a precept started by anatomists and educators but finally receiving the stamp of legislators. Changing views of nature in the eighteenth century pointed at nature as a universal and functional body whereby everything it created had a use and a purpose. Regardless of how much society intervened, it was nature that drove the drafting of laws.

As such, human law interpreted nature's own laws to establish the social order. As the Spanish jurisconsult Antonio Xavier Pérez y López (1736–92) stated in 1785, justice "derives from the nature of things," which ultimately dictated "the true spirit of laws."[12] He thus followed Montesquieu in believing that nature had to guide law. However, law would also help humans to understand nature and to re-establish the natural order once man had attempted to destroy or alter it. The ultimate goal was for human laws to reinterpret nature in order to offer a better understanding of the relationship between nature and humans. By following the law, individuals were able to create order in a world that was prone to disorder and inconsistency. As the political writer José Agustín Ibañez de la Rentería (1751–1826) stated in 1783, "we are slaves to the laws to be truly free."[13] Laws then made humans free by giving them order.

The natural origin of laws while offering authority to the jurist also brought its own challenges, since nature was after all the most immediate expression of the making of the divine. The crime of sodomy made this contradiction all the more evident. Medieval Thomistic notions of natural law based on the doctrine of Saint Thomas of Aquinas had provided a framework for understanding and judging "sins against nature," such as sodomy. To Aquinas, "things act according to their nature, they derive their proper acts and ends according to the law that is written into their nature." This natural law was also a reflection of the eternal law "in their own natures."[14] Natural law guided the legislator in understanding that there were some acts that, regardless of the circumstances, were universally punishable because they threatened the divine law, superior to any other law. Accordingly, eighteenth-century legislators were still unable to disconnect sodomy from its religious roots since sodomy was "a sin against grace, reason, and nature."[15] Sodomy altered the order of nature. But even in this perversion of the natural order, humans were altering their fundamental relationship with the divine. Sodomy threatened the place of the human in the universal order and it also threatened the division of the sexes that guaranteed this universal order in the continuation of the species. The judging of sodomy proved that enlightened views of nature were not disconnected from divine notions of nature. Nature's intention could not be detached from how these judgments reflected God's design.

Sex, Gender and Judgment

In the judgment of crimes lawmakers had to get rid of their own legal fable. Just as anatomists fought the fable of sex change by removing the hermaphrodite from medical discussions, leaving it to the world of fantastic imagination of the populace, equally lawmakers created a body of law that was also formed by clearly defined bodies. In the practice of law, judges and lawyers established a legitimate body, one that was recognized as such before the law as either a man or a woman. This legitimate body was clearly defined in its anatomy. If laws guaranteed the "security of its citizens," only bodies that were labeled male or female could be useful to society and provide for such security. Legislators thus needed to make sure they were able to determine whether the accused was a "perfect man" or woman and, second, once the body was determined then the process of reeducating them had to apply. It was not enough to eliminate an ambiguous body from the courthouse, the body needed to perform and act in accordance with its sex. Education would make possible that reformed criminals would contribute again to the social well-being. However, this did not come easily. Religion and morals were not the only components that affected an individual's sex; lawmakers also had to face the difficulty of judging someone's legitimate body just by observing the facts. Laws could only punish those whose "actions opposed the achievement to such goal."[16] Such functional view of society bore in it the emphasis on judging by actions, rather than condemning personal traits and by establishment of evidence through the interpretations of facts.

Interpreting facts led to evidence. When measuring and valuing evidence, judges had to apply their own discernment, or the ability to identify what was true, important in matters of religion but also in lay tribunals. Acceptable standards of proof, reason, and logic influenced the practice of law and its increasing emphasis on proof. Based on this culture of fact, observation and the seeking for proof provided the basis for any judgment. The theory of legal proof appeared particularly important in continental Europe; unlike in England, which had a system based on the jury, the judge had the ultimate say in the sentence and punishment of a crime. Judges would then read and use legal theory works to guide them. Equally, medical knowledge and evidence were as important in providing evidence for judges. Hence, the rise of medical knowledge as a source of authority permeated the legal arena, with a structure of legal proof that facilitated and welcomed the need for such specialists. Facts, however, were not as tangible as judges wished. Even in the case of sodomy, the judge needed to measure all the components that made up the "logic of the crime," such as the influence of the climate, the character of each nationality and, most of all, the education that the accused had received. Education took a prominent role in correcting sexual behavior; even in cases such as sodomy, a social crime was the product of unleashed passions. Everyone from lawyers to philosophers and religious writers believed that idleness and mendacity fueled all passions that were not directed toward a useful end. The remedy to this problem was to guarantee that children would receive a good education from their early years on. In this respect, writers made an important connection between the sexual division of work and the role of men and women in reproduction. Love of work in childhood would allow grown men to stay out of trouble, and that included becoming the perpetrators of sexual crimes. A good upbringing would guarantee the love of work as an antidote to all morally wrongful passions and deeds.

Spanish lawmakers faced problems similar to the anatomists' as the physical evidence did not match the social part of what it meant to be a man and a woman. Yet, if in theory social norms were meant to be true to nature and its laws, the reality was an increasing awareness of the difficulty of knowing true nature as social norms demanded artifice and "performance."[17] The French philosopher Denis Diderot (1713–84) shared this preoccupation with the Spaniard Benito Jerónimo Feijóo by establishing that appearances, while necessary to regulate social relations, could ultimately hide a person's "true nature." Diderot highlighted the importance of acquiring knowledge through the senses, a main premise of John Locke in his *An Essay Concerning Human Understanding* (1690).[18] To Locke, an author whom Diderot defined as a "comprehensive, penetrating, precise intellect," all thoughts were "innate" ideas coming from tangible sources.[19] However, in addition to observing and judging things based not only on their appearance, the observer also relied on rearing and experience acquired since childhood, and even touch and smell. Diderot agreed with Locke that the senses are everything, and the custom, the habit and the ease with which one perceives things makes the correlation between the thing observed, human senses and the acquisition of knowledge as direct and "natural." Although we experience innate feelings of right and wrong after observation, education can be powerful enough to foster systems of belief that can alter those innate feelings and obscure the truth. According to Diderot, one judges by appearances, which are "the result of the perception of relations and it is in the indetermination of these relations, the ease with which they are perceived," that knowledge is created.[20]

Feijóo, who probably did not read Diderot but read and approved of Locke's empiricism, would have agreed with Diderot about the importance of tangible sources in acquiring knowledge and of the privileged place of medicine as the profession that most relied on observation to reach general theories. Even metaphysics, Diderot wrote, "belongs only to the man who has practiced medicine for a long time, he alone has seen the phenomena, the machine quiet or furious, weak or full of vigor, sound or shattered, delirious or well-regulated, successively imbecile, enlightened, torpid, noisy, dumb, lethargic, acting, living and dead."[21] Diderot and Feijóo both agreed that observation, of which physicians were masters, could guide lawyers to decide what was the product of nature or of education when trying to grasp the workings of such variable human machines. Unlike Diderot, however, Feijóo still believed that some natural and innate feelings had to ultimately guide humans to discern good from bad, even if a bad education and system of beliefs had misled them into falling for deceptive appearances. Physicians could be deceived or worst still they could be deceitful, "fooling almost the entire world." Lawyers who relied on the verdicts of physicians would be deceived as well.[22]

If the essence of knowledge involved being able to distinguish deceitful appearances from truthful reality, this also implied the need to know the essence of things that went beyond their external representation and reflection. As humans, we need to tell apart the true nature of individuals from their external appearances. And yet, we can only discuss nature as appearance, or at least the way it looks to us in our daily life.[23] Experience, Martínez's *experiencia*, is intrinsically connected with the way we experience nature. This realization in the eighteenth century made the Platonic ideal of understanding the view of things as simple reflections in form of what is true and formless even more impossible. If experience is the same as the essence of nature, then experience is nature and vice versa. And thus, as the twentieth-century Spanish philosopher Xavier Zubiri explained, knowledge, although intuitive, is also the product of the experience that sharpens the mental ability to discern. As Zubiri points out, to be able to tell essence from appearance the individual "is not simply in front of things, but he moves among them, deciding in each case about what they are."[24] Therefore, the power of the decision that allows someone to discern the real from what only appears to be real is personal and intimate. This may not have been so unique to the eighteenth century, but rather a continuation of a long-standing preoccupation with truth and authenticity.[25] What is characteristic of the eighteenth century is the uneasiness of living with this precept. There are no bases and tangible proof. Appearances can fool the eye. The impossibility of discovering the essence of things, the substance, appears all the more problematic: if one accepts appearances as true, it may well be only because they appear to be true.

In this context of telling apart what is appearance and what is the truthful "essence" of the individual, the concept of "judgment" becomes crucial. As rational beings, humans have the capacity to judge based on what they perceive. However, it is ultimately judgment, not perception, that can become deceitful. The Portuguese philosopher and translator of Locke's work, Luis António Verney (1713–92), alerted the reader that the soul knows everything, but human knowledge is vulnerable to error: individuals need to make judgments based on evidence acquired through their senses. Many circumstances and conditions can make one person judge something as wrongful while another may decide the action to be good. That is why Verney asked his reader to judge by comparing one idea with the other and act similarly to judges: compare present with past actions and results, based on evidence. Even after this comparison, human judgment can err, because as humans we tend to ignore the essence of things.

Locke posited that humans acquire knowledge of the physical world through their senses. According to Locke, individuals reach general knowledge through the experience and perception of things, which is only deducted by the senses and naming the particular. This knowledge, however, is always incomplete and open to error. Knowledge of God, on the other hand, is certain since this is a knowledge that cannot be perceived through the senses and thus falls into the category of what Locke labeled "substance," where he also placed moral knowledge. According to the Spanish philosopher and royal physician to Ferdinand VI Andrés Piquer (1711–72), we cannot know the essence of things because the origin of human knowledge derives from what we learn through the senses. Piquer, although agreeing with Locke on many points, still believed senses could not reveal "the intimate being of things, but only their forms."[26] Piquer argued this was after all what, long before Locke, Thomas Aquinas had stated in his *Summa Theologica*.[27] If Piquer agreed with Locke on the limits of knowledge and the inability to acquire absolute knowledge, he also believed there is an "intuitive knowledge" of what is "real and truthful." Piquer reached this conclusion by separating reason from "revealed truth." Therefore, the "essence" of things could only be divine. While Locke also thought of two types of knowledge, he still believed that knowledge of material things could only be achieved through the senses. Rather, Piquer concluded that, while there is a level of knowledge of things acquired through the senses, ultimately only God could offer knowledge of the essence of all things. The discussion above reveals the uneasy relationship scientists like Piquer had with the new science. Observation was open to error and, ultimately and reluctantly, Spanish scientists and philosophers who followed the new science had to admit they would not achieve a resolution between them and the old guard, as well as between truth and skepticism.

The importance of judging from experience and the information that the senses give us about things and actions, while open to error, was particularly relevant in the practice of law. The law was ultimately meant to resolve the dilemma of anatomists: the paradoxical relationship between the physical body and the body as it appeared, moved and acted in society. The system of law, therefore, ended up establishing what the twentieth-century sociologist Pierre Bourdieu described as "the inevitable compromise between the real body and the ideal, legitimate body."[28] Lawyers and judges had to be sure their judgments were correct, and that they were not deceived by appearances that were hiding the true essence of an action. Piquer alerted his reader that one comes to wrong judgments because the mind is full of what he called "preoccupations," or preconceptions of the way things are. The rearing and education that parents and family gave individuals shaped such preoccupations. This inadequate judgment not only affected those who needed to judge an action, but also those who engaged in actions that were harmful. The law, however, had to be able to decide in which measure these "preoccupations" compromised someone's ability to be responsible for his or her actions.

The legislation of sex, of determining who was a man or a woman, came from unlawful actions and behaviors, which usually forced the law to intervene to establish the sex of the accused. It was, then, in the practice of law that all the elements discussed up to here came to play: the question of what shaped difference, whether nature or nurture; the moral component in shaping sex difference; and the problematic of discerning truth from appearance. In particular, separating what was natural and what was the product of education in order to judge a crime and its punishment had become an increasingly important aspect of the legislator's job at the end of the eighteenth century. In particular, the new group of jurists followed the ideas of the Italian Cesare Beccaria (1738–94) and his emphasis in determining the reasons why some acted wrongfully to measure the punishment for a given crime.

In a concise work of barely over 100 pages, in *Dei delitti e delle pene* (On Crimes and Punishments) first published anonymously in 1764, Beccaria was able to bring together the essence of the enlightened thought on laws.[29] In it, Beccaria synthesizes some of the major concerns of the Enlightenment, from Montesquieu's system of laws to Rousseau's concept of the social contract.[30] In particular, Beccaria's utilitarian view of punishment and the usefulness of laws, a premise dear to the philosophes, permeated the entire book and is the core element that unites it. The center of Beccaria's treatise, the fairness of punishment and its utility to society resonated in all European court, which almost unanimously welcomed Beccaria's work. Catherine the Great invited Beccaria to be a legal adviser to her penal reform program (an invitation he declined), and the most influential philosophes of the Parisian scene invited the young writer to discuss his work with them. In Spain Beccaria's work also became an instant success.[31] Juan Antonio de las Casas translated it in 1774 into Spanish as *Tratado de los delitos y las penas*. Three years later, in 1777 the Spanish Inquisition included Beccaria's manual on its list of prohibited books.[32] Regardless of the prohibition, Beccaria's work and his "natural rationalistic" approach to the law made him an extremely influential writer among those *ilustrados* who aimed at discarding the scholastic tradition. Beccaria echoes the belief that all judgments had to be valued in their utility. Evidence had to be subordinated to social utility.

Spanish jurists welcomed Beccaria's humanistic approach to punishment combined with a view of the social body, which becomes useful by the way its members interrelate to each other "each and every individual is bound to society which in turn is bound to each of its members, a bond which nature dictates."[33] This humanistic approach was not totally disconnected from a religious component. In spite of the potential heretical component of *Crimes and Punishments* (which was at the center of the Inquisition's prohibition of the book) the truth is that Beccaria acknowledged the divine component of nature and society, a fact that made his argument all the more acceptable to Spanish *ilustrados*. To Beccaria one should not worry much about divine justice since, just like natural justice, both 'are in essence unchangeable and constant, the relationship among them always remains the same." The jurist must let natural and divine justice alone and focus on human justice, which is constantly changing "depending whether the action in question is essential or useful to society." He thus emphasized the need to keep "human justice" separated from divine and natural justice, as the only way for reason to reign in "public affairs." Beccaria then pronounced a sentence that sounds utterly familiar to the Spanish reader, one that Feijóo pronounced four decades before Beccaria: "It is up to the theologian to establish the boundaries of injustice and justice in respect to the intrinsic evil or goodness of an act. It is up to the experts of public law and the State to denote the domains of political justice and injustice – that is what is useful or harmful to society." Did Beccaria read Feijóo? We do not know. What is interesting to point at is that Feijóo established forty years before Beccaria the essence of the mechanism of the legal system of the enlightenment: "Give to Caesar what is Caesar's, and to God what is God's."[34] And yet, as Beccaria himself proclaimed: "everyone understands how much purely political virtue must surrender to the immutable virtue that emanate from God."[35] Regardless of this separation all justice is subordinate to divine law.

Fundamentally, Beccaria's argument will characterize the entire century: crimes had to be judged in relation to social utility, not disconnected from natural and even divine utility. Men and women became useful to society through proper relations with each other. The emphasis on propriety was important, since improper relations were against nature, in the moral aspect of this concept as well as in its social and functional aspects. Beccaria was very much aware of human passions: his goal was not to extinguish them, but instead to limit them by measuring their service to the common good, which was an extension of what nature dictated. Bodies that did not interact according to natural laws jeopardized the harmonic reproduction of nature and endangered the intended balance between nature and society. Adultery was a crime, but one that was rooted in a natural explanation: the natural force that prompted the sexes toward each other. Thus, the "strong attraction that impels one sex towards the other" operates in ways similar "to the gravity, moving force of the universe, because like this one it shortens distances."[36] Intentionally, Beccaria emphasized the usefulness of those relations; their regulation made them useful to society. Punishable as adultery was, it had a natural explanation.

Society's job would be to make sure individuals were educated early on so they could understand how to control and channel those natural instincts within lawful mandates. The job of lawmakers would be to issue laws that redirected the harmful, and yet natural, human instinct to a virtuous one that benefited society. The legal regulation of human reproduction would then direct women's, and particularly men's, unleashed passions toward conservation and increase. This meant the regulation of whom they could marry, and thus with whom they could have sexual relations. Therefore, the laws that involved regulating sexual crimes were founded upon following the law of nature by guaranteeing its preservation. This was the goal of human society and the basis of its wealth. In this regard, any sexual crime that put this premise in jeopardy – from bestiality to sodomy – moved from being a moral sin to becoming a social crime.[37] For that reason, sodomy became the worst crime of all, since it threatened the rightful role of men and women that would guarantee such conservation.[38]

The "Spanish Beccaria," albeit born in Mexico, Manuel Lardizábal y Uribe (1739–1820) was the most renowned jurist to subscribe to Beccaria's "natural rationalism."[39] Lardizábal's treatise *Discurso sobre las penas* (*Discourse on Punishments*) was a short manual aimed at reforming Spain's criminal laws. It earned the praise of foreign writers such as the French diplomat Jean-Françoise, Baron de Bourgoing, who in 1803 compared Lardizábal's book to Beccaria's.[40] In the preface to his work,

Lardizábal takes the essence of Rousseau's contract: "Man is born in society but nature imposes obligations he has to fulfill." To Lardizábal "the code of nature [is] source and origin of all legislation."[41] It is an interesting twist to Rousseau's "Man is born free and everywhere is in chain." To Rousseau, nature offers freedom and it is the wrong social contract that chains him. To Lardizábal, instead, man's natural right is to live in society and nature poses him some inevitable and unalterable obligations. The freedom element so prevalent in Rousseau seems to be absent in Lardizábal's statement. Complying with one's obligation with nature was one's birthright. To this, Lardizábal adds an interesting concept; religion has a social component and as such it needs to enter the equation: religion "is the strongest tie and society's firmest support."[42] Thus, crimes that disturb the religious order are punishable because they are also attempting against the social order. Sodomy was then "punishable not because it is a sin but because it alters the social order."[43] After all, as Juan Álvarez Posadilla stated, "the welfare of the republic is the end of punishment," and the punishment caused needed to be proportional to the amount of damage it inflicted upon society's order.[44] In fact, a number of writers, from Melchor de Jovellanos and Juan Meléndez Valdés (1754–1817) to Lardizábal, Valentín de Foronda, and Juan Sempere Guarinos emphasized "adapting the punishment to the public service," on what later would be known as scientific penology, working on preventing the crime and reforming its perpetrators.[45] In particular, when it came to sodomy the crime would be judged for its offense against social conservation, and "not in what they have as offense to God."[46] The end of the punishment was only to "correct with utility," thus serving Nature and God.

Individuals who used their sex wrongfully threatened the order of society as well as God's, but in the civil court they would be judged only for the harm they inflicted upon the social welfare of the republic. To Lardizábal this was consistent with the judgment of all crimes since "even the religious crimes will be such because religion is the strongest social bond." An individual accused of sodomy threatened nature by preventing reproduction, and the useful order of reproduction in society through marriage. If an accusation of sodomy was accompanied by a claim of hermaphroditism, the sex of the accused had to be determined first. It was the judge's role to determine the sex of a supposed hermaphrodite in order to re-establish the natural order of reproduction and marriage, and the rightful place of men and women in this order. The theory of law relied on this important practical application, which became the paramount aspect of the legislative process. Yet, it was precisely the emphasis on the practice that would reveal the difficulties of matching the legal practice with juridical theory in the eighteenth century. On the one hand, those who theorized on law believed in an abstract and rational view of justice and trusted that, in spite of the differences, it was possible to find a moral order as truthful as the physical order that the law reflected. On the other hand, the challenge was how to put such an orderly theory into the practice of justice in criminal courts. As the Italian jurist Gaetano Filangieri (1752–88) saw it, public utility had to be the focus of the legislator: "the private peace of families, conjugal honor, and public tranquility, are the necessary consequence. Who can avoid observing the utility of such perfect model?" This latest element, utility, made the legislator's journey a remarkable one. This was where theory and practice united: where medical evidence met the law. Both medical and legal contexts increasingly emphasized the importance of tangible evidence, which could offer proof; the ultimate goal was to make sure that citizens performed their proper role in society. There was a "culture of fact" that permeated the European legal system in the eighteenth century.[47] Facts, scientific facts empty of human bias, could become evidence by which the judge would evaluate a crime and its punishment.[48]

The concept "useful" made reference to "the capacity" of things and people that can be "used or benefit from." Individuals' usefulness and productivity was at the core of becoming a legal subject. The *Encyclopédie* article on "idleness" also expressed that only through work could men and women become full humans and recognize their true nature, as "nothing can relieve anyone of this duty, for is one imposed by nature."[49] As the Spanish philosopher, mathematician and musicologist Antonio Eximeno (1729–1808) argued in *Philosophical and Mathematical Institutions* (1796), everything had to apply to the principle of being useful to society; even "the problem with the belief in innate ideas" was not only that it was a false belief, but that is was not "useful" to society.[50] Eximeno, who in 1796 had already left the Jesuit order, denied the existence of all innate ideas, including the idea of God. Like Eximeno, Spanish intellectuals of the second half of the century married philosophical principles with their social, economic and political implications for the "usefulness of the Republic."

Society's ultimate aim was to honor what nature intended for humans. When this did not occur, the legal system stepped in to regulate human behavior to make certain that individuals fulfilled their social obligations not to harm others. Laws were meant to guarantee that women and men performed the tasks that nature had intended for them for the survival of society, from the formation of new citizens to guaranteeing the economic well-being of the nation. The eighteenth-century ideal citizen had to be first of all a useful one. Although in the thought of the Enlightenment women and men were, in principle, equal as subjects before the law, their physical differences – and in particular the differences that geared them toward different roles in generation – made their usefulness distinctive from one another. This contradictory equality based on difference extended as well to differences between races, and even ages.[51] The eighteenth century was, therefore, simultaneously building a new theory of sexual difference and grounding political rights on notions of "the rights of man," which were supposedly innate, natural and sexless.[52]

Contra Natura

Following Montesquieu's *Spirit of Laws*, a work censored and prohibited in Spain but nonetheless accessible to most *ilustrados* – sometimes through the work of Beccaria – jurisconsults understood nature as a system of bodies in interaction.[53] Each body bore its characteristic definition, while always maintaining its place in such a system. Knowledge of nature was crucial to understand the system and its laws. Jovellanos, who was enchanted (*prendado*) by Montesquieu's ideas, agreed that all sciences, law included, had as their end "the knowledge of nature," a knowledge that could only be achieved through observation.[54] An observer would find that relations in nature, from the way animals cared for the offspring to the structure of bees in the beehive, had their parallel in the society of humans. Thus, if the laws of nature were part of large networks of relations connected with each other, the laws that organized society were equally interdependent. This same idea appears at the core of legal writings in the eighteenth century.

The notion of law as part of a universal system cannot be detached from general eighteenth-century notions of how life originated and developed. As we saw in previous chapters, life happened in motion, the product of a set of relations, difficult to separate from all the components that made it possible, from the physical body to social and emotional relations, religion, and place of origin. This concept of life as a whole affected everyone and everything. Living creatures cannot exist in isolation and their mere existence is the result of other creatures' existence. Even the study of the body always appears as the study of relations of the anatomical parts. Martín Martínez argued that everything – from the smallest insect to the largest mountain – must interact with each other following the system of laws that nature displays. As the best-selling author of the educational novel *Eusebio*, Pedro de Montengón pointed out that the natural order is not a given; instead, one needs to understand nature by observing its complex net of relations.[55]

The natural order that operated as a network of relations, male and female, needed to be clearly differentiated, even when it came to fields such as geology. In 1754, the Spanish geologist José Torrubia (1698–1761) observed how "nature operates masterfully, with reliability and order." Just as humans were divided between men and women, some rocks found in Roussillon near the Pyrenees represented "female nature" while others evinced a "male nature." In the mountains, the two kinds were clearly separated: "where there is one kind we do not find the other."[56] It may be difficult to imagine how the male rocks of the Roussillon could ever find their female match, but what Torrubia implied with his observation was that all things, animate and inanimate, had to be separated into female or male. This was the order of nature that society had to emulate; anything else would be acting against nature, or "contra natura."

In the thought of eighteenth-century lawmakers, this relational aspect of nature also had a utilitarian component. Authorities like Buffon reaffirmed this thought. To the French naturalist, the task of observing nature and collecting specimens all had to be studied in relation with one to the other as to reach to generalizations. In the introduction to the translation of Buffon's multi-volume *Histoire naturelle, générale et particulière* (*Natural, General and Particular History*) into Spanish, José Clavijo y Fajardo, after establishing Spain's early role in the study of art and sciences, "when France was still barbarous and rude, [and] it didn't have properly speaking language, arts or sciences," expressed his awe at such a system of natural laws.[57] Clavijo y Fajardo emphasized natural laws' innate utility, with the ultimate purpose to "move us in knowing and glorifying the Creator."[58] To Clavijo y Fajardo, it was the usefulness of nature that took the observer to the divine. The usefulness of nature, reflected in its laws, is also Montesquieu's basic premise in his *Spirit of Laws*. Montesquieu's argument spoke to a growing number of *ilustrados*, such as the jurisconsult Juan Álvarez Posadilla, for whom nothing in nature was superfluous and all was directed to work toward "conservation and increase," which became the basis for the survival of the species. Even the way bodies related to each other had in its end a utilitarian aspect ordered by nature.[59] In this natural system of relations, honored by the laws, all living beings follow "the instinct, tendency or inclination" that they all have "towards its conservation and increase (*conservación y aumento*)."[60] In nature, the motor that unites all the parts of this large body is the urge to reproduce in order to guarantee the survival of each species. In society, the expectation was that individuals worked toward utility by performing the role that their sex and social position mandated. Men and women gained their rightful place in society only by performing their job in the large social network. Therefore, the human species gained its singularity by relating to the other species and man found his place in society by relating to woman. This becomes a natural, social, but also divine mandate.

In the case of wrongful doing, the place of the law and lawyers came as substitute for parents and tutors who had not fulfilled their obligation by educating children in relation to their state. With their authority, then, magistrates became "the truthful tutors of the Republic and fathers of the land."[61] Therefore, men like Lardizábal saw sodomy as a crime that, although the worst of its kind, was still a social malaise which, as such, could be mended. In particular, Meléndez Valdés believed it was fruitless to punish a crime without trying to mend its causes, or else legislators were "multiplying it instead of destroying it."[62] Sodomy, the crime "contra natura," could eventually be redirected so the individual mended his ways and was able to re-establish his place in nature and society in order to become useful to the republic again.

Regardless of the focus on the separation between the realm of religion, society's concerns and those who crafted its laws, sodomy was still a difficult crime for a lay court to judge. The moral and religious component made the separation from its religious aspect challenging. Even from a strictly legal aspect, the judging of sodomy was anything but uniform. In the Crown of Aragon the crime of sodomy fell under the purview of the tribunal of the Inquisition, while in Castile it was under the jurisdiction of the criminal court.[63] It is in this lay context that one would expect to find a more enlightened view in discussions of sodomy. However, as we will see, this was not always the case. Lay judges shared with religious authorities the concerns regarding an act that attacked the very core of the unbreakable bond between God and its creation.

The notion of "contra natura," or against nature, charged with moral connotations throughout the early modern period, took a new meaning toward the end of the eighteenth century. The new understanding of nature, as intimately linked with the social functioning and duties of the individual, became progressively detached from its religious component. God created nature but after that, nature's inner laws were in charge of its own functioning. Sodomy was an act "against nature," but in this case the implicit meaning was that it threatened the harmonic order and functioning of society. "Contra natura," as the physician Andrés Piquer stated, implied an act against the basic premise of human behavior.[64] Men and women needed to "carry themselves in the world to be useful to themselves and to others."[65] As the lawyer Diego Bustos defined it in 1740, sodomy was called "against nature" precisely because "it is against nature itself, which favors reproduction (*propagación*)."[66] Contra natura was an act against reproduction, and the gain and profit for society that reproduction brought.

The separation between the legal setting and its religious component was not totally teased out until the nineteenth century. Still, the Bible appears as a reference in many court cases and divine law permeated some legal discussion. Hence the ambivalence in the theory and practice of law when using the word "crime" in relation to sodomy, and instead going back and forth among "crime," "sin," or "sin against nature."[67] Both social and religious condemnations agreed that the worst case of sodomy was when two men engaged in the act against nature. Sodomy among women did not alter the "economy of creation," since philosophers, physicians, and even lawyers did not consider women as "makers" in the process of reproduction. Sodomy between men and women was less punishable because the natural order of procreation was neither consummated nor altered: the man still performed the duties of a man and the woman those of a woman, albeit via the wrong vessel. Yet, contra natura between men corrupted the natural and social order, as there was the implicit fear of men becoming women. The transformation of men into women was not only a sin, but also a social crime that threatened the entire social structure.

As punishable as the crime of sodomy was, it had some exceptions and regulations. Already in 1676, the lawyer Lorenzo Matheu y Sanz (1618–80), had pointed out, in his *Treaty of Criminal Law*, that any sexual practice that was not directed toward the reproduction of the species was no longer a natural act but an act "against nature."[68] However, not all acts against nature bore the same guilt. This set a series of limitations regarding the guilt of those accused of sodomy. According to this writer, for instance, hermaphrodites could not commit the crime of sodomy because in the case of such hermaphrodites, "the emission of semen [is] done in a way that makes generation not possible." If hermaphrodites were not able to reproduce, their sexual relations would be condemned as sexual misconduct or minor sexual crimes but could never be punished as severely as sodomy. Drawing on previous works of law, Matheu y Sanz pointed out the obvious: No one could be accused of committing sodomy until the sex of the accused was established. Therefore, in cases of accusations of sodomy the judge first had to make sure the accused individual was able to reproduce normally as a male "with the emission of semen."

This essential step – that the sex of the accused had to be established – troubled lawyers and judges. Establishing someone's sex sometimes meant dragging out a long process that involved not only testimonies, but more importantly, surgeons who could offer the professional's final verdict on the matter. Yet, even with the help of not only one, but sometimes two, three or more surgeons, in many instances the results were still inconclusive. For anatomists as well as for lawyers, the lack of complete knowledge of nature left room for deceitfulness. And thus, in 1783, Domingo Vidal, one of the first representatives of forensic medicine in Spain and Europe, wrote that some crimes were so difficult to judge "that not only do we need two or three surgeons, but we also need to consult the classics."[69] Martín de Torrecilla saw how "accidents fog and darken nature," and, Benito Jerónimo Feijóo added, nature was hard to comprehend through intellect alone.[70]

Doubt over the certainty of determining causes had its impact in the medical world, while it was also at the core of the practice of law. In his *Forensic Discourses*, Meléndez Valdés discussed how the lack of certainty made it difficult to decide which punishment someone accused of a crime must receive.[71] Moreover, more troubling was not only the lack of certainty but also the possibility of deception. Feijóo, for instance, worried about false testimonies of anyone who tried to deceive judges as they attempted to determine the causes of a crime.[72] He recommended studying each individual case and its particularities before coming to a conclusion based on reason, rather than the memorization of all past cases, and the use of theory and theology.

Even when the sex of the accused was determined, there were mitigating factors for the crime of sodomy. In 1765, according to the lawyer José Berni y Catalá the one "who has gone against nature commits the abominable crime of sodomy" and yet, if he was crazy and "does not know what he is doing" or he was younger than fourteen, he was exempted from punishment.[73] Berni rarely used the word "sin" in relation to sodomy, and instead saw it as a crime that harmed society and nature. Implicit, however, was that God ultimately established nature. Decades later, in 1797, lawyer Álvarez Posadilla avoided altogether in his *Criminal Practice* the use of the term "sin" in relation to sodomy.[74] By the turn of the century, sodomy seemed to have gained its place in the body of law as a social crime separated from its label as a sin. However, as we will see, the practice of law showed more contradictions than its theory may have revealed.

These contradictions in the practice of law are very much at the core of the case of Sebastián/María Leirado. This was an example of how judges and lawyers had to confront the need to judge and punish the accused while at the same time facing the uncertainty of knowing the crime and the sex of the accused. The first issue at hand for the court's chief senior magistrate, the fifty-seven-year-old Benito Antonio de Barreda y Villa Barreda y Velaverde, was to determine whether the individual "said to be a woman" was indeed a woman or a man. Determining Leirado's sex was important to deciding the guilt, not only of Leirado, but also of the alleged lover, Antonio Fernández. In this case, however, the intention of both lovers was also a crucial component in the trial. It is, then, in the process of the interrogation that the scholar can peel back several layers of meaning. Barreda wanted to establish the social utility of the crime, while Leirado focused more on the natural views, thus casting the seed of a doubt.

There is little information about the man who ran the investigation of Leirado's case, the magistrate Benito Antonio de Barreda. Born in 1712 in Santillana del Mar in Northern Spain, as a young man Barreda had been educated in the colegio mayor of the archbishop Fonseca in Salamanca. Judge of the Royal Chancery of Valladolid since 1760, in 1763 he became the royal magistrate (*corregidor*) of the northern province of Guipúzcoa.[75] Described in 1765 as a "great anti-Jesuit, not very learned and full of vanity," Barreda was also well known for "treating people with contempt."[76] Barreda left his post as royal magistrate in September 1766, two months after a heated conflict arose over how to interpret some of the regional laws of Guipúzcoa, leading to great animosity between Barreda and his body of government in the region.[77] Barreda was also well known as a Thomist. Briefly stated, the late eighteenth-century interpretation of Thomism, originally based on the philosophy of Saint Thomas of Aquinas, separated faith coming from divine authority from reason based on experience and demonstration. Faith and reason were both thought to draw from God, but Thomists believed they had to be seen as separate. As a Thomist, Barreda was probably representative of the new crop of judges who wanted to detach themselves from religious bias. Barreda brought this belief with him in his role as one of Madrid's alcaldes de casa y corte, a job he took in 1766 shortly after he left Guipúzcoa.[78] Three years later he found himself in charge of the case of "the man said to be a woman." In 1771, and after several unsuccessful tries, Barreda became a member of the major judicial power in Castile, the Consejo de Castilla; this post he kept until his death in 1784.[79]

If Barreda wrote about the trials he supervised in his five years as a chief magistrate of the alcaldes de casa y corte, those thoughts have not survived. We only have his interrogations and trial procedures to reveal what he thought about each case. In the case of Leirado's trial, it is interesting to note that Barreda decided not to have the accused testify until he had obtained a full medical report on the acccused. Even after the surgeons' final report on Leirado's sex on November 30, 1769, which confirmed him as a male, witnesses declared that they had heard Leirado was a hermaphrodite. Therefore, although by December 1769 the medical report had confirmed Leirado's male genitalia, Barreda believed he had to investigate Leirado's past to determine the young tavern-keeper's involvement in the events. The medical evidence alone could not condemn the accused. Barreda needed a story of Leirado's life that would reveal not only his intentions but also the possible relapse, a key element in the legal world of the eighteenth century, and both elements had to be considered together. This reveals an important component in the judicial world in early modern Spain: in punishing a crime, judges had to measure the level of responsibility and intention of the perpetrator. And thus, age, mental state, and external conditions that limited the free will had to be considered before inflicting a punishment upon an alleged criminal.[80] Probably because of that, Barreda decided to investigate the case along two parallel lines: one looking at the level of intention the accused could have and the other at how many times the crime occurred.

It was on December 13, 1769, twenty-three days after alcalde Argandoña opened the case, when Leirado was finally brought from the prison cell to testify in front of Barreda, the notary Pedro de los Martínez and the three other alcaldes of the court. The interrogation probably took place in the *sala del crimen* or criminal court, attached to the royal prison (Figure 4.1). The interrogation dragged on for hours at a time, lasting a total of three days and producing thirteen folios (fols. 26–39). Such events were open to the public, but it was not until the 1790s and well into the nineteenth century that trials became real spectacles for Madrid's inhabitants.[81] And yet, the popularity of Leirado throughout Madrid may have attracted some attention, particularly because during the more than three weeks that the accused had been waiting to testify, word must have spread among those who knew Sebastián/María.

Leirado's lengthy testimony reveals different aspects of the accused's legal personae, as well as the way Barreda perceived Leirado's crimes and his legal responsibility. In the practice of law, individuals who were not in control of their actions – a minor, a demented individual or a fool – could not be rendered guilty in the same way as a capable and competent subject. Leirado must have had some sense of holding a chance to appear as someone not in control of their own sexuality and thus not guilty of their own misdeeds. This, while probably not making Leirado innocent, would perhaps make the tavern-keeper's acts less punishable. And thus, in the narrative Leirado tried to be someone whose sexuality others defined. Besides this, Leirado could have used two other factors that would have had legal weight in presenting the accused as less responsible for their acts. One was Leirado's supposed hermaphroditism. In the testimony,

Figure 4.1 "No deceit is safe in its hiding place." Antonio Martínez Salazar, *Colección de memorias y noticias del gobierno general, y político del Consejo* (1764).
Biblioteca Nacional de España, Madrid

Leirado constructed a story that dwelled on the idea that Sebastián may have been a hermaphrodite, just as people consistently perceived this actress-tavernkeeper. In the narration of Leirado's life, the story illustrated a long trail of acts and circumstances suggesting that, regardless of what the surgeons had said, Sebastián was a hermaphrodite. Even after the two surgeons, Juan de Dios López and Manuel Fernández, had concluded Leirado was a "perfect male," the accused persisted in constructing a narrative of a dubious sex. Leirado may have believed a hermaphrodite was less likely to be punished as a sodomite; and may have been right in believing so. As the seventeenth-century lawyer Lorenzo Matheu Sanz (1618–80) wrote in his *Treatise on Criminal Law*, for sodomy to occur between men, both had to be "perfect males."[82] Therefore, if found to be a hermaphrodite, as a woman-to-be Leirado could be guilty of fornication, which entailed a much lesser punishment than the one for sodomy. And thus, whether intentionally or not, Sebastián Leirado wanted to fit into the model of the hermaphrodite to escape legal punishment.

Age, a determining factor in judging the level of responsibility of the accused, was the other consideration Leirado presented to perhaps obtain a milder sentence. From Sebastián's own experience, and the long list of friends and lovers who themselves had been in prison, Leirado must have been very familiar with the practices of the judicial system at the time. The tavernkeeper must have known that sometimes individuals younger than twenty-five received reduced sentences. It is revealing that Leirado lied when declaring to be twenty-two, when in fact by December of 1769 the accused was only four months short of turning twenty-five – the age at which an individual reached full legal responsibility for any crime. Leirado was clearly older than fourteen, the threshold age for any kind of reduced punishment for a crime such as sodomy. As the thirteenth-century Castilian code of law The Seven-Part Code (*Las Siete Partidas*) dictated, men younger than fourteen and women younger than twelve were excused for "crimes of lust" because "they don't have the understanding."[83] Regarding the particular crime of sodomy, the Code excused from guilt a boy younger than fourteen who had been sodomized. In practice, sometimes youngsters up to seventeen and even older were excused. In fact, in his *Political Instruction and Judicial Practice*, published in 1612 and reprinted several times in the eighteenth century, the lawyer Alonso de Villadiego pointed out that although men between seventeen and twenty-five had to be judged as adults, in reality judges were known to reduce the ordinary sentence.[84] This was a practice still maintained in the eighteenth century, as the ordinances of the eighteenth-century *Novísima Recopilación* (New Collection) illustrated.[85]

The age of the accused was particularly important in the judicial system of the late eighteenth century, which valued education as a way to correct and mold the minor who had committed a major crime. Meléndez Valdés found useful the analogy of the pitcher that "conserves for days the taste and smell of the first liquor with which it is filled; so the first age decides forever our character and inclinations."[86] As we saw in Chapter 3, educating children into habits appropriate to their sex and status would allow them to become responsible individuals, useful to the republic. This was the main idea behind the 1740 case of twelve-year-old José Costa from San Ildefonso near Madrid, accused of having committed the crime against nature. In this case, the perpetrator of the sexual act was Antonio Girado, a journeyman in the shoemaker shop of José's father, where José was an apprentice. Girado lived in his master's house and slept in the same bed with another journeyman and José Costa, the master's son. This arrangement, Girado claimed in his defense, was a big mistake since Costa was "a woman who dresses as a man." To have a woman like Costa sleeping with two twenty-year-old men was a mistake, and Costa blamed young José's parents for this. Girado's statement that Costa was a cross-dressed woman prompted Juan Pablo Galeano, who was in charge of the case, to order the surgeon Juan Castaño to examine the twelve-year-old. Although the surgeon concluded José Costa was a male, declarations from the testimonies in the case continued to point out that Costa's external features identified him as a woman. Galeano thus ordered the surgeon to carry out a second examination to verify if José Costa "can perform as a male and a female." The surgeon was apparently annoyed by the judge's request. After finishing his examination and confirming José was indeed a male, he added that if he had found "he had two natures he would have said he was a hermaphrodite" in the first place. The judge initially condemned José to ten years of exile, for having had sex as a passive agent with Antonio Girado. But the city's alcaldes de casa y corte overrode the decision of the judge and instead sent the boy to "his father so he can educate him, and make sure he doesn't allow his son to sleep with anyone."[87]

One is tempted to draw similarities between the cases of Sebastián/ María Leirado and José Costa. Testimonies referred to them as women dressed as men, and in both cases this confusion allowed men to feel entitled to see them as sexually accessible. However, there are important aspects that set the two cases apart and that, in the legal context, were important enough to yield different resolutions. One difference was that both Antonio Girado and the other journeyman suggested the sexual encounter happened only once in the course of one night. Second, an important and determining factor was the age of José Costa; at twelve years old he was clearly a minor, not responsible for such an act. It is important, though, to point out that Leirado's first encounter as a passive agent in a sodomitic act was at age sixteen, when he was forced to have anal sex with his master, an engraver from Naples.[88] Education was also an important part in understanding Leirado's case. In fact, when in July 1766 the bishop of Valencia had the twenty-one-year-old Leirado arrested "for wandering around the city without aim or job and using a woman's dress," the bishop decided to send this youngster back to Madrid and "to the house of his parents with the knowledge that he would be greatly punished if he does the contrary." Leirado was not twelve, but his cross-dressing and vagabond style did not constitute a major crime like sodomy; rather, it was a threat to the social order that, because of Leirado's age, the youngster's parents would still be able to amend.

Even given the ambiguous sexuality and young age, Leirado could be expected to have responsibility for the acts committed. In early modern Spain many judges agreed with religious notions that sinful behavior required a person's willing consent; therefore, a minor who had been forced into sex was not to be condemned. Leirado's Neapolitan master, whom the authorities as well as Leirado's father made all possible efforts to find at the time, had raped the sixteen-year old. Because they could not find him, that case did not proceed. In the trial for the events between Sebastián Leirado and Antonio Fernández on Easter Sunday in 1769, Barreda focused on very different aspects. Given that she had been mistaken for a woman, Sebastián Leirado wanted Benito Antonio de Barreda to pay attention to the actress-tavernkeeper's lack of responsibility for the crimes. Instead, Barreda wanted to investigate what crime had been committed and the degree to which Leirado was responsible for that crime, not so much whether the accused was responsible at all.

By looking at the questions that the alcalde asked Leirado and the other witnesses in the case and what the notary underlined, we may deduce what Barreda believed was important in Leirado's story. For Fernández's testimony, the notary underlined the parts where Fernández first explained why he did not think Leirado was a man: "I didn't feel or see that he had a man's nature and therefore was persuaded that he was a woman." Second, he underlined the detailed explanation of how the sexual act took place and exactly how Leirado "grasped with one of his hands my [Fernández's] member and introduced it between my legs." It was also important that Fernández did not know whether Leirado had ejaculated or not. The judge was also interested in hearing Fernández's account of Leirado's other lovers, such as the tailor Joaquín. The tailor told Fernández how he and Leirado had been together for over a month and "I have been lucky enough that he didn't give me any [venereal illness]." In the testimony of Leirado's servant, the notary underlined the parts about his master's encounters with Joaquín the tailor. The servant also verified that the tailor lived with Leirado for a month and that the tavern keeper also slept that Easter night with Antonio Fernández. Finally, in the surgeon's reports the name of the Italian master who sodomized Sebastián is underlined along with the explanation of how it happened. This same story about the Italian master is also underlined in the testimony of both Sebastián and José Leirado. Yet, it is important to note that in Sebastián's testimony, unlike in that of others, the only part that is underlined is the declaration of the accused's age – twenty-two years old. Perhaps Barreda found what others could tell about Leirado's sexual activities more revealing than what the accused had to say.

Instead of focusing on people's perception of Leirado's sex and gender – something Leirado wanted the judge to focus on – Barreda was moving toward a much more detailed and legalistic aspect of the story. He wanted to know exactly how the sexual encounter between Leirado and Fernández happened, as well as the details regarding the posture and duration of the sexual act. Barreda also wanted to find whether Leirado had deceived Fernández in making him believe Sebastián was a woman and her name was María. In the eighteenth-century judicial system of Castile, judges were particularly meticulous in gathering enough information, not only to condemn the accused but also to establish the degree and nature of the punishment.[89] Yet, because of its intimate nature sodomy was a difficult crime to prove. Ferdinand and Isabella's 1497 royal ordinance regarding the punishment of sodomy established that even when judges could not prove perfect sodomy had taken place, "acts very close and near to its conclusion" would send someone to be burned at the stake.[90]

By 1769 no one had been burned for sodomy, and circumstantial evidence was not enough to condemn someone for such a serious crime. In fact, in practice, judges may have applied a lesser sentence when the act had not been completely executed. Thus, Lardizábal saw that committing a crime had to be condemned less severely than the accomplished crime. As Lardizábal expressed in the prolog of his book, it was the common good of the nation, more than religious or moral concerns that needed to drive the type and severity of punishment of a given crime.[91] And therefore, the individual who repented and did not complete the crime had the potential to be reformed. The ultimate question for the historian is whether Barreda had any doubts about Sebastián Leirado's "legitimate body" and whether, in fact, Leirado was a man. In the legal setting men and women would not only be judged by their sex but also by what we now would identify as their gender traits – the way they acted in an expected way in their role in society. After the surgeon's report there was no doubt that Leirado had the sex of a man, but he also cooked, mended clothes, ironed and did women's hair – all women's jobs – and had sexual relations as a woman.

Sebastián Leirado had been arrested five times before the final arrest for dressing as a woman. In March 1768 Leirado was arrested in Navarra; in July 1768 in Valencia; and a few days later, in July 1768, Sebastián was arrested in Valdemoro, near Madrid. Leirado was arrested a fourth and fifth time in January and March 1769 in the Plaza Mayor in Madrid. The final arrest occurred in November 1769, when Antonio Fernández arrived along with Barreda and his three officials at the Leirados' inn on calle San Ildefonso (see Map 2.1). In previous arrests, Sebastián had been released quickly, but following this final arrest the young tavernkeeper was finally detained. A man who cross-dressed as a woman was guilty of a misdemeanor, for showing an excess, or *exceso*, in his behavior. Such excess was often not punishable. In fact, there are many causes célèbres in early modern Europe involving men who publicly cross-dressed as women, such as the Abbé de Choisy (1644–1735) and Le Chevalier d'Eon (1728–1810).[92] Similarly, in the Spanish legal system, an individual who possessed a prohibited weapon but did not use it was judged differently from the individual who committed a crime with the forbidden weapon. For instance, in 1748 the Spanish monarch issued a royal order prohibiting the cutting down of trees; those who did not obey were guilty of a misdemeanor unless the same person used the wood to produce a fire.[93] Negligence – such as in the case of chopping down trees and inadvertently causing a forest fire – was not condemned as harshly as a crime. The eighteenth-century lawyer Vicente Vizcaino Pérez in his *Code and Criminal Practice* called the first "criminal delinquency" and the second was the "crime itself."[94]

The distinction between "criminal delinquency" and "crime itself" also applied to crimes "against nature," such as sodomy and bestiality.[95] This was nothing new, and probably was based on a long tradition written down in The Seven-Part Code, which distinguished between a complete, or premeditated, crime that involves "guilt," and crime that occurs "by chance." As in the criminal delinquency listed by lawyer Vizcaino Pérez, the crime "by chance" refers to the negligence of those who do not foresee that their acts could cause a crime to occur. In fact, as the jurisconsult Senén Vilanova y Mañes stated at the turn of the century, "without intention there is no crime."[96] The practice of law in each case pronounced whether the "innocent" party was unaware of the nature of the act and had to be punished or not. In 1794, for instance, Tomás Fernández committed bestiality with the most likely innocent she-ass in the town of San Martín de la Vega (Cuenca). The animal was sold and exiled from the town; the owner lost the animal and received the cash resulting from the sale.[97] And thus in the case of sodomy, which created great disruption in the social order, anyone who was not a minor would be punished in one way or another; the crime existed whether the accused was willing or not. In the trial of Sebastián Leirado, his well-known tendency to cross-dress as an actress on and off stage was not punishable in the same way as if his feminine appearance had led him to engage in sodomy. Yet, Leirado could make an argument that there was yet a third possibility: He was only as guilty as the person who chopped down a tree in the forest; it was those who mistook his feminine appearance for real who provoked a fire. What connects one and the other in Leirado's case is the possibility of hermaphroditism, which would remove the willing agency of sodomy.

On April 6, 1770, the four judges, led by Barreda, agreed upon a verdict and sentenced Sebastián Leirado to ten years in prison at the Castillo de la Plaza (Castle of the Plaza) of Pamplona, in Navarra "for committing the unmentionable sin from nine to ten years until now and lately for committing the same crime with Antonio Fernández." As Benito Jerónimo Feijóo had pointed out decades before, three important elements, besides the age of the accused, were necessary to determine the severity of the punishment. The judges had to consider: first, whether they were relapsed criminals or not; second, their awareness of the crime they had committed; and third, whether any reduction of the sentence would "benefit the country or the state," thus making reference to the usefulness to the republic – perhaps if the guilty party had a special job or talent.[98] None of these cases probably applied to Leirado, who appeared to the judges as a relapsing criminal, fully aware of the crime committed and not particularly "useful to the republic." It is interesting to mention that the court decided to include the word "sin" – as in "unmentionable sin" – in the sentence, dispelling any discernible enlightened efforts to separate crime from sin. In the eyes of the judges, Sebastián Leirado was still a "sinner." Besides the crime of sodomy Leirado was also condemned for "other excesses," not spelled out in the sentence but which likely included cross-dressing as a woman. Finally, the court condemned Antonio Fernández, Leirado's fooled lover, to serve in the Spanish navy for four years. The circumstances that surrounded the judgment of Leirado's lover pointed out the problem of assigning blame when no intention was involved. To the judges, Fernández was granted "judicial responsibility" that made him guilty of his actions. Five days after the sentence was issued, on April 25, 1770, Antonio Fernández's mother petitioned the monarch for an indulgence for her son, claiming he was an innocent young man who had been fooled. The same court that had sentenced Fernández answered the petition. María Antonia García saw her plea denied because of the "obscenity of the act" committed by her son and "the mildness of the conviction." Almost a month later, Sergeant Narciso Larrea escorted Sebastián Leirado out of Madrid to the prison in Pamplona, where they arrived on May 18, 1770.

There is an epilog to Leirado's case. Thirteen years later, in 1783, John Howard, a British observer traveling in Spain, gave a brief account of the conditions in the prison at Pamplona. He described Castillo de la Plaza as "an old building in the middle of the city. It has three small courts: the prisoners lie in boxes without mattresses or bedding." The state of the rooms, "very dirty and offensive," seemed to facilitate an "epidemical distemper" that had broken out in 1775, and as a result about eighteen or twenty prisoners had died. A few years later, the viceroy of Navarra, a region with a "singular custom," released all those who survived. If this is true, and if Leirado had indeed survived the 1775 epidemic, the twenty-nine-year-old would have been freed to return to Madrid to Sebastián's parents.[99]

It is difficult to know whether or not the punishment inflicted upon Leirado was representative of other cases of sodomy at the time. The sentences that the tribunal of the Inquisition, which had jurisdiction over sodomy cases in the Crown of Aragon, inflicted upon those condemned for sodomitic practice between 1540 and 1776 ranged from execution (11.66%), galleys (26.84%), exile or confinement (27.96%), and whipping or monetary payment (3.19%).[100] The severity of the punishment varied, depending on the area and the period studied. More sodomites were condemned to be burned in Valencia and Aragon than in Barcelona. Only a minority of sodomy cases deserved capital punishment, according to the Inquisition and lay tribunal alike during the sixteenth and seventeenth centuries.[101] In the eighteenth century the death sentence was extremely rare, whereas Leirado's punishment – confinement in a remote prison – was more common, although the number of years varied. Moreover, both the Inquisition and civil criminal tribunals saw crimes from a technical point of view: for a sodomite to be sentenced to death and burned at the stake, they had to have fulfilled a list of offenses. The majority of cases contained elements of doubt – the accused's intention to offend the church, in the Inquisition's case; or, in the criminal court, their threat to the social well-being, which was also a reflection of the divine order.

For inquisitors and lay judges alike, of primary importance was whether sodomy had been perfect – that is, semen had been spilled into the wrong vessel – and to understand the intention behind the act. Prosecutors had to prove whether the guilty party bore the intention to upset the natural order, whether they believed their act was not a sin and perverted the order of God and nature. And, as Francisco Tomás y Valiente put it, by altering "the economy of creation [the sodomite] prevents the possibility of a collaboration of men with God."[102] This simple fact, interfering with what God intended, going against nature, made sodomy a sin in both the religious and the civil contexts, particularly in the society of the Spanish Enlightenment. The economic waste, the seed that could not be invested in the production of a new human being, became a "social sin" in a society that equated its wealth with the number of its productive citizens.

Sodomy was not only morally punished by the church but it also jeopardized the enlightened agenda that followed Adam's Smith's *An Inquiry into the Nature and Causes of the Wealth of Nations* in proclaiming that a fertile nation had no room for unproductive citizens.[103] Argument against "unproductive sex" developed along with political discourses at the end of the eighteenth century about the potential threat of depopulation. Spanish reformers believed lack of population growth was the root of Spain's main economic and social problems. In fact, Pedro Rodríguez de Campomanes (1723–1802), minister for Spain's Charles III and one of the most influential economists and politicians of eighteenth-century Spain, saw the "greatest civil happiness of a republic" grounded on its large population, "for a large population is the greatest wealth that a kingdom can have."[104] The minister's active pursuit to educate all groups and to eliminate vagrants from Spanish cities reflects this emphasis on productivity and happiness.[105] This quest for productivity went along with the removal of all waste, economic, and otherwise. The metaphor about "waste" worked for both money and sex when people believed that human beings, and their work to transform nature into useful things, accounted for the origin of wealth. In this understanding, reproductive sex was the ultimate valuable activity. Sexual confusion threatened the whole schema.

This important economic pursuit of many of the European nations and their empires resonated in other institutions and areas of society, in particular in the legal field. It was, after all, what the Irish writer and economist established in Spain, Bernard Ward (?–1779), labeled the "Economic Project."[106] This project did not simply involve economic premises; the economic pursuit could only function if all other aspects of society were coordinated with the goal of the Spanish and European Enlightenment: social utility. Social utility became a central element in the work of Ward and other Spanish economists, and it was also central to understanding lawmaking at the end of the eighteenth century. An individual's service to society would become not only an economic but also a political strength of a nation. Individuals became visible and gained their value in society by performing their tasks in a productive way.

The economic project was intimately connected to the work of political economists such as Rodríguez de Campomanes, for whom education was a central concern. The work of Rodríguez de Campomanes, a lawyer himself, also had an impact on the way lawmakers understood the functioning of the law in the making of their society. In the minister's view, social construction, guided by nature's prescription, determined the utility of an individual. Thus, a person's value derived and had to be judged from his or her actions. The political and legal subjects were those judged by the rightful and useful performance of their jobs. What remained for debate was who had to determine what those jobs were, whether they followed what nature prescribed and in which measure they were or were not altered by the education the individual had received. This was part of the discussion of how the subject was constructed in eighteenth-century Europe, as the product of such an intimate relationship with the laws of nature. This view of society not only was a reflection of nature but also had to guarantee two fundamental precepts of the Enlightenment agenda: progress and human happiness.

The heavy weight given by economists like Rodríguez de Campomanes and Ward to social rules and education in the formation of the individual brought the debate regarding whether society could alter nature outside the medical and philosophical realms into the areas of politics, law, and economics. In fact, another key intellectual of the later part of the eighteenth century, the lawyer and minister Gaspar Melchor de Jovellanos (1744–1811), saw in the construction of language a basis for all reality.[107] To Jovellanos, an avid reader of Locke, language summarized and reduced all thoughts. Although all ideas come from individuals' perception of nature, the social interpretation of nature aided by language created reality. Immanuel Kant also perceived it this way at the end of the eighteenth century. The body not only had to be understood as the physical body alone, something that Spinoza had pointed out, but the perception of the body could alter the formula and give us a result that was far from the same physical body.[108] Although Kant did not express it directly, the result of this premise was that in many ways the perception of the body became so imbedded with the physical body that one could alter the other: the social perception that emanated from a natural given could ultimately alter nature. This idea of the body retained at its core the intention behind discussions of sex and gender in the eighteenth century in places as unexpected as economic debates. The fact was that eighteenth-century economists' and lawmakers' expectation that gender mirrored sex resulted in the assumption of heterosexual complementarities that affected, not only the reproduction of the species, but also the economic and political well-being of the nation.[109]

The effeminate sodomite called into question the position of men as complete legal, economic, and social subjects useful to the republic. If their social role fell into what it was expected from women, their biology still required them to be judged as males. Yet, some individuals like Leirado tried to question this separation. The surgeons may have concluded he had the sex of a male, but friends, lovers, and mere acquaintances still saw and treated him as a woman. As such, Leirado claimed the resulting confusion about Sebastián's gender absolved the actress-tavernkeeper of some responsibility in the punishable actions. The judge accepted the final medical report and determined that Sebastián Leirado was a man responsible for his acts, and that his actions upset the natural urge and social duty of men to procreate.

Ultimately, sodomy called into question the enlightened core of eighteenth-century legal reforms that separated religious from social elements, and sin from crime. In cases of sodomy, lawyers still had to consider the religious implications of a crime that, more than any other, could not discard its sinful implications. Yet, the case of Sebastián/María Leirado shows that perhaps social elements such as how useful and necessary the accused was within the community or whether they had threatened the social well-being were as important as the moral components that surrounded the case. However, there was unanimous condemnation of the crime Leirado committed, and Barreda's thorough investigation also made it clear that the mitigating factors that could have reduced the sentence may not have been considered. Leirado's ambiguous gender was clearly disrupting each social context in which Sebastián was immersed. Because of age, Leirado would not have been seen as eligible for education or reform, regardless of whether the feminine tendencies were natural or not. Altogether Leirado did not seem to be an individual that could greatly contribute to the social well-being of his community. Although the judge did not express it in those terms, in fact the religious condemnation of Leirado's crime seemed only to reaffirm the accused inability to become a useful citizen of the republic, demonstrated by the fact that Leirado performed the wrongful role in the sexual act and in the work carried out.

5   Sex and Gender: Reconsidering the Legacy of the Enlightenment

In 1779 the Spanish diplomat José Nicolás de Azara (1730–1804) labeled the 1700s "the century of restlessness,"[1] when "arts, sciences, politics, the fortune of individuals and nations, even the domestic life," all were "in continuous movement and agitation."[2] Despite the difficulties of discarding the antiquated beliefs of the past, many intellectuals like de Azara realized theirs was a century of change and certain restlessness. One of the areas that provoked the most restlessness, even anxiety, was the need to comprehend the natural world, expressed in terms of "victory over nature." The key to that victory was in understanding its system of laws. Laws rightfully positioned the individual in a universal system of relations, making them "dependent to a system of universal norms that apply equally to all its members."[3] Universal laws became concrete in the way the individual related to surroundings, education and experience, which were all the more important in shaping the human experience.[4] Thus, individuals' social interactions with others had to be an extension of these harmonic universal and natural laws since just as nature operated by a system of relations, so did human behavior.[5] At the very center of both nature and society lay the relationship between men and women in procreation.

In their view of two separate sexes operating according to "a system of universal norms," writers of the Enlightenment provided future ways of looking at sex and gender in the modern world. The first was by establishing a strict separation of the sexes that had to explain the relation between nature and society. The division of the sexes allowed society to serve nature in fulfilling its ultimate goal, the survival of the species. This basic tenet of the natural law translated among humans into social utility. Bodies needed to be useful and the body's social expression – that is, the individual's actions and social practices – had to be in harmony with the natural system. Yet, in supporting this definition, these same thinkers forced upon nature notions and concepts that betrayed a political agenda directed to satisfy governmental needs. It was a call to see in nature the reflection of society's own virtues, which included notions of what a man and woman, should or should not be; how they should or should not act.

The second aspect, which emanated from the first, was that the individual body was in fact made up of two bodies that remained separate: the legitimate (legal) body and the real (physical) body.[6] Both were intended to fit into one. The legitimate body offered a juridical view of the real body by which there was always a separate and a superior level of organization (society) that ordered and regulated an immanent level (nature) in order to "produce 'culture' or 'civilization'." The overarching discourse over how nature and society shaped the individual made impartiality impossible. No matter how flexible, permeable and impermanent the real body was, it was ultimately the legitimate body that would define and guide where and how the individual needed to fit into nature and society. As we saw in previous chapters, a real body was expected to eventually transform, alter, and become – having a marked sex identified by a certain and stable gender identity. Beyond the expectation that sex and gender must be in agreement was the belief that gender led the way in shaping and accommodating sex into its proper social expression. Ultimately, by directing sexual difference toward guaranteeing reproduction, eighteenth-century authors were turning the legitimate body into a heterosexual body.

At the basis of the relationship between the real and legal bodies, we find the linguistic construction of the categories of men and women. Both categories became subordinated to the more powerful and general category of "man," a definition that in the minds of the thinkers of the Enlightenment had to encompass all human beings. This effort, which bore political meaning, was meant to create a universal citizen for their new society, in theory equal to each other and not bound by sexual differences.[7] This universal and equal principle established the politics of recognition for the sexes. Ultimately, the division of the sexes was going to ensure equality by bringing nature and society in harmonic coordination. Yet, in spite of this claim of equality, in fact, thinkers of the Enlightenment constructed an individual that in his ideal characteristics was always a man who had an anatomically distinctive masculine body, and who had to relegate anything feminine to a secondary and subordinated position. Definitions of "human" in the French *Encyclopédie* as well as eighteenth-century Spanish dictionaries confirmed that referring to "that which belongs to man or is characteristic of man." This ideal male citizen had political meaning since the rethinking of space, and the "new symbolic politics," was overtly masculine.[8]

Contemporary feminist theorists have retaken the challenges inherited from the Enlightenment to find new ways to understand sex and gender. One of the areas of study has been the relationship between nature and society, nature and nurture, and whether sex and gender are both culturally constructed. This was part of the dialectic between nature and society that characterized the debates over sex formation in the eighteenth century. To this other questions followed, is gender, as socially and culturally constructed, also shaped by nature? Is sex the product of nature alone? To measure how natural and social forces shape subjects and, in particular, the bodies that subjects inhabit becomes problematic because bodies are the result of a dense network of relations that involve both natural and social agents. Instead of difference many feminists are retaking the pre-Enlightenment thought of sameness as a way to explain human behavior. This is an aspect of sex that eighteenth-century observers, from anatomists to philosophers, were also aware of. How can one separate nature and society if both are so intimately interrelated? When observers label something a human body, they arrive "at this determination through a web of sticky associations that corrupt its claims to autonomy."[9] There are no unique entities; instead entities are the results of the interaction of their multiple parts that act through networks. Notions of the body are constructed through social relations and relations of power. Even the body's physical processes do not work in isolation because cells rearrange themselves in constant collective work.

It is altogether in the rethinking of the place of the body – and in particular of the female body – in relation to notions such as nature and society, sameness and difference, that one can undo and redo the legacy of the Enlightenment in establishing modern notions of sex and gender. New notions of the body also require a new language, different from the male-centered language of the Enlightenment. Instead of a male-centered language of the human body some feminists have wanted to retake the production of meaning by establishing the female body as the principal denominator and the political implications that this may have. Renaming the language of the sexes also allows theorists to rename the relations between nature and society. Other feminists have abandoned the body as grounds for identify sex and gender and instead focus on gender as the guide to understand how bodies are culturally and socially constructed. Still, whether it is focus on sameness, the female body or gender construction at the core of contemporary discussions of sex and gender remain unsolved dilemmas regarding the exact relationship between nature and society, the place of the individual in society and the nature of the subject.

Nature/Nurture: The Debate Revisited

Eighteenth-century anatomists and philosophers focused on the differences between men and women, casting away ambiguous bodies that the figure of the hermaphrodite represented. To these authors, the immense power of education could only redirect nature to its original intention always directed towards making men and women socially productive. In this dialectic between nature and society sameness had a dangerous, unproductive even unpatriotic component. Both nature and society built their relationship on difference so as to make human, social and cultural reproduction possible. Past references on sameness – expressed by the sameness of male and female organs – were discarded. The relationship between nature and society was therefore not built on their collaboration but singular differences.

When studying nature, eighteenth-century anatomists, as well as natural philosophers, focused on difference in nature rather than sameness, from difference between male and female to difference among climates or crops from region to region. Yet, there is as much evidence of difference in nature than sameness. Eighteenth-century entomologists acknowledged that much.[10] But it was the sexual difference, for instance, in the way the queen bee sought sexual gratification from the worker bees, what instead became the focus of attention.[11] The question is, then, why such emphasis on difference? The answer lies in the importance to any discourse of prioritizing reproduction in order to understand nature. An intrinsic part of any understanding of nature is the belief that nature's fundamental raison d'être is to reproduce itself. This premise takes us to the assumption that all beings are predisposed and wired to reproduce the species. The body is fundamentally designed for reproduction, regardless of the particular individual situation. Reproduction is a "natural" potential granted to all beings. It, moreover, defines the essence of humanity for it is through reproduction that humans perpetuate the species.

Implicit in the debates over sexual difference in the eighteenth century were those shifting understandings of humans and their role in society. Albeit acknowledging the divine presence in nature, writers of the Enlightenment sought for the explanation of how humans had to behave and relate to each other and their environment from a dialectical perspective. On one hand there is nature, on the other we have the lives of those who inhabit the natural world. In this relationship, nature has a "moral authority" difficult to escape.[12] At the end of the day, one must bow to nature and its internal laws. Such authority became all too powerful in the eighteenth century, as it seemed to proclaim sexual difference was the key for its own survival. Many faults could be forgiven but not the one that altered the sexual difference because in it laid the danger of destroying the natural order. This is not a story characteristic only of the eighteenth century. Writers of the Enlightenment constructed a narrative based on traditional views of nature. Everything that happens in nature ultimately must be directed to perpetuating each of its species.

In an apparent contradiction, nature's sameness produces difference to perpetuate itself. The difference between male and female is what allows the species to reproduce itself, thus preserving the natural world. Accordingly, for eighteenth-century writers it was necessary to overlook sameness in order to emphasize the differences between the two sexes that ensured reproduction. The apparently harmless premise that sexual difference is necessary to guarantee the survival of the species bore and still bears political meaning. As Monique Wittig pointed out in 1978, any definition of humanity always works in the interest of preserving the heterosexual contract.[13] Sex is the construct of gender discoveries and practices that seek to ground themselves in pre-discursive nature that intrinsically crafts its own survival by perpetuating the species. An understanding of nature in its relations to society will also maintain this assumption. In this sense, the plasticity of nature becomes rigid when it meets human reproduction. The reproductive body, grounded on a sexual difference, is no longer "natural." It is, in fact, the materialization of the legitimate body. The real body gains its legitimacy as a body recognized and accepted in society when it functions as it should to reproduce.

Feminist theories have suggested that perhaps the emphasis in the eighteenth century on sexual difference was the result of a view of nature and society as opposite. Instead, the relationship between the two could be a construction: there may be no differences between them. Networks of relations connect the natural and social in a close and intimate union between nature and society, which turns the space between them into nothing but a "mirage."[14] Evelyn Fox Keller, in particular, has described the "illusion" of a separation between nature and society, "so deeply entrenched in our thinking" and "resistant to dissolution."[15] To Keller, the two do not need to be constructed in opposition. Nature shapes society and vice versa; the former does not exist without the naming of its parts by social interaction. It might be, as Matt Ridley has recently stated, "nature via nurture" rather than "nature versus nurture." Nature depends upon nurture to be realized. It is no longer a dialectic relationship. Education, rearing and, in general, the social context of an individual can eventually have a drastic impact on the body. The cumulative effect is also significant. Scientists have now pointed at the fact that over generations these factors external to the body can even allow nature to alter the initial function of some genes.[16] Therefore, nature is outside ourselves as well as an integral part of ourselves; a part that allows us to connect with other human beings. It is always a work in progress through which one becomes.[17] This is a concept that some eighteenth-century writers grasped. Even though anatomists focused on their dissections of the physical body, they still believed in the power of education. Physicians writing on children's health also saw how the minds of children could be as malleable as their bodies. Rightful and repetitive habits – and the repetition was important – could alter natural predispositions. More than two centuries later, the realization of how much nurture shaped nature has prompted questions regarding the ever-omnipotent role of nature and even the intrinsic component of nature as stable and predictable. Nature's stability depends on the illusion of a society that is also stable.

Discussions of the role of nature and society in the construction of gender and sexual difference ultimately hide conflictive notions of the idea of nature and difference itself. Because the role of society is always established from our perception of what natural is, both nature and society are temporary and readily manipulable.[18] This manipulable and mutable element is in part connected to the fact that the relation between nature and society is historically and politically shaped, serving as Kate Soper pointed out, an "ideological service."[19] And thus, as we saw, in eighteenth-century as well as in contemporary notions of sexual difference, the discourse appears as an overarching force that allows people to articulate difference. This is particularly true in the area of medicine where social and cultural biases have impacted the way scientists carry out their experiments and analyze the results. In the twenty-first century, imaging technology has served to perpetuate gender traits by grounding them on physical and scientific evidence.[20] The mapping of the brain may now tell the scientist whether an individual is predisposed to have certain behavior, including gender-related characteristics and sexual orientation. This social – and scientifically grounded – model of nature sometimes appears to justify social practices. If nurture can alter nature, it can also be that nature gives us the clues to understand social behavior. The exact relationship between nature and nurture remains unresolved.

The eighteenth-century quest to find the exact links that form the bridge between what is natural and social reveal the obsession of the writers of the Enlightenment to find order and predictability in human behavior. Some feminist theorists have pointed at the need humans have of finding certainty in spite of the knowledge that relationships and their nomination are in constant flux.[21] Despite our awareness of the relationship between nature and nurture, and our inability to tell them apart, we are always seeking a definite answer. In the same way that the anatomists searched for certainty in the division of the sexes they found in human anatomy, modern scientists, guided by social interests, also reveal a search for certainty. Any desire to find coherence where there is none, or predictability where there is uncertainty, also reflects anxiety and unease regarding our inability to fully grasp the exact mechanisms of the formation of the subject. This reflects the uneasiness in acknowledging the constantly changing elements that form the subject. According to Kate Soper, then, if the nature–nurture division "is theorized as entirely politically instituted, and hence indefinitely mutable," it cannot be fully comprehended and we may begin to question whether such a division truly exists.[22] The mutable, culturally and historically constructed, and politically shaped notion of nature may render Nature, in capital letters, absent.[23] Nature, in fact, appears as a reality only in practice; any attempt to theorize or generalize nature acts as light upon shadows.[24] It makes them disappear.

To feminist thinkers, if nature and society are so deeply connected, the question is whether the physical body can live outside the nurturing part of the equation, which "inscribes its specific and mutable gender text."[25] Is nature ever a reality or an idea that cannot be understood outside discourse? If nature and society shape each other does this mean that both work in the same way? Is nature as mutable as nurture? Or, to the contrary, is it only gender, as the product of society that can shape human behavior, while nature appears as uniform and immutable? The answer is probably that nature must be as mutable and variable as nurture; otherwise, as Carrie Hull has argued, "the wide variability in gender becomes nearly inexplicable." We cannot hold the argument, then, that a "static sex binary is at the root of sex inequality," if both sex and gender are part of a complex network. When any of the parts of the network move, they also alter the relationship and the meaning of both sex and gender.[26] Given this, it seems futile to ask which one – nature or society – impacts the other, since they are constantly shaping each other as relations are rearranged.

Language and the Webs of Significance

The new perspectives on sameness have also made theorists rethink the Enlightenment's efforts to understand the human body in connection with its social purpose and political implications. On the one hand, regardless of the social context, the division between male and female genitals was always tangible and palpable. On the other hand, the anatomists constructed a sexed body that could not exist without its place in society and its notion of utility. They were compelled to look at the naked body through what Clifford Geertz has called "webs of significance," made of symbolic and mythical images that shape individuals' knowledge of themselves and their surroundings.[27] Even anatomical parts of the body were and are imbued with symbolic values that connected them to larger issues in society. Many elements create those webs of significance; one of them, and probably the one that has received the most attention in feminist studies, is how the way language inscribes itself on a sexed body to create a "culturally constructed set of signifying surfaces."[28] The "naming of the body" was crucial in the anatomists' observations and construction of a two-sexed system. The separation of the sexes went along with the nomination of the female genitalia different than the male. Those names worked together with a production of knowledge that connected them with views of society where by men and women were separated but complementary. Language, thus, was, and still is, the bridge that links body to society. Language, such a powerful component in the way anatomists constructed the division between the sexes, has allowed some feminist theorists to question the division of the sexes itself. Some theorists have seen how language, culturally established, constructs our notions of gender and sex. Others, have used the symbolism of language, and in particular the symbolism of the mother, to recover the sexual difference of the Enlightenment and alter it: the default human is the female to which the male needs to be subordinated.

In the eighteenth-century, as well as in modern feminist thought, language operates through webs of significance to create notions of sex and gender, and their relations. It is a process similar to Ferdinand de Saussure's explanation of how words interact to construct a language system.[29] Saussure understood language, first of all, as a system of relations; words have meaning only when positioned in relation to one another in this system. To explain his theory of language and meaning Saussure used the analogy of the chess game. In the chess game pieces gain their value by the way they are positioned on the chessboard.[30] To understand what each piece means one must know the role this particular piece plays in the game, otherwise it is meaningless. Equally, in language a sign becomes part of a system of signs and their relationships. The content of a word and its capacity to refer to an idea is determined by this relationship.[31] Saussure's analogy parallels sex difference and its gender interpretation. In this interpretation sex never exists without gender; in fact, just as speech and thought are interdependent, the king piece and its movements on the chessboard are the same. Thus, gender becomes the vehicle of sex.[32] Like a word that is not spoken, sex renders itself invisible without gender. The bodies the anatomists observed could only come to the surface when they were part of those webs of significance that in themselves could alter the immutable physical conditions that separated the sexes.

When we perceive the body itself as part of the webs of significance, as a cultural locus of gender meanings, it becomes unclear what aspects of this body are natural or free of cultural imprint.[33] The body we inhabit becomes, as Simone de Beauvoir saw it, a "cultural situation," shaped by the surrounding cultural and social components where it is situated.[34] Gender "is a way of inhabiting in one's body," and therefore this way of existing needs to be measured in relation to "a field of cultural possibilities," which are obtained from the outside but also reinterpreted. There is no other way to live our lives, to exist in our own bodies, than to do it as an expression of gender. As a result, according to Judith Butler, "both gender and sex seem to be thoroughly cultural affairs."[35] It may be that the only reality we can speak for is the one we construct through language, which interprets nature and society and their relations. It is not so much that the close relation between nature and society makes any separation a mirage, but that even nature and society are concepts that need to be rethought. They are just part of the webs of significance or pieces of the chess game. These webs of significance allow us to see ourselves and what is around us in a meaningful way that becomes a reality only through the experience of recognition that makes us "socially viable beings"[36] Someone needs to play the chess game to turn it into a reality. Therefore, someone needs to recognize an individual as a man or a woman for that person to be one or the other.

The relations between the sexes, expressed in gender terms, must be understood in dichotomy because the rules of the chess game ask us to do so. The rules of the game also respond to any political agenda behind the chess movements. Just by naming a body part and deciding whether or not it is a sexual organ, one is making a distinction that usually emphasizes the difference and dichotomy between the sexes. This naming – how, when and to whom – bears yet another layer of meaning that has an ideological component. Butler also points out the political consequences of this distinction, since "a political and linguistic network that presupposes and hence requires that sex remain dyadic" will inevitably work toward perpetuating such difference.[37] Men and women are political categories, and their linguistic construction responds to political needs. The political component behind the playing of the chess game, behind the naming of the parts of the body, and ultimately the recognition of someone as a male or a female, is the one that transforms the "real" body into the "legitimate" body. The webs of significance are void of political action until someone uses them to further a cause.

The political component of the division of the sexes was an important aspect in the eighteenth century – with its emphasis on utility – but also in contemporary feminist thought. In fact, in the work of the feminist of the theory of sexual difference, implicit is that the questioning of the bases of the division of the sexes can bring in a political revolution.

The theory of sexual difference asserts that there are innate biological and ontological differences between men and women that shape the way they experience the world and interact in society.[38] To these feminists the problem is seeing difference as detrimental to women by separating "the Subject" from "the Other," as Simone de Beauvoir did.[39] Instead, men and women can be two different groups, with their own empowering values. The solution is then to provide women with a symbolic history that gives them authority and value, which will not come from men's symbolic world, but women themselves will generate. In a way, the feminist theorists of sexual difference are trying to solve the Enlightenment paradox by celebrating anatomical difference and minimizing – to the point of denying – the impact of nurture, which is irrelevant in comparison to nature. Suggesting that the human default is the woman rather than the man presents the real political challenge. Following the theories of the French philosopher Luce Irigaray and her understanding of sexual difference, these authors argue that women's recognition as full human beings starts when the individual mirrors herself in the image of the mother. Knowledge of the body needs to be understood in those terms.[40] A girl acts in ways that imitate the mother, who helps her honor what is natural and immutable in women. This image of the female body offers to viewers what is eternal and omnipotent by reflecting the "chain of life, the continuity of being."[41] The body of the woman is then the producer of symbolic meaning. The female body takes over the webs of significance to establish a set of symbolic relations dictated by women for women. According to these feminists, taking over the webs will eventually translate into changing the "rules of the game," or to use the analogy of the chess game, altering the way the pieces move and ultimately giving all the power in the game to the queen instead of the king.

To Spanish and Italian feminist theorists of sexual difference, to honor one's womanhood is to honor one's body and the one who has given us life: the mother. In particular, according to Milagros Rivera, the patriarchal order has destroyed the "maternal house." Women can only be free when they restore this maternal house in society, the "order of the mother" that will replace the "patriarchal order." The "order of the mother" only becomes a reality when it is lived and felt. It is the practice of living in the body, the lived experience from the sexed body that puts the symbolic into practice, a practice that can be political. Following Irigaray and her *Ethic of the Sexual Difference*, Rivera defines sexual difference as a "political practice" and a relation.[42] Women's relations with each other, and the practice of these relations in honoring each other's desires, becomes political.[43] They create the symbolic link that takes all women to the origin – the mother and her symbolic order. With this emphasis on practice, and in particular political practice, Rivera makes a point in marrying theory and practice, an element that has become characteristic of Spanish and Italian feminism.

The theory of sexual difference seems to bring back some of the ideals of the Enlightenment by highlighting the natural and immobile component of the difference between the sexes. Critics of the theory of sexual difference claim that, from this perspective, the female body imposes the tyranny of a prescribed femininity upon women.[44] Moreover, by reducing women's experience to a philosophical and symbolical level, women's suffering becomes a creation of the mind, a mind that does not yet know how to liberate itself from the masculine yoke. Once liberated it is a mind always grounded on a female body that has no history, since the entire past was lived within the male symbolic framework that demolished the feminine until women themselves were ready to unearth it, recover it, and own it again. Yet, and in spite of its limitations, some of the points of the theory of sexual difference may be useful to understand the triad that sexual difference, nature and society has become.[45] The body is an overarching presence in the history of humanity: from the concept of the body in the Greek polis, where the polis was "a body" for its citizens, to the body in Christianity, wherein the origin of the body is in God not in the city.[46] Overall, in this historical understanding, the body appears not so much as a tangible identity, but as a symbol. Without questioning how this body is constructed – and by whom, whether it is society or nature or both – these feminists see the body as the only symbolic way to exist. Negating the body has its own intrinsic punishment since "faking not having the body one has is the road towards poverty or symbolic misery."[47] The body offers a symbolic language through which women and men can exist in the world.

The symbolism imposed upon a sexed body leads to two key concepts for understanding sexual difference. First, it acknowledges the key role of human desire in the shaping of one's identity as a man or a woman and in the construction of meaning. Second, it shows how "this desire to be" always accompanies the practice of being. In other words, desire does not become a philosophical and abstract concept, but instead appears as a political tool for action and change. Human desire inevitably translates into a bodily form. Bodies, and the way each individual sees and understands desire in relation to other bodies, must mediate all desires, from the desire for food and sex, for love and warmth, or power and recognition. It is an omnipresent desire – from a psychoanalytic point of view a lack that only the recognition of the mother can fulfill. According to the theory of sexual difference, for a woman to be emancipated, and thus equal to man, she needs to be at once a woman and a man. Many women find this impossible and have to give up their womanhood to be free. Thus, only as transvestites can they find equality and liberation.

Theorists of sexual difference draw their support from both men and women. However, it is women, engaged in relationships with each other, who carry the entire weight of the practice of difference. What moves them and their practice is the desire to be, "the practice of relationships makes the realization of one's own desire possible, the female desire intervenes with the symbolic and then names fragments of that reality that were chaotic."[48] In this respect, Milagros Rivera seems to agree with Judith Butler on the importance of recognition in the production of the sexed subject. In Rivera's theory, however, only the authority of women, and more particularly of the mother, can recognize this subject, either male or female, by acknowledging and honoring their desire to be in the world and to cohabit with others. The link that unites the relationship with the mother and the establishment of a "symbolic order" is the word, the maternal word. Thus, the mistake lies with those who search for this recognition of the "desire to be" in the figure of the father instead of the mother.[49] With this approach, Rivera wants to erase all binary dichotomies that draw from a rationalist approach to the body that contemporary society has inherited from the Enlightenment. Eighteenth-century writers famously put a seal on the division of body and mind, reason and sentiment, not without its contradictions and struggles.[50] One only needs to think of Samuel Richardson's, or Rousseau's, sentimental novels to grasp the essence of this internal fight between reasonable virtue and passionate sentiment. Rivera sees the work of the feminists of the theory of sexual difference as a bold response, an alternative to the body that the writers of the Enlightenment created, a body not only detached from its mind but a body that rejects the mother. Instead, if the body is seen as a continuation of the maternal body, then the dichotomies of body and mind, body and soul, nature and nurture, masculine and feminine are overcome. It is a "liberatory practice" that the Italian philosophers Emma Baeri and Luisa Muraro call the "circle of flesh," or "virtuoso circle," a maternal and feminine circle mediated by women's bodies.[51] In this circle, body and word are one; one finds its origin in the other, and vice versa.

The feminists of the theory of sexual difference are taking concepts that were central in the thought of the Enlightenment, such as human desire, fantasy, practice and social utility, to recast established notions of sex and gender. Desire and practice are also elements at the core of the work of feminists of different backgrounds, such as Simone de Beauvoir, Judith Butler, Luce Irigaray, or Joan Scott. In these points, the theorists of the sexual difference find common ground with those theorists who have been critical of their approach. Desire, and most particularly female desire, may represent a way to escape the webs of significance, of wondering who wins in the relation between nature and nurture, and whether in this relation gender precedes sex. Sexual difference appears ultimately as the product of human desire, which goes beyond definitions of humanity that are constructed as masculine. Desire cannot be trapped in a gendered definition; it becomes the production of the subject who, although sometimes grounded on sexual desire, becomes ultimately sexless. Culture can only offer a set of values for such difference, but the elements that set the difference are ultimately pre-social.

Desire becomes, along with yet another element, imagination, also part of the Enlightenment discourse on sexual difference, key in dismantling eighteenth-century notions of sex and gender. As we saw in Chapter 3, eighteenth-century physicians understood when social utility guided imagination it could alter the male body turning into a breast-feeding body and erasing sexual differences. In contemporary feminist thought imagination also becomes all-powerful when we apply them to either political practice or the practice of creating one's own story and narrative. The narratives rearrange meaning to create identities that are the product of a complex web of references. Butler and Scott make reference to "construction of narratives" as we approach gender and sex, narratives that construct meaning, such as how the words "man" or "woman" develop in different stories. Joan Scott, in particular, argues that ideas evolve in the practice of understanding, in the construction of narratives and application of concepts and categories.[52]

Ideas evolve through paradoxes; practice shows us and makes us use the gray areas, which confuse and challenge us to find new meanings. Scott uses the example of eighteenth-century France to elaborate on the concept of paradoxes in relation to French feminism. In particular, in her chapter on the French revolutionary Olympe de Gouges, Scott analyzes the essence of the thought of the Enlightenment on sexual difference. Imagination, a concept applied differently to men and women, exemplifies those paradoxes. De Gouges in particular took on the concept of imagination to offer an interesting perspective on the contradictions of the Enlightenment in the construction of meaning. Claims of an active, and therefore "masculine," imagination offered De Gouges a place in the new French republic as a "citizen." De Gouges' political activism sought to bring down the barriers and dichotomy that public versus public created, and with it also questioned the parallel sexual division. Olympe de Gouges defied the creation of meaning of the French Enlightenment, as expressed in the political practices of the revolutionaries. De Gouges was able to turn around the meaning of "woman" by establishing practices that identified politically active men. More than two hundred years later, this practice of searching for meaning, despite the difficulties of understanding established categories, has political implications. It moves individuals to search for solutions that often have a legal component, especially when people mobilize to guarantee rights for those who lack legal visibility. In this sense, the practice of sex and gender appears to be founded on both political and legal bases of what individuals recognize to be "woman" and "man."

Recognizing someone as a man or a woman appears to be the result of a socially negotiated agreement, with political consequences. In fact, "it is only through recognition by others that man can constituted itself as a person."[53] Some writers have suggested that this socially constructed and gendered view of the individual is so powerful as to pre-date the physical body. The discourse comes first, before we see the body; thus, one can never see the body in all its nakedness because it has been clothed since birth in a series of concepts, symbols, and ideas that precede the body. The series of discourses, from medical to legal, and educational, which "act on and through the body," can create an imaginary self, a fantasy of coherent identity.[54] Because of this element of fantasy, of hopeful invention, we may argue, as Joan Scott has done recently, that a cohesive and well-defined identity as a "woman" appears as a fantasy, a necessary historical construction devised for political purposes.[55] A fixed identity as a woman, or any other form of identity as belonging to a particular group rather than another, becomes a "fantasy," necessary for certain political groups to justify changes.[56] In particular, sexual difference may in fact be an expression of this construction and the product of anxiety, a quest for certainty where there is none. And thus, we need to ask ourselves how, under what conditions, and with what fantasies the identities of men and women – which so many historians take to be self-evident – are articulated and recognized. Accepting the fantasy is the first step in revealing its workings and significance.

The notion of "woman" may not only be a fantasy, but also the result of an amalgam of relationships – social, political, and cultural – which in themselves bear contradictions. These relationships are articulated in relations of power, and changes in those relations of power alter the meaning of women (and men). In fact, we may see individuals as "a 'degree of power' (a capacity to affect) in the midst of other bodies," which both affect, and are affected by, other individuals.[57] These networks of relations of balancing powers are, in fact, part of a subject production, which is always constructed in relation to people and things. Therefore, bodies need to be understood in their capacity to "affect and be affected" in a series of relations and encounters,[58] and how these relations bear political meaning.[59] This form of entanglement tells us that the very essence of any body, and any individual, becomes the result of these relations. Thus, entities of any kind do not exist before these particular and multiple relationships that create them. Subject production is then a process bounded by and enhanced by historical and embodied limitations.

The means and effects of subject production vary with time and circumstance, but subject production is also contained in the site of the body that functions as a symbolic and physical place. There through different "ways of knowing [and] modes of truth," the human is recognized as a sexed and gendered being.[60] The body becomes, in Moira Gatens' words, an "imaginary body" that is "socially and historically specific in that is constructed by: a shared language; the shared psychical significance and privileging of various zones of the body ... and common institutional practices and discourses (medical, juridical and educational) which act on and through the body."[61] In this regard, the body becomes real in the symbolic world of a group that recognizes a given body as such. Recognition becomes a circular process regarding how the legal discourse interrelates with other fundamental discourses – the medical and political – in order to construct knowledge of sex and gender. For instance, the medical notion of the subject predates the legal subject in most cases. The legal existence of a newborn begins after the medical community recognizes her as a female, after which a birth certificate can be issued. The symbiotic relationship between the medical and legal aspects of the construction of the subject is difficult to undo. One depends on the other. Because of such interdependence, Drucilla Cornell believes that it is by reshaping notions that have political and legal impact, such as the concept of the binary division between public and private, that individuals may have an impact on the imaginary or symbolic domain and recover some agency.[62]

The legal discourse has a definitive impact on how a society understands gender relations. It is a system that legitimizes the subject while limiting its power to evolve by limiting gender identity to a certain and tangible definition. It suppresses cultural fantasies by "limiting people's freedom to see themselves as sexual beings" that are not the ones within the legal domain. Thus, by rethinking the legal system and its symbolic power, Cornell is asking us to reconceptualize the person and human freedom in relation to sexual difference. She connects sex, gender, and notions of the subject directly with Immanuel Kant's theories, which argue the person is not a fixed and rigid board upon which discourses work. Instead, from a Kantian perspective, the individual is "a possibility, an aspiration which...can never be fulfilled once and for all."[63] Far from the stable entity presumed by the traditional subject of philosophy, this "person" is understood as an ideal for which we all struggle. The construction of the subject is the result of a process, a struggle, built through constant contradictions and paradoxes. In this process, we must search for the "imaginary domain," a space for "re-imagining who one is and who one seeks to become" that respects the person's element of possibility.[64] Sex is the basic identification in the imaginary domain. It is an identification that is meant to offer freedom and possibilities for women within the diversity of difference rather than sameness.[65]

Conclusion: Sex and Gender

Reverting to language, psychoanalysis or performance, scholars are still debating the exact position of the sexed body in the creation of gender. Does the subject pre-exist the construction of sex and gender? Does sex exist at all before gender? Are there natural foundations for sex? If, instead, everything is the result of tepid networks of constantly flowing and indefinable relations, why is sexual difference still central in the construction of sex and gender? These are questions that ultimately take us to fundamental debates ignited during the eighteenth century: the search for certainty and order sought in natural laws, and the way to achieve this by constructing a separation – and a correlation – between the social and the natural. Nature and society have to be separate, while at the same time society must also be a reflection of what nature intended. Therefore, although the natural and social are separate one needs the other. Without society nature would be purposeless, and without nature the social world would lack the solid fundament of the natural world. All these concerns bring us to the core of the production of the subject and how human beings inhabit the body and their specific role in society.

In the difficult relationship between nature and society and the construction of the subject, some scholars have found the concept of gender empowering.[66] It is empowering because it erases sex, or at least a view of sex as rigid and limiting. Gender not only liberates men and women from their own sexed bodies but also takes them outside cultural constraints. From a psychoanalytical perspective of gender, what we become is what we have always been.[67] Taking gender beyond oppositions would thus always constitute a return to the pre-Oedipal ambiguity, which would take us outside culture, as we know it. Therefore, the body appears as dynamic, as a mode of desire, which may reveal the influence, sometimes not so obvious, of psychoanalytical theories in Judith Butler's and Joan Scott's work. As Butler stated, "the body is not a static or self-identical phenomenon, but a mode of intentionality, a directional force and mode of desire."[68] To her own question "Does one choose one's gender?," she answers: "To choose a gender is to interpret received gender norms in a way that reproduces and organizes them anew"; it is an act of reformulating that liberates us from our own self. In Butler's world, therefore, there is a sense of constant movement and reshifting: "Gender is a tacit project to renew a cultural history in one's own corporeal terms."[69] Gender appears as a link to binary separations, nature and culture, society and the self.

Gender also allows us to make sense of the instable and volatile historical context that sets relations of sexual difference. In particular, Joan Scott points out how, through the study of gender, we can grasp "at the relationship between the psychic and the normative," settling "the confusions associated with sexual difference by directing fantasy to some political or social end."[70] Still anchored in the idea of "fantasy," which incidentally recalls the powerful place of imagination in Olympe de Gouge's self-representation, Scott suggests that because both, the psychic and the normative, are in fact constructions of the mind, unfulfilled wishes of what the self desires and what society as a group wishes, gender also becomes a fantasy that unites them both. Scott lays this out very well in her book *The Fantasy of Feminist History*. She describes the transition in feminist thought, which has moved from a "sex/gender system" that mirrors a nature/nurture dichotomy to a view of gender as the product of complex relations that involve mainly, but not exclusively, nature.[71] The body is only one of the points of departure for gender relations; others are social relations and relations of power. It is also questionable that there is a direct link between sex, and its more static presence, and gender as cultural and socially constructed.

Gender, as a concept, moves away from the rigidity of an eighteenth-century construction of the body, guided by anatomical definitions, to offer a higher plasticity to a body shaped by human relations and desires. Both the physical and social selves are constructions that can and will change with time and place. But, while gender liberates the self from the constraints of a rigid and static body, it may also create the illusion of malleability and flexibility. The problem with a gendered approach to sexual difference is that it intends to liberate, to eliminate sexual difference by in fact eliminating sex, since gender is sex and all is gender. It creates a fantasy of some kind, and the belief that there is nothing tangible we can ground ourselves on. Our view of the world from birth is through a series of socially constructed codes, signals and symbols that help us make sense of what we see. Everything, from what we touch to what we smell and see, is processed by the brain and given a category we identify. The body we inhabit is therefore constructed by those symbols and we can never shed the gender cover that we wear. There is no certain knowledge of a reality that is always mutable.

The conception of the body as constantly being inscribed with a gender meaning is not new. In the late eighteenth century, Immanuel Kant had already stated that our knowledge of the world through the senses is always mediated by, not only our ability to name what we see but also our comprehension of its meaning. Kant himself was ready to accept that our mental picture of the world could eventually even alter the world we see itself. Yet, the German philosopher never thought the physical reality of the external world to be irrelevant in the construction of human thoughts and ideas. In fact, any mental activity of the natural world had to emanate first from the natural world itself. By turning all that we see and touch into the product of a social construction, some scholars have transformed gender into the magical riddle that will solve all problems and answer all questions regarding sexual difference. According to Kate Soper, by making gender the answer to all our prayers, we forget that human beings are part of a much larger natural world and have much more in common with animals than we are ready to recognize. This does not eliminate the possibility that nature and culture are different names for the same thing. And, for that matter, "What if Nature is that same force field of articulation, reinventions and frisson that we are used to calling Culture?."[72] How are we so sure that which we call "culture" is not in fact part of nature, just by another name? Then we may not need "gender" since gender may be an aspect of the natural world.

Responding to the challenges represented by gender as an omnipotent term, some authors have revived the concept of "sexual difference," rethinking its limits and possibilities. Although it is uncertain and difficult to pin down in its physicality, sex appears to offer a way to understand differences among human beings that is richer than the gender system in which they appear to be inserted.[73] First, as we have seen, there is a need to rethink the concept of nature that lies behind definitions of sex. We need to view nature in its own erratic and sometimes unpredictable functioning, rejecting a view inherited from the Enlightenment of seeing systems everywhere, particularly in nature. Nature's cyclical component does not preclude a rational and predictable event. As Steven Asma pointed out, it is "the mediation of our knowledge [that] may prevent perfect reflections of nature's exact contours, but nature does come to us in discreet forms." Therefore, we should allow nature to remain undefined, rather than burdened with sex categories, "because we can't be certain about our perception of males and females."[74] The existence of sexual ambiguity does not exclude the possibility that dividing human beings into "man" or "woman" is perhaps the most accurate and practical way of understanding difference. What Asma suggests is allowing the category of man/woman to respond to a natural world, which in itself is open to a number of variations and alterations. This appears as a more viable solution than stating that physical differences between the sexes – different genitals or chromosomes – do not exist. Arguing that sexual differences are constructions of the mind does not make them go away. Sex can in fact be as mutable as gender, and as liberating or as limiting. It all depends on which set of relations is established.

A possible solution to the dilemma presented by the relation between sex and gender may be in keeping the different categories – sex, gender, nature, and culture – while paying more attention to the networks that unite them, and that make the mutual influences possible. As we saw at the beginning of this chapter, relations among mutable categories are what keep categories from breaking apart, and what allow us to make sense of the "webs of significance." In 1994, Iris Marion Young pointed out the importance of those relations and the need for feminists to think of women as a group.[75] Seeing women as a group has political purposes, which, if we remember Joan Scott's argument, are a "fantasy" of coherence. Thinking in terms of the group, however, needs to come with accepting the singular differences among women themselves. Borrowing Jean-Paul Sartre's concept of "serial collectivity," Young defined these series as collectives "whose members are unified passively by the relation their actions have to material objects and practico-inert histories … Membership in the series does not define one's identity."[76] People come together and form part of a group that shares common goals, but that does not proclaim that they all share much more than those goals ahead. According to Young, there are external elements that bring women together to form a "series." Two basic ones are the sexual division of labor and compulsory heterosexuality. Young thus agrees with Scott that "woman" is a political construction that does not coincide with the reality of many women. For Young, "series" is a better way to express how women see their group and their identity in the group. The category of woman is then built from relations that are historically constructed, politically motivated and that can be reshaped spatially.

Young's approach to sex and gender has its own problems. For instance, what happens to women who do not fall into the prescribed and expected heterosexuality? Does it mean they are no longer women? This is, in fact, what Monique Wittig proclaimed in her article "One is not Born a Woman."[77] To Wittig, women whose objects of desire are other women, rather than the prescribed heterosexual norm, are no longer women, since they reject the basic elements that to society make them women. Yet, many lesbians have disagreed with this statement, claiming that their sexuality does not turn them into non-women. Still, a lesbian would fit with difficulty into the series "woman," as Young conceives it. In fact, believing that it is completely optional for women to belong to the series that "woman" represents seems a bit naïve. Being part of a series may indeed be optional, but it appears far more challenging to renounce one's body and proclaim oneself a "man" while having physical traits that identify one as a woman. In part, this is one of the main limitations of Young's argument: the place of the body in her series. To Young, bodies "are only one of the practico-inert objects that position individuals in the gender series."[78] They do not seem to be central or determinant in the "woman" series. This seems to disregard the fact that the series is constructed by each of the members themselves, while at the same time they also bear public recognition by outsiders. A member of the series who has the apparent body of a man may find acceptance into the series difficult. Still, what makes Young's argument attractive and useful is the way she articulates the concept of "woman," first as a construction, and second as the result of a number of relations in space and time. Focusing on relations unites the human experience to other species that find group relations crucial to their survival. As Rebecca Jordan-Young has stated, "being male or female is not simply determined at one moment for any individual organism, but is the result of a multiple-step process." Even the production of an organism responds to a tepid series of relations that can be altered and transformed by internal and external events at any time during gestation.[79]

In these series of relations, with their combinations which form a subject that can be seen as a "woman," it is important to measure in which ways the law interacts with the construction of the subject. In other words, how does the subject begin its lawful existence? As Michel de Certeau pointed out, the process by which "the subject authorizes its own existence is a different labor from the one in which he is allowed to exist."[80] The institutional legitimatization of the subject makes its production all the more difficult in shifting parameters that lack the certainty on which the legal system feeds. One could alternate between the series of "man" and "woman," but it would take a lot of effort to shift from one category to another in the legal system, as anyone who has tried to legally change his or her gender identity can attest. As Michel Foucault saw it, "the modern subject is always open, never finally delimited, yet constantly transversed." A subject is always constituted by actions, institutions and languages that precede him, and that have been previously institutionalized.[81] This is why women as much as men are the product of what came before them. The legal subject sums up the symbolic mapping of the subject, with its historical component, and the expectations of what men and women must do to become useful citizens.

Definitions of "man" and "woman" bear a historical component, not only of the time in which these categories operate, but also of past definitions, difficult to tear away. The ideal of Rivera and the feminists of the theory of sexual difference to start anew, to "start from oneself" (*partir de sí*) and walk away from centuries of a shared symbolic world with men, seems difficult to achieve. Although Joan Scott has alerted us to the fantasy of the concept of "woman," the truth is that we cannot escape this fantasy, as the body may be the main point of reference we have to create the meaning of gender. We need to ask the question that Denis Riley posed in 1988 – whether woman is a "historically and discursively constructed" category, always changing and evolving in relation to other categories that also change – and then see what weight this question bears in twenty-first-century definitions. Is it possible to eliminate binary categories of man/woman set in opposition? What can history teach us in this respect? Despite the efforts of eighteenth-century physicians and lawmakers, the diverse and mutable categories of "man" and "woman" made dualistic, and opposed, categories difficult to settle. Mutable categories of men and women were (and are) part of the production of the subject, "a subject-in-process" that is never completely finished.[82] In particular, woman is a category, as Rosi Braidotti has seen it, in permanent metamorphosis. It is a difficult-to-grasp category that nonetheless needs to be stable so it can have a legal and political meaning. As the feminist theorists of sexual difference have argued, this woman has a body that – despite its nomadic element – is grounded on "a field of intersecting material and symbolic forces; it is a surface where multiple codes (race, sex, class, age, etc.) are inscribed."[83]

To acknowledge the mutable element of the category of woman, one also needs to recognize that the webs of significance are also mutable, themselves. The symbolic mapping of the body and the subject is constantly altered by those same categories that interrelate and change themselves in space and in time. In a kaleidoscopic way, the different parts of the subject are different and diverse but connected, linked as well to the subject's webs of significance. This way of approaching body and mind questions a dualistic relationship, since both body and mind are equal parts of this composition that is the subject. In the same way, the relation between sex and gender appears as close and more symbiotic. It is irrelevant which of the two precedes the other.

Eighteenth-century anatomists were aware of these webs of significance. Their firm belief in universal systems, all connected and mutually dependent, shaped their views on the human body and sexual difference. We found their legacy, and its limitations, in precisely those universal systems that seek order and consistency. At the same time, it is in the thought of the Enlightenment that we also find the grounds for a different understanding of sex and gender. As the preceding chapters have shown, eighteenth-century anatomists, and the influence of their theories on lawyers and philosophers, were never at ease with their own convictions for a clear-cut separation of the sexes. They hesitated. It is in this hesitation one finds hope for change. The declaration of physician Narciso Esparragosa at the turn of the century expressed it all – the ambiguous sex of some individuals was in fact "the effect of those pranks with which nature usually seems to disturb its laws."[84] Esparragosa's laws were the laws the Enlightenment had produced and were already well established by 1803, when the physician wrote his report on "the supposed hermaphrodite" Juana Aguilar. In his report, Esparragosa reaffirmed the statement of the anatomist Martín Martínez, who saw the populace was prompted to believe in the existence of hermaphrodites; a belief philosophers, anatomists and physicians had fueled by "ennobling that faked ghost" that the hermaphrodite was. Aguilar, who was missing both complete sexual organs, was a "rare phenomenon that only the anatomic knife could unveil." But since Aguilar was still alive in 1803 and an autopsy could not be performed, Esparragosa had to be left with the uncertainty of a body that was "neutral," similar to "the neutrality of certain bees." Albeit accepting nature's "games," the physician remained steady in refusing to label Aguilera as a "hermaphrodite" and instead seeing it more as a "neutral bee."

The same implicit contradiction that the Enlightenment bore – the creation of a system of laws that could never fully be proven – appears in the discourse of the newspaper editor and Thomas Jefferson's supporter, James Callender, a contemporary of Esparragosa. When, during the election campaign of 1800, Callender accused the incumbent President John Adams of displaying a "hideous hermaphroditical character, which has neither the force and firmness of a man, nor the gentleness and sensibility of a woman," he was implicitly drawing from the imaginary of past centuries and the symbolic force of the hermaphrodite in an area already free of sexual ambiguity.[85] Interestingly, in both cases, the physician and the journalist were unearthing the figure of the hermaphrodite that eighteenth-century anatomists had buried decades ago: hermaphrodites were entities that lacked the characteristic of both sexes, rather than having them at the same time.[86] Sameness was still in their mind, but it could only weaken society and bring it to its certain demise. Perhaps it is this perspective of the late Enlightenment that can offer some responses, continuities and possibilities for change. As a form of resolution Esparragosa and Callender both embraced the contradictions of the Enlightenment and expressed the reality that, no matter how hard we try, ultimately one cannot really get to know nature. Once we think we do, it plays another prank on us, and we are left unsure – who is a man and who is a woman?

Notes

Introduction

1 William Shakespeare, *The Tempest* (Toronto and New York: Bantam Books, 1988 [c.1611]), Act 5, Scene 1.

2 Aldous Huxley, *Brave New World* (New York: Harper Collins, 2004 [1932]), 18.

3 Kenneth Fitzpatrick Russell, *British Anatomy: 1525–1800. A Bibliography* (Melbourne: Melbourne University Press, 1963), xxi.

4 Mary Lindemann, *Medicine and Society in Early Modern Europe* (Cambridge, UK: Cambridge University Press, 1999).

5 Matthew Landers and Brian Muñoz eds., *Anatomy and the Organization of Knowledge, 1500–1850* (London and New York: Pickering and Chatto, 2012).

6 "Organic economy" as used by Charles Bonnet, *Contemplation de la nature* (1764), quoted in Lorraine Daston, "Attention and the Values of Nature in the Enlightenment," in *The Moral Authority of Nature* eds., Lorraine Daston and Fernando Vidal (Chicago: The University of Chicago Press, 2004), 120.

7 *Diccionario de Autoridades* (Madrid: Editorial Gredos, 1963 [1726–39]).

8 Landers and Muñoz eds., *Anatomy and the Organization of Knowledge*.

9 Peter R. Anstey and John A. Schuster eds., *The Science of Nature in the Seventeenth Century: Patterns of Change in Early Modern Natural Philosophy* (Dordrecht, UK: Springer, 2005). The study of nature and humans went hand in hand. We only need to look at the interest in which botanists observed the sexual life of plants, anthropomorphizing their efforts to reproduce; see Marjorie Swann, "Vegetable Love: Botany and Sexuality in Seventeenth-Century England," in *The Indistinct Human in Renaissance Literature* eds., Jean E. Feerick and Vin Nardizzi (New York: Palgrave MacMillan, 2012), 139–58.

10 In Europe, see for example the work of the German Jesuit Athanasius Kircher and the Danish scientist Nicolas Steno; Horacio Capel, "Religious Beliefs, Philosophy and Scientific Theory in the Origin of Spanish Geomorphology, 17th-18th centuries," *Organon, Polish Academy of Science, Warsaw, special issue "La pensée géographique"* 20/21 (1984/1985): 219–29.

11 This is the case of José Antonio González de Salas (1588–1651), see Francisco Pelayo, *Del diluvio al megaterio: los orígenes de la paleontología en España* (Madrid: Consejo Superior de Investigaciones Científicas, 1996).

12 José Vicente del Olmo, *Nueva descripción del orbe de la tierra* (Valencia: Ioan Lorenço Cabrera, 1681).

13 In particular along with the musician and mathematician Félix Falcó de Belaochaga, del Olmo was one of the principal members of the 1685 series of literary salons hosted by the conde de Alcudia.

14 Olmo, *Nueva descripción.*

15 Lindemann, *Medicine and Society.*

16 Jean Sarrailh, *La España Ilustrada de la segunda mitad del siglo XVIII* trans. Antonio Alatorre (Mexico City: Fondo de Cultura Económica, 1957).

17 André du Laurens, *Les Oeuvres de Me André du Laurens* ed., G. Sauvageon (Paris: Chez Iean Petit-Pas, 1639 [1621]), 357; quoted in Katherine Crawford, *European Sexualities, 1400–1800* (Cambridge and New York: Cambridge University Press, 2007), 100.

18 Juan Huarte de San Juan, *Examen de Ingenios para las ciencias* ed., Guillermo Serés (Madrid: Cátedra, 1989 [1575]).

19 Crawford, *European Sexualities,* 110.

20 Francis Clifton, *État de la médecine ancienne et moderne: avec un plan pour perfectionner celle-ci* (Paris: Chez Quillau, 1742), viii.

21 Thomas Laqueur, *Making Sex: Body and Gender from the Greeks to Freud* (Cambridge, MA: Harvard University Press, 1990), 149.

22 Michael Stolberg, "A Woman Down to Her Bones: The Anatomy of *Sexual Difference* in the Sixteenth and Early *Seventeenth Centuries,*" Isis 94 (2003): 274–99; see also Katharine Park and Robert A. Nye, "Destiny is Anatomy," (review of Thomas Laqueur, *Making Sex: Body and Gender from the Greeks to Freud) New Republic* (February 18, 1991): 53–7; To Lyndal Roper, for instance, the case of persecution of witches shows how gender in early modern Europe encompassed much more than the social perception of a sexed body. The body of the witch went beyond gender expectations to engage with notions of fantasy and emotion that also shaped notions of the body; see Lyndal Roper, *The Witch in the Western Imagination* (Charlottesville: University of Virginia Press, 2012); Helen King, *The One-Sex Body on Trial: The Classical and Early Modern Evidence* (Aldershot, UK: Ashgate, 2013).

23 Jesús Pérez Magallón, *Construyendo la modernidad: la cultura española en tiempo de los novatores (1675–1725)* (Madrid: Consejo Superior de Investigaciones Científicas, 2002).

24 José Pardo Tomás and Àlvar Martínez Vidal, "El tribunal del protomedicato y médicos reales (1665–1724): entre la gracia real y la carrera profesional," *Dynamis* 16 (1996): 59–90.

25 Sachiko Kusukawa, *Picturing the Book of Nature: Image, Text, and Argument in Sixteenth-Century Human Anatomy and Medical Botany* (Chicago: The University of Chicago Press, 2012).

26 Anthony Clifford Grayling, *The Age of Genius: The Seventeenth Century and the Birth of the Modern Mind* (New York: Bloomsbury, 2016).

27 Diego Gavira y León, *Varias dissertaciones médicas, theoretico-prácticas, anatómico-chirúrgicas y chymico-pharmacéuticas enunciadas y públicamente defendidas en la Real Sociedad de Sevilla* (Seville: Imprenta de las Siete Revueltas, 1736), 41.

28 Ole Peter Grell and Andrew Cunningham eds., *Medicine and Religion in Enlightenment Europe* (Aldershot, UK: Ashgate, 2007); Pardo Tomás and Martínez Vidal, "El tribunal del protomedicato."

29 OlgaVictoria Quiroz-Martínez, *La introducción de la filosofía moderna en España: el eclecticismo español de los Siglos XVII y XVIII* (Mexico City: Colegio de Mexico, 1949), 15–29.

30 Italian doctors would establish contact with physicians of Seville, who in their turn appeared to make the connection of theory and practice real by having also relationships with prominent apothecaries. One of the best-known physicians of the new science, Diego Mateo Zapata worked closely with apothecary Félix Palacios, and physician Juan Muñoz y Peralta with the apothecary Juan Fernández Lozano; José Pardo Tomás and Àlvar Martínez Vidal, "Un siglo de controversia: la medicina española de los novatores a la Ilustración," in *La Ilustración y las ciencias: para una historia de la objetividad* eds., Josep Lluís Barona Vilar, Javier Moscoso, and Juan Pimentel (Valencia: Universitat de València, 2003), 107–35.

31 Blas Beaumont published *Exercitaciones anatómicas y essenciales operaciones de cirugía: con un breve resumen de los instrumentos y vendages* (Madrid: Imprenta del Convento de Nuestra Señora de la Merced, 1728). He dedicated the book to the French surgeon, royal physician to the Spanish monarch, Juan Baptista Legendre.

32 Joel Mokyr, *The Gifts of Athena: Historical Origins of the Knowledge Economy* (Princeton: Princeton University Press, 2002); Maxine Berg, "The Genesis of 'Useful Knowledge'," *History of Science* 45 (2007): 123–33.

33 Thomas Laqueur, *Solitary Sex: A Cultural History of Masturbation* (New York: Zone Books, 2003).

34 Immanuel Kant, *Anthropology from a Pragmatic Point of View* ed., Robert B. Louden (Cambridge, UK: Cambridge University Press, 2006 [1785]), 212.

35 Immanuel Kant, "What Is Enlightenment?" in *Introduction to Contemporary Civilization in the West* trans. Peter Gay (New York: Columbia University Press, 1954), 1071–76.

36 William Leiss, *The Domination of Nature* (Montreal: McGill-Queen University Press, 1994 [1972]).

37 Daniel Defoe, *The Life and Strange Surprizing Adventures of Robinson Crusoe* (London: Printed for W. Taylor, 1719), 206.

38 María del Carmen Iglesias Cano, *Razón y sentimiento en el siglo XVIII* (Madrid: Real Academia de la Historia, 1999).

39 María del Carmen Iglesias Cano, *Razón, sentimiento y utopía* (Barcelona: Galaxia Gutenberg, 2006).

40 Michel Foucault, *Madness and Civilization: A History of Insanity in the Age of Reason* trans. Richard Howard (London and New York: Routledge, 2001 [1961]).

41 Landers and Muñoz, *Anatomy and the Organization of Knowledge.*

42 Michel Foucault, *The Order of Things: An Archeology of the Human Sciences* trans. Alan Sheridan (New York: Vintage Books, 1994 [1966]), 157–60.

43 As Joan Scott has alerted us one should not reinscribe "the naturalized terms of difference (sex) upon which systems of differentiation and discrimination (gender) have been built, analysis begins at an earlier point in the process, asking how sexual difference is itself articulated as a principle and practice of social organization," Joan Wallach Scott, *Gender and the Politics of History.* Revised Edition (New York: Columbia University Press, 1999), 207. On

the Enlightenment efforts to "name" the body parts, see Rebecca Haidt, *Embodying Enlightenment: Knowing the Body in Eighteenth-Century Spanish Literature and Culture* (New York: St. Martin's Press, 1998).

44 Pierre Bourdieu, *Le Sens Pratique* (Paris, 1980), 366 quoted in Joan Wallach Scott, "Gender: A Useful Category of Historical Analysis," *The American Historical Review* 91, 5 (December 1986), 1069.

45 Federico Garza-Carvajal, *Butterflies Will Burn: Prosecuting Sodomites in Early Modern Spain and Mexico* (Austin, TX: University of Texas Press, 2003).

46 Susan Stryker, *Transgender History* (Berkeley: Seal Press, 2008).

47 Judith Butler, *Undoing Gender* (New York and London: Routledge, 2004), 57.

1 The Anatomy of Sex

1 The century started with the War of Spanish Succession (1701–14), the political conflict fought between the Habsburg Grand Alliance and the Franco-Spanish Alliance over the succession to the throne of Spain following the death childless of Charles II of Spain.

2 Anatomy held the promise of bringing this form of scientific revolution in Spanish soil.

3 Diego Mateo Zapata, *Disertación médico-teológica, que consagra a la serenísima señora princesa del Brasil* (Madrid: Don Gabriel del Barrio, 1733); quoted in Luis S. Granjel, *Anatomía española de la Ilustración* (Salamanca: Ediciones del Seminario de Historia de la Medicina Española, 1963).

4 Martín Martínez, *Anatomía completa del hombre con todos sus hallazgos, nuevas doctrinas y observaciones raras hasta el tiempo presente y muchas advertencias necessarias para la cirugía, según el método que se explica en nuestro theatro de Madrid* (Madrid: Imprenta Bernardo Peralta, 1764 [1728]), prolog.

5 Universities were still the place where anatomists and physicians received their formal instruction based on the teaching of the works of Galen and Aristotle, Carlos del Valle-Inclán, "El léxico anatómico de Porras y de Martín Martínez," *Archivos Iberoamericanos de Historia de la Medicina* 4 (1952): 141–228 (142); María Victoria Cruz del Pozo, *Gassendismo y cartesianismo en España: Martín Martínez médico filósofo del siglo XVIII* (Seville: Universidad de Sevilla, 1997), 16; Ramón Ceñal "Cartesianismo en España. Notas para su historia (1650–1750)," *Revista "Filosofía y Letras" de la Universidad de Oviedo* (1945): 1–95.

6 One of such tertulias was the *Veneranda Tertulia Médica Hispalense Médico-Química, Anatómica y Matemática*, established in 1697 in Seville. This tertulia provided the basis for the later Royal Society of Medicine and other Sciences of Seville, Antonio Hermosilla Molina, *Cien años de medicina sevillana: la Regia Sociedad de Medicina y Demás Ciencias de Sevilla, en el siglo XVIII* (Seville: Diputación Provincial de Sevilla, 1970); for the new medical literatura available and probably read in those tertulias, *see* María Esther Alegre Pérez and María del Mar Rey Bueno, "La biblioteca privada de Juan Muñoz y Peralta (ca. 1655–1746)," in *Estudios de historia de las técnicas, la arqueología industrial y las ciencias: VI Congreso de la Sociedad Española de Historia de las Ciencias y de las Técnicas, Segovia-La Granja, 9 al 13 de septiembre de 1996* eds., Juan L. G. Hourcade, Juan M. Moreno Yuste, and Gloria Ruíz Hernández

(Valladolid: Junta de Castilla y León, Consejería de Educación y Cultura, 1998), 385–90.

7 Jesús Pérez Magallón, *Construyendo la modernidad: la cultura española en el tiempo de los novatores (1675–1725)* (Madrid: Consejo Superior de Investigaciones Científicas, 2002). Physicians and anatomists were educated to university level, while surgeons usually acquired training and were certified by the guild. Many, but not all, physicians became anatomists and focused on the study of the body in its anatomy.

8 Quoted in Juan Carrete Parrondo, Fernándo Checa Cremades, and Valeriano Bozal eds., *El grabado en España: Siglos XV al XVIII* 32 vols. (Madrid: Espasa-Calpe, 1988), 1: 317.

9 José María López Piñero, "Crisóstomo Martínez. El hombre y la obra," in *El atlas anatómico de Crisóstomo Martínez* (Valencia: Ajuntament de València, 1982), 19–68 (76); Antonio Mestres Sanchis, "La Ilustración Valenciana en España y Europa," in *Ilustración, ciencia y técnica en el siglo XVIII español* eds., Enrique Martínez Ruíz and Magdalena de Pazzis Pi Corrales (Valencia: Universitat de València, 2008), 41–62.

10 Nuria Valverde, "Small Parts: Crisóstomo Martínez (1638–1694), Bone Histology, and the Visual Making of Body Wholeness" *Isis* 100 (3) (September 2009): 505–36; Raúl Velasco Morgado, "Nuevas aportaciones documentales sobre el grabador Crisóstomo Martínez y su atlas de anatomía," *Asclepio. Revista de Historia de la Medicina y de la Ciencia* 64 1 (January–June 2012): 189–212.

11 *Discurso político y phísico*, in Jorge M. Ayala, *Pensadores aragoneses: Historia de las ideas filosóficas en Aragón* (Saragossa: Institución Fernando el Católico, 2001), 369.

12 Granjel, *Anatomía española*, 14.

13 A group of scientists and intellectual had founded the Society in 1697 as the *Veneranda Tertulia Médica Hispalense Médico-Química, Anatómica y Matemática* to receive royal approval in 1700.

14 Quiroz-Martínez, *Introducción de la filosofía moderna*, 23.

15 Diego Mateo Zapata, *Crisis médica sobre el antimonio y carta responsoria a la Regia Sociedad Médica de Sevilla* (Madrid: s.n., 1701), appeared in *Table méthodique des Mémoires de Trévoux (1701–1775)* (Paris: Auguste Durand, 1865).

16 Hermosilla Molina, *Cien años*.

17 Martínez never held a teaching position at a university.

18 He became a professor of anatomy, a personal physician to Philip V of Spain, and was examiner of the royal tribunal of the *Proto-Medicato* – the royal institution that regulated health practitioners in the Spanish empire. For Martín Martínez's biography, see Cruz del Pozo, *Gassendismo y cartesianismo*, 21–9.

19 Martín Martínez's major works were *Anatomía compendiosa y noches anatómicas* (Madrid: Lucas Antonio de Bedmar, 1717), *Medicina sceptica y cirugía moderna: con un tratado de operaciones chirurgicas* (Madrid: Imprenta de Gerónimo Roxo, 1722) the second volume of this work was published in 1725, *Compendio y examen nuevo de cirugía moderna* (Madrid: Don Gabriel del Barrio, 1724), *Anatomía completa del hombre con todos los hallazgos, nuevas doctrinas y observaciones raras hasta el tiempo presente, y muchas advertencias necessarias para la cirugía: según el methodo con que se explica en nuestro theatro de Madrid* (Madrid: Imprenta Bernardo Peralta, 1764 [1728]), *Philosofia*

escéptica, extracto de la physica antigua y moderna, recopilada en diálogos, entre un aristotélico, cartesiano, gasendista, y escéptico, para instrucción de la curiosidad española (Madrid: s.n.,1730).

20 Tullio Gregory, *Scetticismo ed Empirismo: Studio su Gassendi* (Bari, Italy: Laterza, 1961), 165.

21 Particularly in Martínez's *Medicina scéptica.*

22 Francis Bacon, championed in the European eighteenth-century as one of the predecessors of the Enlightenment's emphasis on order, progress and utility, became an influential thinker for Spanish scientists and philosophers in the early 1700s; Lewis Pyenson and Susan Sheets-Pyenson, *Servants of Nature: A History of Scientific Institutions, Enterprises and Sensibilities* (New York: W.W. Norton & Company, 1999), 400–24.

23 Martín Martínez, *Medicina scéptica* t. I: 86.

24 Grayling, *Age of Genius.*

25 Martín Martínez, *Noches anatómicas.*

26 The same structure is also characteristic of the Portuguese priest Teodoro de Almeida's *Philosophical Recreation,* which takes place over a series of afternoons.

27 In particular *Anatomía completa del hombre,* see John Tate Lanning, *El Real Protomedicato. La reglamentación de la profesión médica en el imperio español* (Mexico City: Facultad de Medicina, Instituto de Investigaciones Jurídicas-UNAM, 1997), 473; Verónica Ramírez Ortega and María Luisa Rodríguez Sala, "La influencia de las obras médicas europeas en la renovación de las disciplinas de la salud en México (1770–1833)," in *XV Encuentro de Latinoamericanistas Españoles* eds., Esther Campo García, José Carpio Martín, et al. (Madrid: Trama editorial, 2013), 1157–63.

28 For an analysis of Martín Martínez's work, see Haidt, *Embodying Enlightenment,* 13–62.

29 In his *Teatro crítico universal* 9 vols. (Madrid: Imprenta de L. F. Mojados, 1726–40) vol. 1, Benito Jerónimo Feijóo discusses his views on medicine (see *discurso* no. 5).

30 Martínez, *Anatomía completa,* 188.

31 Haidt, *Embodying Enlightenment,* 19–43.

32 José de Ortega, *Elogio histórico del Sr. Dr. Joseph Cerni leído a la Real Academia Medicina Matritense en 30 de marzo de mil setecientos quarenta y ocho* (Madrid: En la imprenta del Mercurio, 1748).

33 Martínez was an anatomist and physiologist, marrying the physical observation of the practice of the human body with its functioning.

34 On the "foundation of sexual difference" in eighteenth-century Spain, see Richard Cleminson and Francisco Vázquez García, *Sex, Identity and Hermaphrodites in Iberia, 1500–1800* (London: Pickering and Chatto, 2013), 76–81.

35 Faramerz Dabhoiwala, *The Origins of Sex: A History of the First Sexual Revolution* (Oxford: Oxford University Press, 2012), 97.

36 Martínez, *Anatomía completa,* Chapter I, lesson IV.

37 Ian Maclean, "Evidence, Logic, the Rule and the Exception in Renaissance Law and Medicine," *Early Science and Medicine* 5, 3 (2000): 227–57.

38 Charlotte Witt, *Ways of Being: Potentiality and Actuality in Aristotle's Metaphysics* (Ithaca and London: Cornell University Press, 2003).

39 Martínez, *Anatomía completa.*

40 It was not the same with effeminate men, since Aristotelian philosophy saw the progression from man to woman as unnatural, but not the other way around.

41 *Relación verdadera de una carta que embió el padre Prior de la orden de Santo Domingo, de la Ciudad de Úbeda, al Abbad mayor de San Salvador de la Ciudad de Granada, de un caso digno de ser avisado, como estuvo doze años una monja professa, la qual avía metido su padre por ser cerrada, y no ser para casada, y un día haziendo un ejercicio de fuerza se le rompió una tela por donde le salio la naturaleza de hombre como los demás, y lo que se hizo para sacalla del convento. Agora sucedió en este año de mil y seys ciento y diez y siete* (Granada, Spain: s.n., 1617), Biblioteca Nacional de España (Madrid) "Informe sobre Magdalena Muñoz dominica profesa de la Coronada, de Úbeda, que se convirtió en hombre y tomó el nombre de Gaspar Muñoz" by Licenciado Moreno, manuscript number 12179; see also Francisco Rafael de Uhagón y Guardamino (Marqués de Laurencín), *Relaciones históricas de los siglos XVI y XVII* (Madrid: Impr. de la viuda é hijos de m. Tello, 1896), 335–7.

42 Sherry Velasco, *Male Delivery: Reproduction, Effeminacy, and Pregnant Men in Early Modern Spain* (Nashville, TN: Vanderbilt University Press, 2006), Craig Felton and William B. Jordan, *Jusepe de Ribera: Lo Spagnoletto, 1591–1652* (Fort Worh: Kimbell Art Museum, 1982), 129–31.

43 Juan Huarte de San Juan, *Exámen de ingenios para las ciencias* ed., Guillermo Serés (Madrid: Cátedra, 1989 [1575]), 634.

44 Luis Fernández, *Historia de animales y phisiognomía* (written in 1591 and circulated in manuscript form but printed in 1650), Josette Riandière la Roche, "La physiognomie, miroir de l'âme et du corps: à propos d'un inédit espagnol de 1591," in *Le corps dans la société espagnole des XVI et XVIIe siècles* ed., Augustin Redondo (Paris: Publications de la Sorbonne, 1990), 51–62.

45 Originally published as *De humana physiognomonia.* On the influence of della Porta's work among Spanish artists and intellectuals, see María del Mar Albero Muñoz, "La fisiognomía y la expresión de las pasiones en algunas bibliotecas de artistas españoles en el siglo XVII," *Cuadernos de Arte de la Universidad de Granada* 42 (2011): 37–52.

46 Giambattista della Porta, *La fisionomia dell'huomo et la celeste* (Milano: Gruppo editoriale Castel Negrino, 2006 [1652]), 508–509. Della Porta died in 1615. Years after his death, in 1652, the book was reedited as *La fisionomia dell'humo et la celeste.*

47 Archivo Histórico Nacional de España (Madrid): Inquisición, Tribunal de Valencia, libro 941, fol. 350–8 (1651). This case is discussed in Cristian Berco's *Sexual Hierarchies, Public Status: Men, Sodomy, and Society in Spain's Golden Age* (Toronto and Buffalo: University of Toronto Press, 2007), 30–1, in Rafael Carrasco's *Inquisición y represión sexual en Valencia* (Barcelona: Laertes, 1985), 146–8, and in François Soyer, *Ambiguous Gender in Early Modern Spain and Portugal: Inquisitors, Doctors and the Transgression of Gender Norms* (Leiden and Boston: Brill, 2012), 96–124.

48 In parts of the document 1646 appears as the date while in others the year given for his marriage is 1647.

49 In the kingdom of Valencia sodomy, the unspeakable crime, fell under the purview of the "Holy Tribunal of the Inquisition."

50 Almost a century earlier, in 1578, testimonies in the trial of the Bishop of Salamina, described the bishop's lover as a "little page of blue eyes and soft voice" or "effeminate voice," Francisco Núñez Roldán, *El pecado nefando del Obispo de Salamina: un hombre sin concierto en la corte de Felipe II* (Seville: Universidad de Sevilla, 2002), 25, 29.

51 Aristotle, *On the Generation of Animals* trans. Arthur Platt (Adelaide: The University of Adelaide, 2007), 267.

52 Jenny Mann "How to Look at a Hermaphrodite in Early Modern England," *SEL Studies in English Literature 1500–1900* 46,1 (2006): 67–91. In the sixteenth and seventeenth centuries, the job of physicians was to measure which of the two sexes of a hermaphrodite nature had initially intended to create. In combination with the gender traits displayed, the individual was allowed to choose the sex that would legally and socially be part of their identity for the rest of their lives.

53 Lorraine Daston and Katharine Park, "The Hermaphrodite and the Orders of Nature: Sexual Ambiguity in Early Modern France," *GLQ: A Journal of Lesbian and Gay Studies* 1, 4 (1995): 419–38.

54 Jaime Alcalá y Martínez, *Disertation médico-chirúrgica sobre una operación cesárea executada en muger y feto vivos, en esta ciudad de Valencia* (Valencia: Viuda de Geronymo Conejos, 1753), 11.

55 On the removal of the hermaphrodite in early modern Spain, what the authors call "the expulsion of the marvelous," Richard Cleminson and Francisco Vázquez García, "Subjectivities in Transition: Gender and Sexual Identities in Cases of 'Sex Change' and 'Hermaphroditism' in Spain, c. 1500–1800," *History of Science* 48 (2010): 1–38.

56 Palmira Fontes da Costa makes this argument for eighteenth-century England; Palmira Fontes da Costa, "'Mediating Sexual Difference': The Medical Understanding of Human Hermaphrodites in Eighteenth-Century England," in *Cultural Approaches to the History of Medicine: Mediating Medicine in Early Modern and Modern Europe* eds., Willem de Blécourt and Cornelie Usborne (New York: Palgrave MacMillan, 2004), 127–48.

57 Kathleen Long, *Hermaphrodites in Renaissance Europe* (Aldershot, UK: Ashgate, 2006).

58 Fontes da Costa, "'Mediating Sexual Difference'," 127–48.

59 The term "vulgar" embraced not only ordinary people without education or ability to offer a rational judgment but also all of those who did not follow a method of empirical observation and rational judgment; María del Carmen Iglesias Cano, *El pensamiento de Montesquieu: Ciencia y filosofía en el siglo XVIII* (Barcelona: Galaxia Gutenberg, 2005).

60 Anne Fausto-Sterling, *Sexing the Body: Gender Politics and the Construction of Sexuality* (New York: Basic Books, 2000), 32–6.

61 Patrick Gaille, *Les hermaphrodites au XVII et XVIII siècles* (Paris: Les Belles Lettres, 2001), 12.

62 The spectacle of hermaphrodites was also part of the tradition of the popular new gazettes in early modern Spain. They were known in Spain as "*avisos y relaciones.*"

63 Roy Porter, *Enlightenment: Britain and the Creation of the Modern World* (London: Penguin Press, 2000). In particular, at the end of the sixteenth

century a taste for the strangeness of the stories of hermaphrodites turned into a genre of its own, the *Relations of Hermaphrodites*. The goal of these publications was entertaining while informing in a pseudo-scientific way; Antonia Morel d'Arleux, "Las relaciones de hermafroditas: dos ejemplos diferentes de una misma manipulación ideológica," in *Las relaciones de sucesos en España: 1500–1750. Actas del primer Coloquio Internacional (Alcalá de Henares, 8, 9 y 10 de junio de 1995)* eds., Henry Ettinghausen, Víctor Infantes de Miguel, Augustin Redondo, and María Cruz García de Enterría (Madrid: Servicio de Publicaciones de la Universidad de Alcalá, 1996), 261–74.

64 Alice Dreger has shown how, even in the nineteenth century physicians still debated the existence of hermaphrodites and their place in the medical world; see Alice Dreger, *Hermaphrodites and the Medical Invention of Sex* (Cambridge, MA: Harvard University Press, 1998).

65 Judith Butler, *Giving an Account of Oneself* (New York: Fordham University Press, 2005), 6.

66 It is surprising, however, that although the anatomist admits there was a wide range of difference between the organs of different men or between women, he did not grade some as being "more perfectly masculine" or others as "more perfectly feminine," nor did he give parameters for doing so.

67 Juan Cabriada was one of the founders of the Royal Society of Medicine and Other Sciences of Seville.

68 Nicolás Fernández, "The Body of the Letter: Vital Force and the Practice of Spanish Medicine in Juan de Cabriada's Carta Filósofica, Medico-Chymica (1687)," *Revista Hispánica Moderna* 68, 2 (2015): 109–24.

69 Diego Mateo Zapata, *Crisis médica sobre el antimonio, y carta responsoria a la Regia Sociedad Médica de Sevilla* (Madrid: s.n., 1701); see also Diego Mateo Zapata, *Disertación médico-teológica, que consagra a la serenísima señora princesa del Brasil* (Madrid: Don Gabriel del Barrio, 1733) and *Ocaso de las formas Aristotélicas* (Madrid: Imprenta del Hospital General, 1745). The latter was printed and distributed posthumously. Zapata's *Disertación médico-teológica* provoked an immediate response among his critics; see Francisco Perena, *Conclusiones teológico-médico-legales contra la disertación médico-teológica de Diego Mateo Zapata* (s.l. s.n., 1733).

70 José Pardo Tomás, *El médico en la palestra: Diego Mateo Zapata (1664–1745) y la ciencia moderna en España* (Valladolid: Junta de Castilla y León, 2004).

71 Anatomy theaters were first founded in the sixteenth century. In Spain, the first anatomy theater, and one of the oldest in Europe, was established in 1554 in Salamanca; José Pardo Tomás, *Un lugar para la ciencia: escenarios de práctica científica en la sociedad hispana del siglo XVI* (Tenerife, Spain: Fundación Canaria Orotava de Historia de la Ciencia, 2006).

72 "Informe sobre el establecimiento del Colegio de Cirugía de Madrid, dado por D. Antonio de Gimbernat en Madrid, a 14 de Julio de 1780," in *Biblioteca clásica de la medicina española: Obras de Antonio de Gimbernat* ed., Enrique Salcedo y Ginestal 2 vols. (Madrid: J. Cosano, 1926-28), 1: 145–54 (146); see also Granjel, *Anatomía española*, 28.

73 José Pardo Tomás and Àlvar Martínez Vidal, "Los orígenes del teatro anatómico de Madrid, (1689–1728)," *Asclepio* 44 (1997): 5–38; José Pardo

Tomás, "El primitivo teatro anatómico de Barcelona," *Medicina e Historia* 65 (1996): 8–28.

74 Antoni de Gimbernat, *Oración inaugural que para la abertura de los estudios, celebrada en el Real Colegio de Cirugía de Barcelona el dia 5 de octubre de 1773* (Barcelona: Francisco Suriá y Burgada, 1773).

75 Manuel de Porras, *Médula de cirugía y exámen de cirujanos* (Madrid: s.n. 1691).

76 Manuel de Porras, *Anatomía galénico-moderna* (Madrid: en la imprenta de música, por Bernardo Peralta, 1716).

77 Antonio Bonet Correa, *Fray Matías de Irala: grabador madrileño* (Madrid: Ayuntamiento de Madrid, 1979).

78 Martínez, *Anatomía completa*, 156, 177.

79 Martínez, *Anatomía completa*, 188.

80 Jonathan Sheehan and Dror Wahrman, *Invisible Hands: Self-Organization and the Eighteenth Century* (Chicago and London: The University of Chicago Press, 2015).

81 Sebastián de Covarrubias Orozco, *Diccionario El Tesoro de la Lengua Castellana o Española* (Madrid: Imprenta Luis Sánchez, 1611).

82 Baruch Spinoza, *Ethics* (Champaign, IL: Project Gutenberg, 1999 [1677]), book 2, propositions 12, 13, 21; Michael della Roca, *Representation and the Mind–Body Problem in Spinoza* (New York and Oxford: Oxford University Press, 1996), Chapter Eight.

83 Pierre Bayle, *Dictionnaire Historique et Critique* (Rotterdam: Reinier Leers, 1697); Martín Martínez defended Feijóo from his critics in "Carta defensiva sobre el primer tomo del Teatro crítico universal," in Benito Jerónimo Feijóo, *Teatro crítico universal* 9 vols. (Madrid: Joaquin Ibarra, 1779 [1726–40]), 2: 322–52.

84 Guillermo Ricca, "Ilustración radical y drama intelectual: Spinoza, Feijoo y las matrices diversas," *A Parte Rei. Revista de Filosofía* 55 (January 2008): 1–12; Atilano Domínguez ed., *Spinoza y España. Actas del Congreso Internacional sobre "Relaciones entre Spinoza y España" (Almagro, 5–7 noviembre 1992)* (Cuenca, Spain: Ediciones de la Universidad Castilla-La Mancha, 2004).

85 Pauline Phemister, *The Rationalists: Descartes, Spinoza and Leibniz* (Cambridge, UK and Malden, MA: Polity Press, 2006).

86 Spinoza, *Ethics* Part 1, Concerning God Propositions, 21–9.

87 Royal Spanish Dictionary (*Diccionario de Autoridades*), entry for *albedrío*.

88 Biblioteca Nacional de España (Madrid): Mss. 12966-20: *Noticia y Relación individual del suceso occurrido en el convento de Religiosas de las Madres Capuchinas de la ciudad de Granada en el año 1792*, 6 fols.; this case has been analyzed by María José de la Pascua Sánchez, "¿Hombres vueltos del revés? Una historia sobre la construcción de la identidad sexual en el siglo XVIII," in *Mujer y deseo: representaciones y prácticas de vida* eds., María José de la Pascua, María del Rosario García-Doncel Hernández, and Gloria Espigado Tocino (Cadiz, Spain: Universidad de Cadiz, 2004), 431–44.

89 "Todo en la Medicina es disputado: luego todo es dudoso," Feijóo, *Teatro crítico* 1:14 (discourse on "Medicine").

90 Francisco Sánchez-Blanco, *La mentalidad ilustrada* (Madrid: Taurus, 1999), 61–122.

91 Robin George Collingwood, *The Idea of Nature* (Oxford: Oxford University Press, 1960 [1945]), 113.

2 Medical Theory versus Practice: The Case of Sebastián/María Leirado

1 Most of the anatomists of this generation were also surgeons, or "anatomist-surgeons."

2 Judith Butler, "Appearances Aside," *California Law Review* 88, 1 (January 2000): 55–63; "Doing Justice to Someone: Sex Reassignment and Allegories of Transsexuality," *GLQ: A Journal of Lesbian and Gay Studies* 7, 4 (2001): 621–36.

3 Thomas Abercrombie has analyzed the fascinating case of Antonio Yta (born María) for the late colonial Spanish America. Yta's wife accused her husband of being "a woman dressed as a man." The trial reflects yet another aspect of how authorities dealt with cases of individuals with ambiguous gender and the social consequences this could have; Thomas Abercrombine, "Una vida disfrazada en el Potosí y la Plata Colonial: Antonio-nacido-María Yta ante la Audiencia de Charcas (un documento y una reflexión crítica)," *Anuario de Estudios Bolivianos, Archivísticos y Bibliográficos* 11(2008): 3–45.

4 Lorraine Daston, "Marvelous Facts and Miraculous Evidence in Early Modern Europe," in *Questions of Evidence: Proof, Practice, and Persuasion across the Disciplines* eds., James Chandler, Arnold I. Davidson, and Harry Harootunian (Chicago: The University of Chicago Press, 1994), 274.

5 The entire trial of Sebastián Leirado and documents belonging to the case are housed in Archivo Histórico Nacional (Madrid), Consejo 5373, Causas Criminales, n. 4 "Madrid Causa criminal contra Sebastian Leyrado sobre pecado nefando," 1769.

6 *La vida de Lazarillo de Tormes y de sus fortunas y adversidades* ed., Aldo Ruffinatto (Madrid: Clásicos Castalia, 2001 [1554]).

7 On the construction of a literary person in *El Lazarillo*, see Arnold Weinstein, *Fictions of the Self: 1550–1800* (Princeton: Princeton University Press, 1981), 20.

8 That must have been around 1757 since Sebastián Leirado was born in 1745; Archivo Parroquial de San Sebastián (Madrid) Libro de Bautismos año de 1745, 9-abril-1745, fol. 8.

9 Marta V. Vicente, "Staging Femininity in Early Modern Spain," in *The Early Modern Hispanic World: Transnational and Interdisciplinary Approaches* eds., Kimberly Lynn and Erin Rowe (Cambridge, MA: Cambridge University Press, 2017), 339–59.

10 Emilio Cotarelo y Mori, *María Ladvenant y Quirante, primera dama de los teatros de la corte* (Madrid: Sucesores de Rivadeneyra, 1896), 45.

11 In a former declaration in 1766 he provides the name as D. Juan de Chaure, capitan of the Africa regiment.

12 Archivo Parroquial de San Sebastián (Madrid) Libro de Defunciones año de 1767.

13 Luis Belmonte Bermúdez, *El diablo predicador y mayor contrario amigo* (Madrid: Ayuntamiento de Madrid, 2013 [1653]). The play was first represented in 1623.

14 The play had been prohibited by the Tribunal of the Inquisition for its criticism of the clergy, Antonio Roldán Pérez, "El diablo predicador una comedia cuestionada. El consejo de la Inquisición contra el Tribunal de Sevilla," in *El centinela de la fe: estudios jurídicos sobre la Inquisición de Sevilla en el siglo XVIII* ed., Enrique Gacto Fernández (Seville: Universidad de Sevilla, 1997), 399–469.

15 Cruz del Pozo, *Gassendismo y cartesianismo.*

16 López was a young student at Alcalá during the 1730s. By then Martín Martínez had already become an authority in the field of anatomy. He was professor of anatomy in the General Hospital of Madrid until 1734, the year of his death.

17 José Antonio Díaz Rojo, "La biblioteca del Ilustrado Juan José de Arostegi, cirujano del Hospital de San Bernabé (1799)," *Publicaciones de la Institución Tello Téllez de Meneses* 66 (1995): 107–18. Luis S. Granjel, "La obra anatómica de Manuel de Porras y Juan de Dios López," *Medicamenta* 38 (1962): 289–92.

18 Juan de Dios López, *Compendio anatómico dividido en cuatro partes* 4 vols. (Madrid: s.n., 1750–52).

19 López's *Compendio* was one of the main books in the library of the school of surgery of the General Hospital at the end of the eighteenth century; see Juan Manuel Núñez Olarte, *El Hospital General de Madrid en el siglo XVIII: actividad médico-quirúrgica* (Madrid: Consejo Superior de Investigaciones Científicas, 1999), 144–5. By the mid-nineteenth-century, the work of López was already dismissed as merely a poor translation of César Verdier's manual *Abrégé de L'anatomie du corps humain* (Bruxelles: Jean Leonard, 1752 [1734]); Manuel Hurtado de Mendoza, *Tratado elemental complemento de anatomía general* (Madrid: Imprenta de García, 1830), 3, 17; and Lorenzo Boscasa, *Tratado de anatomía general, descriptiva y topográfica* 3 vols. (Madrid: Librería de los Señores Viuda é Hijos de Antonio Calleja, 1844–5), 1, part 2, 357. Boscasa accused Juan de Dios López of corrupting the core of "our scientific language" in his *Compendio* for its poor translations and many Gallicisms. However, this is not entirely true. López's work differs considerably from Verdier's manual. In fact, the library of a surgeon from Girona (Spain) from the 1790s had both the work of Verdier in its two Spanish translations as well as López's *Compendio anatómico*; see Anastasio Chinchilla, *Anales históricos de la medicina en general, y biográfico-bibliográficos de la española en particular* (New York: Johnson Reprint Corp, 1967 [1843]), 154, and Antonio Hernández Morejón, *Historia bibliográfica de la medicina española* 7 vols. (Madrid: Jordán, 1842–52), 7: 190.

20 Frederik Ruysch, *Thesaurus anatomicus* (Amsterdam: Apud Joannem Wolters, 1701–6); Jacques-Bénigne Winslow, *Exposition anatomique de la structure du corps humain* (Paris: Guillaume Desprez, 1732); on López's influence by European anatomists, see Granjel, *Anatomía española*, 57–61.

21 López, *Compendio anatómico*, I, 1.

22 López, *Compendio anatómico*, I, 1–2.

23 Jerónimo Cortés, *Fisonomía y varios secretos de naturaleza* (Valencia: Librería Paris, 1992 [1598]); Emilio Palacios Fernández, studies this work in his "Las fábulas de Félix María de Samaniego: Fabulario, bestiario, fisiognomía

y lección moral," *Revista de Literatura* LX, 119 (January–February 1998): 79–100.

24 Ludmilla Jordanova, "The art and science of seeing in medicine: physiognomy, 1780–1820," in *Medicine and the Five Senses* eds., William F. Bynum and Roy Porter (Cambridge, UK: Cambridge University Press, 1993), 122–33.

25 Esteban Pujasol, *El sol solo, y para todos sol, de la filosofía sagaz y anatomía de los ingenios* (Madrid: Magalia Ediciones, 2000 [1637]), 84.

26 Giambattista della Porta believed that a man doing women's jobs could have a tendency to pursue "the unspeakable sin."

27 Buffon's main work, translated into Spanish in 1773 and 1785, was central in shaping the view of Spanish philosophers on nature and natural monsters.

28 Jean-Pierre Guicciardi, "Hermaphrodite et le prolétaire," *Dix-Huitième Siècle* 12 (1980): 49–77.

29 James R. McGuire, "La representation du corps hermaphrodite dans les planches de l'Encyclopédie," *Recherches sur Diderot et sur L'Encyclopédie* 11 (1991): 109–29.

30 Palmira Fontes da Costa, "Albrecht von Haller e o debate sobre a existência de seres humanos hermafroditas" *Revista Portuguesa de Filosofia* 66 (2010): 70–80.

31 Deirdre Coleman, "Entertaining Entomology: Insects and Insect Performers in the Eighteenth Century," *Eighteenth-Century Life* 30, 3 (Fall 2006): 107–34.

32 Ludmilla Jordanova, *Nature Displayed: Gender, Science and Medicine 1760–1820* (London: Longman, 1999), 160.

33 *Diccionario de Autoridades.*

34 Pierre Jean George Cabanis, *Rapports du physique et du moral de l'homme* 2 vols. (Paris: Crapart, Caille et Ravier, 1802), 1: 315–316.

35 Rebecca Haidt, "Fashion, Effeminacy, and Homoerotic Desire (?): The Question of the Petimetres," *Letras Peninsulares* 12 (Spring 1999): 65–80.

36 For a study of the petimetre's ambiguous sexuality Haidt, *Embodying Enlightenment* and Haidt, "Fashion, Effeminacy," 65–80.

37 Haidt, *Embodying Enlightenment*, 116.

38 The dangers of wasted discharge are analyzed by Laqueur, *Solitary Sex.*

39 According to Torres Villarroel, quoted by Haidt, *Embodying Enlightenment*, 168 (I am quoting Haidt's translation from the Spanish).

40 Antonio Manuel Ruíz, *Memorial de las damas arrepentidas de ser locas al tribunal de las juiciosas i discretas* (Madrid: s.n., 1755).

41 Francisco Mariano Nipho, *El amigo de las mujeres traducido del francés por D. Francisco Mariano Nipho* (Madrid: s.n., 1771). Nipho also translated the fifteenth-century French poet Alain Chartier's work and adapted it for an eighteenth-century audience.

42 *Diario curioso, erudito, económico y comercial* (Madrid: Librería de Arribas, carrera de San Gerónimo, 1786).

43 Archivo Histórico Nacional (Madrid), Alcaldes de Casa y Corte, fols. 770–4: "Copia de Tonadilla a Solo: La Humorada de Garrido, Censura: Madrid, 14 de noviembre de 1786, estando el Sr. D. Josef Miguel de Flores del Consejo de Alcaldes de Casa y Corte en el coliseo del Príncipe donde se representaba la obra *La Religión Española y Musulmán Nobleza*, advirtió que la tonadilla

primera cantado por el gracioso Miquel Garrido vestido de muger tenía algunas expresiones malsonantes e indecorosas."

44 María de Zayas y Sotomayor, *Desengaños amorosos* (Madrid: Aldus, 1950 [1647]), see Margaret Greer, *María de Zayas Tells Baroque Tales of Love and the Cruelty of Men* (University Park, PA: Pennsylvania State University Press, 2000).

45 Michael Shapiro, *Gender in Play on the Shakespearean Stage: Boy Heroines and Female Pages* (Ann Arbor: University of Michigan Press, 1994).

46 Tirso de Molina, *El vergonzoso en palacio* (Madrid: Real Academia Española, 2012 [1624]); Tirso de Molina, *Don Gil de las calzas verdes* (Madrid: Cátedra, 2009 [1635]). Although first published in 1624 and 1635 respectively, both plays were performed years before their publication, 1611 or 1612 for *El vergonzoso* and 1615 for *Don Gil*.

47 Peter E. Thompson, *The Triumphant Juan Rana: A Gay Actor of the Spanish Golden Age* (Toronto: University of Toronto Press, 2006), 65.

48 Patricia Simons, *The Sex of Men in Premodern Europe: A Cultural History* (Cambridge, UK: Cambridge University Press, 2011), 152–57.

3 Nature, Nurture, and Early Modern Sexuality

1 Not having a separate field of pediatrics, children's health was part of the area of gynecology and obstetrics.

2 Yet, the 1792 case of Mother Fernanda, related in Chapter 1, still fueled the imagination of many at the turn of the century.

3 John Locke, "Some Thoughts Concerning Education [1693]," in *The Educational Writings of John Locke* ed., John William Adamson (London: E. Arnold, 1912), 33–4, 64, 175–89; see Adrian Johns' discussion on Locke, Adrian Johns, *The Nature of the Book: Print and Knowledge in the Making* (Chicago, IL: The University of Chicago Press, 1998), 405–8.

4 Pierre Bourdieu, *The Logic of Practice* trans. Richard Nice (Stanford: Stanford University Press, 1990), 73.

5 Bourdieu, *Logic of Practice*, 70.

6 *Diccionario de Autoridades*.

7 Juan de la Cerda, *Libro intitulado vida política de los estados de las mugeres: en el qual se dan muy prouechosos y Christianos documentos y auisos, para criarse y conseruarse deuidamente las mugeres en sus estados …: con vn Indice Alphabetico muy copioso de materias, que siruen de lugares comunes* (Madrid: Alcalá de Henares, 1599), 5.

8 *Plain Reasons for the Growth of Sodomy in England: To which is added, The Petit Maitre, an Odd Sort of an Unpoetical Poem, in the Troly-lolly Stile* (1730), reprinted in Alexander Pettit and Patrick Spedding eds., *Eighteenth-Century British Erotica* II, 5 vols. (London: Pickering & Chatto, 2004), 5: 189–218.

9 The text actually reads "stroked up *before…*"

10 Lawrence Stone already saw this in the context of the family; see Lawrence Stone, *The Family, Sex and Marriage in England, 1500–1800* (New York: Harper & Row, 1979).

11 Paul Schuurman, Jonathan Walmsley, and Sami-Juhani Savonius-Wroth eds., *The Continuum Companion to Locke* (New York: Continuum, 2010). In particular, the translation, *L'éducation des enfants*, was based on the fifth edition of Locke's work.

12 The publisher and translator Pierre Coste translated Locke's major educational works into French. In Spain, the work was published as *La educación de los niños* and translated from the French.

13 Locke, "Some Thoughts," 1.

14 Locke, "Some Thoughts," 46, 179.

15 Locke understood knowledge "as the perception of the connection and agreement or disagreement and repugnancy of any of our ideas;" John Locke, *An Essay Concerning Human Understanding in Four Books* (London: Printed by Eliz. Holt for Thomas Basset, 1690), 4: 525.

16 Locke, a philosopher usually studied for his non-religious ideas, in fact grounded education in a moral behavior linked to his theories on the certainty of knowledge of God and moral behavior.

17 José Manuel López Gómez, "El manuscrito 148 de la biblioteca pública del estado de Burgos: 'Enfermedades de Mujeres de Agustín Ginesta'," *Gimbernat* 23 (1995): 135–48.

18 Other Spanish physicians writing on obstetrics were Francisco Canivell (1721–97) and Juan de Navas, *Elementos del arte de partear* (Madrid: Imprenta Real, 1795).

19 Agustín Ginesta, *El conservador de los niños* (Madrid: Imprenta Real, 1797).

20 Manuel Jesús García Martínez, "Los cuidados pediátricos a finales del siglo XVIII: El Conservador de los Niños una obra sobre autocuidados," *Híades. Revista de Historia de la Enfermería* 7 (2000): 327–54.

21 José Clavijo y Fajardo, *El Pensador. Pensamiento LXIII* (Madrid: Imprenta de Joachin Ibarra, 1763–7), 109.

22 Jean-Jacques Rousseau, *Émile: ou de l'éducation* (Paris: Garnier-Flammarion, 1966 [1762]), 258.

23 In 1763, the Mexican friar Cristóbal Mariano Coriche wrote a scathing response to Rousseau. Cristóbal Mariano Coriche, *Oración vindicativa del honor de las letras, y de los literatos* (Puebla: Imprenta del Colegio Real de San Ignacio, 1763).

24 On the influence of Rousseau's work in Spain, see François Lopez, "Aspectos específicos de la Ilustración Española," in *II Simposio sobre el Padre Feijóo y su siglo* (Oviedo: Centro de Estudios del Siglo XVIII, 1981), 38. *Émile* was, in fact, the inspirational text for *Eusebio*, Pedro de Montengón's Spanish version of Rousseau's ideal pupil. In his 600-page book, Montengón discussed the issues of "nature versus nurture." Distributed in four parts from 1786 through 1788, Eusebio became a bestseller in Spain, with 70,000 copies sold in its first edition. Pedro de Montengón, *Eusebio* (Madrid: Cátedra, 1998 [1786–8]); for a comparison between the work of Montegón and Rousseau's, see Pedro Santonja, *El "Eusebio" de Montengón y el "Emilio" de Rousseau: el contexto histórico (Trabajo de literatura comparada)* (Alicante, Spain: Consejo Superior de Investigaciones Científicas, Instituto de Cultura, 1994), and Ana L. Baquero Escudero, *El viaje y la ficción narrativa española en el siglo XVIII* (Alicante, Spain: Biblioteca Virtual Miguel de Cervantes, 2009).

25 Olegario Negrín Fajardo, "Locke y Rousseau en *El Pensador* de Clavijo y Fajardo," in *Estudios dieciochistas en homenaje al profesor José Miguel Caso González* 2 vols. (Oviedo, Spain: Instituto Feijóo de Estudios del Siglo XVIII, 1995), 2: 181–94.

26 Early Spanish physicians like the sixteenth-century author Luis Mercado and his work on women and children's health also influenced Agustín Ginesta; see José María López Piñero and Francesc Bujosa i Homar, *Los tratados de enfermedades infantiles en la España del Renacimiento* (Valencia: Cátedra de Historia de la Medicina, 1982), 109–30.

27 Valentín de Foronda, *Cartas sobre la policía* (Madrid: Imprenta de Cano, 1801), 212.

28 See Elena del Río Parra, *Una era de monstruos: representaciones de lo deforme en el Siglo de Oro español* (Madrid: Iberoamericana, 2003), 73.

29 *Diccionario de Autoridades*.

30 Pseudonim for Andrés Ferrer de Valdecebro, *El porque de todas las cosas* (Madrid: Andres García de la Iglesia, 1668), 8.

31 Saint Thomas Aquinas, *Commentary on Aristotle's Physics* (New Haven: Yale University Press, 1963), 131.

32 Margrit Shildrick, *Embodying the Monster: Encounters with the Vulnerable Self* (London: Sage Publications, 2002).

33 Aristotle, *On the Generation of Animals* trans. Arthur Platt (Adelaide: The University of Adelaide, 2007), 19.

34 Masturbation was also regarded as a waste, see Laqueur, *Solitary Sex*.

35 Saint Augustine, Bishop of Hippo, *Confessions* trans. Edward B. Pusey (New York: Modern Library, 1999), book eight.

36 Del Río Parra, *Era de monstruos*, 37–42.

37 *Diccionario de Autoridades* (1780, 1787).

38 Biblioteca Histórica de la Universidad de Alcalá (BHUA): "Observación sobre las circunstancias encontradas en un pretendido hermafrodito," manuscript by Agustín Ginesta (Madrid, 1798), June 21–8. Ginesta, *Conservador de los Niños*.

39 Iglesias Cano, *Razón y sentimiento.*

40 Pierre Boaistuau, *Histoire prodigiouses* (1560), translated into Spanish as "Historias prodigiosas y maravillosas de diversos sucesos acaescidos en el mundo escritas en lengua francesa por Pedro Bouistau, Claudio Tesserant y Francisco Belforest," ed., Enrique Suárez Figaredo, *Lemir* 17 (2013 [1574]): 126–447. The text was translated into Spanish in 1636 by Andrea Pescioni.

41 Erasmus' *Manual of a Christian Soldier* was translated and published in Spain in 1526, while his *Hand Book on Good Manners for Children* (*De civilitate morum puerilium libellus*) (1530), dedicated to the young Prince Henry of Burgundy also became a reference work on early modern pedagogy; see Merridee L. Bailey, "In Service and at Home: Didactic Texts for Children and Young People, c. 1400–1600," *Parergon* 24, 2 (2007): 23–43, and Jacques Revel et al., "Forms of Privatization," in *A History of Private Life* 5 vols., eds., Philippe Ariès and Georges Duby (Cambridge, MA: Harvard University Press, 1989), 3: 174.

42 *De Tratendis Disciplinis* (1531); see León Esteban Mateo and Ramón López Martín, *La escuela de primeras letras según Juan Luis Vives: estudio, iconografía y textos* (Valencia: Universitat de València, 1993), 38–43.

43 Jerónimo Gómez de Huerta, *Historia Natural de Plinio* (Madrid: Pedro Madrigal, 1599–1629).

44 Saint Augustine, Bishop of Hippo, *On Christian Doctrine* (New York: Bobbs-Merrill, 1958), book three, Chapter XXXVI.

45 San Vicente Ferrer, *Sermones del bienaventurado san Vicente Ferrer: en los quales avisa contra los engaños de los dos Antichristos y amonesta a los fieles Christianos que esten aparejados para el Juicio final* (Burgos: en casa de Philippe de Junta, 1577).

46 De la Cerda, *Libro intitulado*, 8.

47 Francesc Baucells, *Font mystica y sagrada del Paradis de la Iglesia* (Figueres, Spain: I. Porter, 1760, [1704]), 203.

48 Cissie Fairchild, *Domestic Enemies: Servants and their Masters in Old Regime France* (Baltimore: Johns Hopkins University Press, 1984).

49 Marta V. Vicente, "Staging Femininity in Early Modern Spain," in *The Early Modern Hispanic World: Transnational and Interdisciplinary Approaches* eds., Kimberly Lynn and Erin Rowe (Cambridge, MA: Cambridge University Press, 2017), 339–59.

50 Sylvie Steinberg, *La confusion des sexes: Le travestissement de la Renaissance à la Révolution* (Paris: Fayard, 2001), 91–130. It could also be argued that both Le Chevalier d'Eon and Pierre Aymond Dumoret were transgender individuals; see Gary Kates, *Monsieur d'Eon Is a Woman* (Baltimore: Johns Hopkins University Press, 2001).

51 Rousseau, *Émile*, book I.

52 Nina Felshin, "Clothing as Subject," *Art Journal* 54, 1 (Spring, 1995): 20–9; see also Álvaro Molina and Jesusa Vega, *Vestir la identidad, construir la apariencia* (Madrid: Ayuntamiento de Madrid, 2004).

53 Susan Crane, *The Performance of the Self: Ritual, Clothing and Identity during the Hundred Years Wars* (Philadelphia: University of Pennsylvania Press, 2002).

54 On the meaning of the sambenitos and their symbolic value for the Inquisition, see Luis R. Corteguera, *Death by Effigy: A Case from the Mexican Inquisition* (Philadelphia: University of Pennsylvania Press, 2012).

55 "Sobre cuánto contribuye a la salud pública, la regulación physica de los vestidos," in *Memorias academicas de la Real Sociedad de Medicina y demás Ciencias de Sevilla* ed., Real Sociedad de Medicina (Seville: Imprenta de D. Josef Padrino y Solis, 1786), 4: 381–410 (406).

56 William Buchan, *El conservador de la salud de las madres y los niños* (Madrid: Imprenta de D. Fermin Villalpando, 1808), 14.

57 Haidt, *Embodying Enlightenment*, 107–20.

58 Lorenzo Hervas y Panduro, *Historia de la vida del hombre* 6 vols. (Alicante, Spain: Biblioteca Virtual Miguel de Cervantes, 2007 [1789]), 1: 207.

59 *Diccionario de Autoridades*.

60 Luis R. Corteguera, "King as Father in Early Modern Spain," *Memoria y Civilización* 12 (2009): 49–69; This model of the artisanal family with the father-figure (the master) at the head provided the basis for the organization of the first factories in eighteenth-century Spain, see Marta V. Vicente, *Clothing the Spanish Empire: Families and the Calico Trade in the Early Modern Atlantic World* (New York: Palgrave MacMillan, 2006).

61 Leslie Tuttle, *Conceiving the Old Regime: Pro-Natalism and the Politics of Reproduction in Early Modern France* (Oxford: Oxford University Press, 2010), 181. This was not a singular feature of the eighteenth century. Charlene Villaseñor-Black has shown how in the seventeenth century the increasing popularity of St. Joseph made him a loving father at the center of a "happy

family," *Creating the Cult of St. Joseph: Art and Gender in the Spanish Empire* (Princeton: Princeton University Press, 2006). This phenomenon of the loving father crucial to the well-being of the family intensifies in the eighteenth century.

62 Jean-Claude Bonnet, "La malédiction paternelle," *Dix-Huitième Siècle* 12 (1980): 195–208.

63 Jen-Claude Bonnet, "De la famille à la patrie," in *Histoire des pères et de la paternité* eds., Jean Delumeau and Daniel Roche (Paris: Larousse, 2000 [1990]), 245–67.

64 BHUA "Observación del lechero Antonio Lozano hecha por D. José Castellar médico y cirujano del Real Hospital de Cumaná" (1786), 5 fols.

65 *El tiempo ilustrado de la medicina*; quote from Dr. Castellar in his report on Antonio Lozano.

66 Archivo General de Indias (AGI) Estado, 62, n. 3, 13 fols.

67 For information regarding Juan Mercier, see Luis Navarro García ed., *José de San Martín y su tiempo* (Seville: Universidad de Sevilla, 1999), 348.

68 AGI Estado, 62, n.3, 3 r.

69 BHUA José Castellar, "Observación de un hombre que crío a sus pechos uno de sus hijos (Observación del Lechero Antonio Lozano)," October 1790.

70 Manuel Ossorio y Bernard, *Progresos y extravagancias. Apuntes para un libro* (Madrid: Imprenta de Moreno y Rojas, 1887), 65.

71 María del Carmen Iglesias Cano, "Educación y pensamiento ilustrado," in *Actas del congreso internacional sobre "Carlos III y la ilustración"* ed., Ministerio de Cultura, vol. III Educación y pensamiento (Madrid: Ministerio de Cultura, 1989), 1–30. Michael Burke argues this focus on utility set aside the Spanish Enlightenment from the French less concerned about the practical aspects of usefulness; Michael E. Burke, *The Royal College of San Carlos: Surgery and Spanish Medical Reform in the Late Eighteenth Century* (Durham, NC: Duke University Press, 1977), 5. On the distinctive character of the Spanish Enlightenment, see also George Klaeren, "Encountering the Enlightenment: Science, Religion and Catholic Epistomologies across the Spanish Atlantic" (PhD dissertation, University of Kansas, 2017).

72 *Diccionario de Autoridades*.

73 Gail Kern Paster, Katherine Rowe, and Mary Floyd-Wilson eds., *Reading the Early Modern Passions: Essays in the Cultural History of Emotions* (Philadelphia: University of Pennsylvania Press, 2004), 1–21; see also Stephen Gaukroger ed., *The Soft Underbelly of Reason: Passions in the Seventeenth Century* (New York and London: Routledge, 1998).

74 Susan James, "Explaining the Passions: Passions, Desires, and the Explanation of Action," in *Soft Underbelly*, 17–33.

75 Jean Francois Senault, *The Philosophy of the Passions; Demonstrating Their Nature, Properties, Effects, Use and Abuse* trans. Henry Earl of Monmouth (London: Printed for J. Almon, 1772 [1651]), Sir Edward Reynolds, "A Treatise on the Passions and Faculties of the Soul of the Man," in *The Whole Works of the Right Rev. Edward Reynolds*, 6 vols. (London: B. Holdsworth, 1826 [1640]), 6: 10.

76 Maurizio Ferraris, *L'Immaginazione* (Bologna: Il Mulino, 1996).

77 Gary Tomlinson, "Five Pictures of Pathos," in *Reading the Early Modern Passions*, 192–214.

78 Antonio Mestre Sanchis, *Apología y crítica de España en el siglo XVIII* (Madrid: Marcial Pons, 2003), 353–72.

79 Stephen T. Asma, *On Monsters: An Unnatural History of Our Worst Fears* (Oxford: Oxford University Press, 2009), 141–62.

80 Valeria Finucci, "Maternal Imagination and Monstrous Birth: Tasso's Gerusalemme liberata," in *Generation and Degeneration: Tropes of Reproduction in Literature and History from Antiquity to Early Modern Europe* eds., Valeria Finucci and Kevin Brownlee (Durham, NC: Duke University Press, 2001), 41–77; see also Jan Bondeson, *A Cabinet of Medical Curiosities* (Ithaca, NY: Cornell University Press, 1997), 144–69.

81 It is what Adrian Johns has labeled "a habituated passion;" Johns, *Nature of the Book*, 405.

82 Judith Butler, *Gender Trouble: Feminism and the Subversion of Identity* (New York: Routledge, 1990), 139.

83 Butler, *Gender Trouble*, 139.

84 Burke, *Royal College of San Carlos*, 25.

85 Sigmund Freud, The *"Uncanny,"* in *The Standard Edition of the Complete Psychological Works of Sigmund Freud, Volume XVII (1917–1919): An Infantile Neurosis and Other Works* (London: Vintage, 2001), 217–56.

86 *Relation historique du voyage aux régions équinoxiales du nouveau continent* ed., Hanno Beck 3 vols.(Stuttgart: F. A. Brockhaus, 1970 [1814]), 1: 376–8. Written with Aimé Bonpland. The exact same text appears in English in *The Analectic Magazine* vol. XII (July–December, 1818): 509–11. The 1818 translation of Humboldt account is found in George Paxton, *Illustrations of the Holy Scriptures* (Edinburgh: Sterling & Kenney, 1825).

87 Humboldt, *Relation historique*, 377.

88 Roberto Lionetti, *Latte di padre: Vitalità, contesti, livelli di lettura di un motivo folklorico* (Brescia, Italy: Grafo, 1984), 122.

89 Joan Wallach Scott, *Only Paradoxes to Offer: French Feminists and the Rights of Man* (Cambridge, MA: Harvard University Press, 1996), 209.

90 Barbara Newman, *From Virile Woman to Woman Christ: Studies in Medieval Religion and Literature* (Philadelphia: University of Pennsylvania Press, 1995).

91 Giana Pomata, "Menstruating Men: Similarity and Difference of the Sexes in Early Modern Medicine" in *Generation and Degeneration*, 109–52; John L. Beusterien, "Jewish Male Menstruation in Seventeenth-Century Spain," *Bulletin of the History of Medicine* 73 (1999): 447–56; Cathy McClive, "Masculinity on Trial: Penises, Hermaphrodites and the Uncertain Male Body in Early Modern France," *History Workshop Journal* 68 (Autumn 2009): 45–68.

92 On the consequence that mothers not breastfeeding their own children had for society, see Jaime Bonells, *Perjuicios que acarrean al género humano y al Estado las madres, que rehusan criar á sus hijos: y medios para contener el abuso de ponerlos en ama* (Madrid: Miguel Escribano, 1786); Carmen Sarasúa, *Criados, nodrizas y amos: el servicio doméstico en la formación del trabajo madrileño 1758–1868* (Madrid: Siglo Veintiuno Editores, 1994), 187–96.

93 Ignacio Beteta, *Gazeta de Guatemala* (1797–1816); this case has been studied by Martha Few, "'That Monster of Nature': Gender, Sexuality, and the Medicalization of a 'Hermaphrodite' in Late Colonial Guatemala,"

Ethnohistory 54, 1 (Winter 2007): 159–76; and more recently by María Elena Martínez "Archives, Bodies, and Imagination: The Case of Juana Aguilar and Queer Approaches to History, Sexuality, and Politics," *Radical History Review, Special Issue on "Queering Archives"* 120 (Fall 2014): 159–82.

94 Georges Louis Leclerc, comte de Buffon, *Natural History* trans. William Smellie 9 vols. (Edinburgh: Printed for William Creech, 1780–85), 2: 242. Esparragosa made his findings public by publishing them in the *Gazeta de Guatemala*, aware of the expectations and publicity the case had received.

95 Martínez, "Archives, Bodies."

96 María Elena Martínez, "Sex, Race, and Nature: Juana Aguilar's Body and Creole Enlightened Thought in Late Colonial New Spain," paper presented at the *Race and Sex in the Eighteenth-Century Spanish Atlantic World*, Symposium USC, Los Angeles, CA, April 12–13, 2013.

97 Martínez, "Sex, Race, and Nature," 40.

98 Mary K. Bloodsworth-Lugo, *In-Between Bodies: Sexual Difference, Race, and Sexuality* (Albany, NY: SUNY Press, 2007).

99 Ilona Katzew, *Casta Painting: Images of Race in Eighteenth-century Mexico* (New Haven: Yale University Press, 2004).

4 The Body of Law: Legislating Sex in Eighteenth-Century Spain

1 The practice of separating crime from sin reflects general changes in the jurisdiction of the European Enlightenment. Unlike England, where judgment of crimes involved a popular tribunal, in France, Germany, and Spain the judge bore the ultimately application of the law in a given case.

2 Wilhelm von Humboldt, *Los límites de la acción del Estado* ed. and trans. Joaquín Abellán (Madrid: Tecnos, 1988 [1792]), 149.

3 *My Thoughts* (*Mes Pensées*), 1, 1234; quoted in Brian Singer, *Montesquieu and the Discovery of the Social* (New York: Palgrave MacMillan, 2013), 144.

4 In his text "Of the Crime against Nature," he makes this more explicit; Montesquieu, "Of the Crime against Nature," in *The Spirit of Laws* trans. Thomas Nugent (Chicago: Encyclopædia Britannica, 1758 [1748]), book 12, Chapter 6, section 6: "A crime which religion, morality and civil government equally condemn."

5 "El Teólogo examina la malicia intrínseca del acto; el Jurista considera las consecuencias que tiene para el Público," Feijóo, *Teatro crítico*, III, discurso 11, "Balanza de Astréa, o recta administración de la Justicia."

6 Francisco Tomás y Valiente, "El crimen y pecado contra natura," in *Sexo barroco y otras transgresiones premodernas* ed., F. Tomás y Valiente et al. (Madrid: Alianza Universidad, 1990), 33–56.

7 Martín de Torrecilla, *Encyclopedia canónica, civil, moral, regular y orthodoxa, utilíssima no solo para abogados y jueces, ni solo para canonistas y legistas, sino también para theologos, moralistas y para todos los confessors dispuestas por las letras del alphabeto* (Madrid: Blas de Villa Nueva, 1721), 53.

8 For women and sodomy, see Sherry Velasco, *Lesbians in Early Modern Europe* (Nashville, TN: Vanderbilt University Press, 2011).

9　Pierre François Muyart de Vouglans, *The Criminal Laws of France in Their Natural Order* (1780), excerpts in Jeffrey Merrick and Bryant Ragan eds., *Homosexuality in Early Modern France: A Documentary Collection* (New York: Oxford University Press, 2001), 22.

10　Martínez, *Philosofía escéptica*.

11　Daniel H. Nexon, *The Struggle for Power in Early Modern Europe: Religious Conflict, Dynastic Empires and International Change* (Princeton: Princeton University Press, 2009).

12　Antonio Xavier Pérez y López, *Principios del orden esencial de la naturaleza, establecidas por fundamento de la moral y la política y por prueba de la religión* (Madrid: Imprenta Real, 1785), 34. About Pérez y López, see Mario Méndez Bejarano, *Historia de la filosofía en España hasta el siglo XX* (Madrid: Renacimiento, 1929), 366–77.

13　José Agustín Ibañez de la Rentería, *Discursos que Don Joseph Agustin Ibañez de la Rentería presentó a la Real Sociedad Bascongada de los Amigos del País* (Madrid: Pantaléon Aznar, 1790), 131. The lectures compiled in this work were delivered between 1780 and 1783.

14　Saint Thomas Aquinas, *The Summa Theologica* (Chicago: Encyclopaedia Britannica, 1952) "The Various Kinds of Laws."

15　Mark D. Jordan, *The Invention of Sodomy in Christian Theology* (Chicago: University of Chicago Press, 1998), 126.

16　Humboldt, *Límites de la acción*, 149.

17　Jorge Arditi, *A Genealogy of Manners: Transformations of Social Relations in France and England from the Fourteenth to the Eighteenth Century* (Chicago: University of Chicago Press, 1998).

18　Locke understood knowledge "as the perception of the connection and agreement or disagreement and repugnancy of any of our ideas;" John Locke, *An Essay Concerning Human Understanding in Four Books* (London: Printed by Eliz. Holt for Thomas Basse, 1690), 4: 525.

19　Robert Cru, *Diderot as a Disciple of English Thought* (New York: Columbia University Press, 1913), 170.

20　Cru, *Diderot as a Disciple*, 406.

21　Quoted in Cru, *Diderot as a Disciple*, 280.

22　José Gazola, *El mundo engañado por los falsos médicos* (Valencia: Ant. Bordazar, 1729).

23　Sarah Chatwin, "Habeas Corpus: Theories of Embodiment in the Philosophy of Maurice Merleau-Ponty and Contemporary Feminism" (PhD dissertation, University of Essex, 1994).

24　Xavier Zubiri, *Naturaleza, Historia, Dios* (Madrid: Editora Nacional, 1963 [1942]), 38.

25　Jeremy Robbins, *Arts of Perception: The epistemological mentality of the Spanish Baroque, 1580–1720* (New York: Routledge, 2007).

26　Andrés Piquer, *Lógica moderna o Arte de hallar la verdad y perficionar la razón* (Valencia: en la oficina de Joseph García, 1747), 35. See also his *Discurso sobre la aplicación de la philosophía a los assuntos de religión* (Madrid: Joachin Ibarra, 1757).

27　Thomas of Aquinas, *Summa Theologica*, question 29.

28　Bourdieu, *Logic of Practice*, 72.

29 Beccaria's work was written upon the advice and influence of two Italian brothers, Pietro and Alessandro Verri.
30 Bernard E. Harcourt, "Beccaria's 'On Crimes and Punishments': A Mirror on the History of the Foundations of Modern Criminal Law" (Coase-Sandor Institute for Law & Economics Working Paper No. 648, 2013).
31 Cesare Beccaria, *On Crimes and Punishments* trans. Graeme R. Newman and Pietro Marongiu (New Brunswick and London: Transaction Publishers, 2009 [1764]), vii–lxviii.
32 Angel Toro, "Beccaria y la Inquisición Española," *Anuario de Derecho Penal y Ciencias Penales* 24 (1971): 391–416; see also Alejandro Agüero and Marta Lorente, "Penal Enlightenment in Spain: From Beccaria's Reception to the First Criminal Code," in *The Spanish Enlightenment Revisited* ed., Jesús Astigarraga (Oxford, UK: Voltaire Foundations, 2015), 235–63.
33 Beccaria, *On Crimes and Punishments*, 13, 245.
34 *King James Bible* (Cambridge: Chadwyck-Healey, 1996), Mark 12:17.
35 Beccaria, *On Crimes and Punishments*, 5.
36 Beccaria, *On Crimes and Punishments*, 180.
37 Tomás y Valiente, "Crimen y pecado."
38 Beccaria, *On Crimes and Punishments*, 94–9. Beccaria was heavily influenced by Montesquieu as well as the French lawyer Guillaume-François Le Trosne.
39 Luis Prieto Sanchís, "La filosofía penal de la Ilustración española," in *Homenaje al Dr. Marino Barbero Santos in memoriam* ed., Luis Arroyo Zapater and Ignacio Berdugo Gómez de la Torre (Cuenca: Ediciones del Universidad de Castilla-La Mancha, 2011), 489–510.
40 "On peut le lire avec plaisir et profit, meme après celui de Beccaria" (It can be read with pleasure and profit, even after Beccaria's), Jean-François, baron de Bourgoing, *Tableau de l'Espagne moderne* 3 vols. (Paris: Chez Levrault frères, 1807 [1788]), 1: 344.
41 Manuel de Lardizábal y Uribe, *Discurso sobre las penas, contrahido á las leyes criminales de España* (Madrid: Don Joachin Ibarra 1782), vii.
42 Lardizábal, *Discurso sobre las penas*, 98.
43 Lardizábal, *Discurso sobre las penas*, 94–5. A judge had to evaluate what area the crime attempted against: either religion, customs, against peace and against the public or private safety; Lardizábal, *Ibid*, 32.
44 Juan Álvarez Posadilla, *Práctica criminal por principios o modo y forma de instruir los procesos criminales de las causas de oficio de justicia contra los abusos introducidos* (Madrid: Viuda de Ibarra, 1797), diálogo VIII, 182.
45 Joaquín Alonso Pacheco, "El pensamiento penológico de Lardizábal (Breve comentario al 'Discurso sobre las penas')," *Revista de la Escuela de Estudios Penitenciarios* (February 1953): 64–71; Manuel de Rivacoba y Rivacoba, *Lardizábal, un penalista ilustrado* (Santa Fe, Argentina: Imprenta de la Universidad Nacional del Litoral, 1964); José Antón Oneca, "El derecho penal de la Ilustración y D. Manuel de Lardizábal," *Revista de Estudios Penitenciarios* 174 (July–September 1966): 595–626; Jesús María Silva Sánchez and Baldo Lavilla, "La teoría del delito en la obra de Manuel de Lardizábal," *Estudios de Derecho Penal y Criminología: en homenaje al profesor José María Rodríguez Devesa* 2 (1989): 345–72.

46 Lardizábal y Uribe, *Discurso sobre las penas*, 97–8. This author follows legislator Hugo Grocio (1583–1645) as he states that "crimes against religion must be punished only because of the utility they bring to society" ("los delitos contra la religión solo han de ser penados por la utilidad que la religión reporta a la sociedad"), quoted in Manuel de Rivacoba y Rivacoba, "Los iusnaturalistas clásicos y el pensamiento penal," in *Estudios en memoria de Jorge Millas* (Santiago de Chile: Sociedad Chilena de Filosofía Jurídica y Social, 1984), 372.

47 Barbara J. Shapiro, *A Culture of Fact: England, 1550–1720* (Ithaca: Cornell University Press, 2000).

48 Lorraine Daston, "Marvelous Facts and Miraculous Evidence in Early Modern Europe," in *Questions of Evidence: Proof, Practice and Persuasion across Disciplines* eds., James Chandler, Arnold I. Davidson, and Harry Harootunian (Chicago: The University of Chicago Press, 1994), 243–74.

49 Quoted in Lieselotte Steinbrügge, *The Moral Sex: Woman's Nature in the French Enlightenment* (New York: Oxford University Press, 1995), 25.

50 *Institutiones philosophicae et mathematicae* (Madrid: Ex Typographia Regia, 1796). A century later the philosopher Marcelino Menéndez y Pelayo still believed "all what man does, feels, meditates and wants, has to refer to as its ultimate term to its utility and conservation," *Historia de los heterodoxos españoles* 3 vols. (Madrid: Librería católica de San José, gerente V. Sancho-Tello 1880–81), vol. 5, Chapter 4.

51 Londa Schiebinger, *Nature's Body: Gender in the Making of Modern Science* (New Brunswick, NJ: Rutgers University Press, 2004).

52 Lynn Hunt, *Inventing Human Rights: A History* (New York: Norton & Co., 2007); Carole Pateman, *The Sexual Contract* (Stanford: Stanford University Press, 1988).

53 Montesquieu was translated and commented by the attorney general of the *Sala de Casa y Corte* of Madrid, José Garriga, *Observaciones sobre el espíritu de las leyes* (Madrid: Imprenta de González, 1787). Montesquieu was banned from being read by the Inquisition but nevertheless his texts reached Spain and its main authors. For instance, Juan Meléndez Valdés read Montesquieu and his *Spirit of the Laws* as a student in 1774; Leopoldo Augusto de Cueto (marqués de Valmar), *Biblioteca de Autores Españoles. Poetas Líricos del siglo XVIII* (Madrid: M. Rivadeneyra, 1869), 63: 80. Among the books confiscated from Pablo Olavide in 1766 one also finds Montesquieu; François Lopez "El libro y su mundo," in *La República de las Letras en la España del siglo XVIII* eds., Joaquín Álvarez Barrientos, François Lopez, and Inmaculada Urzainqui Miqueleiz (Madrid: Consejo Superior de Investigaciones Científicas, 1995), 78, 97.

54 *Biblioteca de Autores Españoles. Obras publicadas é inéditas de D. Gaspar Melchor de Jovellanos* ed., Cándido Nocedal (Madrid: M. Rivadeneyra, 1859), 50: 1325–30; see also María del Carmen Iglesias Cano's analysis of Montesquieu, Iglesias Cano, *Razón y sentimiento*, 365–422; as well as Gaspar Melchor de Jovellanos, "Discurso sobre el estudio de la geografía histórica pronunciada en el instituto de Gijón," in *Obras publicadas é inéditas* (Madrid: M. Rivadeneyra, 1859), vol 46, discurso 20. This was first observed in the function of the human body, and in fact, many philosophers and lawmakers had been first, like Montesquieu, interested in the study of anatomy.

55 Montengón, *Eusebio;* for a study of Montengón, see Rogelio Blanco Martínez, *Pedro Montengón y Paret (1745–1824): Un ilustrado entre la utopía y la realidad* (Valencia: Universitat Politècnica de València, 2001).

56 José Torrubia, *Aparato para la historia natural española* (Madrid: Impr. de los Herederos de don A. de Gordejuela y Sierra, 1754), 44.

57 José Clavijo y Fajardo, *Prólogo a la traducción de la "Historia Natural" del Conde de Buffon* (La Orotava, Tenerife: Fundación Canaria Orotava de Historia de la Ciencia, 2001 (1785)), 46.

58 Clavijo y Fajardo, *Prólogo*, 56.

59 Álvarez Posadilla, *Práctica criminal*, 185–206, and his *Comentario a las Leyes de Toro* (Madrid: Joachin Ibarra, 1794), 10. As lawyer, Juan Álvarez Posadilla pointed at the social utility aspect of what he understood to also be a natural prescript.

60 According to the definition of the *Diccionario de Autoridades* (1780).

61 Lardizábal, *Discurso sobre las penas*, 206–09.

62 Lardizábal, *Discurso sobre las penas*, 247.

63 William Monter, *Frontiers of Heresy: The Spanish Inquisition from the Basque Lands to Sicily* (Cambridge and New York: Cambridge University Press, 1990), 279.

64 Andrés Piquer, *Philosophia moral para la juventud española* (Madrid: Joachin Ibarra, 1755).

65 Piquer, *Philosophia moral*, 115. He quotes Huarte de San Juan: "What is important is to know the useful job to which each person's nature incline them (to do)" (*Importa trabajar en que cada qual conozca el ejercicio útil a que le inclina la propia naturaleza) Ibid.*, 116.

66 Archivo Histórico Nacional (AHN) Criminal 1740, "Caso contra Antonio Girado y Joseph de Costa sobre el crimen nefando," fol. 598v.

67 Helmut Puff, "Nature on Trial: Acts "Against Nature" in the Law Courts of Early Modern Germany and Switzerland," in *Moral Authority of Nature*, 232–53.

68 Lorenzo Matheu y Sanz, *Tractatus de Re Criminali* (1676), quoted in Tomás y Valiente, "Crimen y pecado," 54.

69 Domingo Vidal, *Cirugía forense ó Arte de hacer relaciones chirurgico-legales* (Barcelona: Carlos Gibert y Tutó, 1783), 28.

70 Torrecilla, *Encyclopedia canónica*, entry "Naturaleza," 2.

71 Juan Meléndez Valdés, *Discursos forenses* (Madrid: Imprenta Nacional, 1821).

72 Feijóo, *Teatro crítico* III, "El engaño," discurso undecimo.

73 José Berni y Catalá, *Práctica criminal con nota de los delitos, sus penas, presunciones y circunstancias, que los agravan, y disminuyen* (Madrid: Cívitas, 1995 [1749]).

74 Álvarez Posadilla, *Practica criminal*, on the same year, however, Vicente Vizcaino Pérez still calls sodomy a "sin," *Codigo y práctica criminal arreglado a las leyes de España* (Madrid: En la Imprenta de la Viuda de Ibarra, 1797), 78.

75 Vicente de Cadenas y Vicent, *Caballeros de la orden de Calatrava que efectuaron sus pruebas de ingreso durante el siglo XVIII* (Madrid: Hidalguía, 1986), 3:145.

76 Archivo General de Simancas, Gracia y Justicia leg. 254 (590) "Noticias de los ministros que componen el Consejo Supremo de S.M. y de otros

dentro y fuera de esta Corte," Madrid, August 12, 1765, document transcribed in Rafael Olaechea, "El anticolegialismo del gobierno de Carlos III," *Cuadernos de Investigación. Geografía e Historia* 2 (1976): 79–90.

77 Pablo de Gorosábel, *Noticia de las cosas memorables de Guipuzcoa ó Descripción de la provincia y de sus habitadores: exposición de las instituciones, fueros, privilegios, ordenanzas y leyes: reseña del gobierno civil, eclesiástico y militar, etc.* (Tolosa, Spain: Imprenta de E. López. 1899–1901).

78 He became one of the *alcaldes de casa y corte* of Madrid.

79 María del Carmen Irles Vicente, "Tomismo y Jesuitismo en los tribunales Españoles en vísperas de la expulsion de la Compañía," *Revista de Historia Moderna* 5 (1996): 73–99.

80 Tomás y Valiente, "Crimen y pecado," 334.

81 Fabio López Lázaro, *Crime in Early Bourbon Madrid (1700–1808): An Analysis of the Royal Judicial Court's Casebook* (Lewiston, NY: Edwin Mellen Press, 2008).

82 Lorenzo Matheu Sanz, *Tractatus de re criminali* (1686), 376–82; quoted in Francisco Tomás y Valiente, "Crimen y pecado," 54.

83 Quoted in Tomás y Valiente, "Crimen y pecado," 41.

84 Alonso de Villadiego, *Instrucción política y práctica judicial* (Madrid: Juan de la Cuesta, 1612), 71–75.

85 *Novísima Recopilación de las Leyes de España* (Madrid: s.n. 1805).

86 Meléndez Valdés, *Discursos forenses*, 90, 173.

87 AHN Criminal 1740, "Caso contra Antonio Girado y Joseph de Costa sobre el crimen nefando."

88 Italian cities were notorious for their alleged vice and promiscuity, see Nicholas Sinclair Davidson, "Sodomy in Early Modern Venice," in *Sodomy in Early Modern Europe* ed., Thomas Betteridge (New York: Manchester University Press, 2002), 65–82. Antonio Girado was not from Naples but from the city of Alicante, part of the kingdom of Valencia, which had an important number of people accused of sodomy throughout the early modern period; Carrasco, *Inquisición y represión sexual.*

89 Fabio López Lázaro, "'No Deceit Safe in its Hiding Place': The Criminal Trail in Eighteenth-Century Spain," *Law and History Review* 20, 3 (2009): 449–78.

90 *Real Pragmática Acerca de los Reos de Pecado Nefando*; the document is transcribed in Garza-Carvajal, *Butterflies will Burn*, 219 note 16.

91 Lardizábal y Uribe, *Discurso sobre las penas*. Lardizábal's work was inspired by Montesquieu and Beccaria.

92 Paul Scott has recently questioned Choisy's memoirs were in fact a recount of his life, but rather Choisy's literary construction, see Paul Scott, "Authenticity and Textual Transvestism in the Memoirs of the Abbé de Choisy," *French Studies* LXIX, 1 (2015): 14–29.

93 Tomás y Valiente, "Crimen y pecado," 212.

94 "Delito criminal" and "delito propiamente dicho," see Vizcaino Pérez, *Código y Práctica.*

95 Torrecilla, *Encyclopedia canónica*, differentiates "culpa teológica" (theological guilt" from "culpa jurídica" (juridical guilt). Culpa teológica was equal

to sin, see Celestino Carrodeguas Nieto, *La sacramentalidad del matrimonio: doctrina de Tomás Sánchez* (Madrid: Universidad Pontificia Comillas, 2003).

96 Senén Vilanova y Mañes, *Materia criminal forense ó tratado universal teórico práctico de los delitos y delincuentes en género y especie* 4 vols. (Madrid: Imprenta de Tomás Albán, 1807), 1:312.

97 Tomás y Valiente, "Crimen y pecado," 231, 298.

98 Feijóo, *Teatro crítico*, tomo VI, discurso 1, 12.

99 John Howard, *The State of the Prisons* (London and Toronto: E.P. Dutton & Co., 1929 [1784]), 124–25.

100 We do not know the outcomes of the trials for the remaining of the cases.

101 Cristian Berco, *Sexual Hierarchies, Public Status: Men, Sodomy, and Society in Spain's Golden Age* (Toronto and Buffalo: University of Toronto Press, 2007), 76. For sodomy cases under the Inquisition tribunal, see Monter, *Frontiers of Heresy*. As the study of Mary Elizabeth Perry for seventeenth-century Seville has shown the criminal court did not hesitate to severely punish the sodomite by burning them at the stake. In fact, from 1567 through 1616 seventy-one men were burned guilty of sodomy; Mary Elizabeth Perry, "The 'Nefarious Sin' in Early Modern Seville," *Journal of Homosexuality* 16, 1–2 (1988): 67–89.

102 Tomás y Valiente, "Crimen y pecado," 38.

103 Adam Smith, *An Inquiry into the Nature and Causes of the Wealth of Nations* (Chicago: Encyclopaedia Britannica, 1977 [1776]).

104 Quoted in Richard Herr, *Rural Change and Royal Finances in Spain at the End of the Old Regime* (Berkeley: University of California Press, 1989), 52. Campomanes was minister of finances under Charles III.

105 Rodríguez de Campomanes was an admirer of Adam Smith and saw the increasing wealth of the Spanish nation in the growth of population. In particular, citizens of a society became useful individuals when their work was beneficial to the whole; Pedro Rodríguez de Campomanes, *Discurso sobre el fomento de la industria popular* (Madrid: Imprenta de Antonio de Sancha, 1774); and his *Discurso sobre la educación popular de los artesanos y su fomento* (Madrid: Imprenta de Antonio de Sancha, 1775).

106 Bernard Ward, *Proyecto económico en que se proponen varias providencias, dirigidas á promover los intereses de España, con los medios y fondos necesarios para su plantificación* (Madrid: J. Ibarra, 1779 [1764]), 79–92.

107 Gaspar Melchor de Jovellanos, *Memoria sobre la educación pública, o sea tratado teórico-práctico de enseñanza con aplicación a las escuelas y colegios de niños* (Madrid: Biblioteca Nueva, 2012 [1802]), 233.

108 As Kant later wrote in his *Critique of Pure Reason* trans. Paul Guyer and Allen W. Wood (Cambridge, UK: Cambridge University Press, 1998 [1781]): "We can only have knowledge of 'appearances' of the object, but not of the object."

109 Judith Butler, *The Psychic Life of Power: Theories in Subjection* (Stanford: Stanford University Press, 1994), 23.

5 Sex and Gender: Reconsidering the Legacy of the Enlightenment

1 He did so in his introduction to the edited works of his friend the painter Antonio Rafael Mengs. Mengs is the author of a penetrating portrait of

Azara, since 2013 hanging in the Museo del Prado in Madrid. He was brother to the well-known naturalist of South America, Félix de Azara; see Stephan F. Schröder and Gudrun Maurer, *Mengs & Azara: el retrato de una amistad* (Madrid: Museo Nacional del Prado, 2013).

2 "El nuestro será quizás distinguido en la posteridad por el siglo de la inquietud. Las artes, las ciencias, la política, la fortuna de las naciones y de los particulares y hasta la vida doméstica, todo está en un continuo movimiento y agitación," José Nicolás de Azara, prolog to *Obras de D. Antonio Rafael Mengs, primer pintor de Cámara del Rey* (Madrid: Imprenta Real de la Gazeta, 1780 [1773]), 1. One needs to say it was also the century of incertitude, not only in Spain but all over Europe, as a characteristic of the Enlightenment; Joaquín Otero Sendra, "Domingo Vidal y Abad, cirujano español del siglo XVIII," *Medicina & historia: Revista de estudios históricos de las ciencias médicas* 35 (May 1974): 7–26.

3 Iglesias Cano, *Razón y sentimiento*, 158.

4 Jerrold Seigel, *The Idea of the Self: Thought and Experience in Western Europe since the Seventeenth Century* (Cambridge, UK: Cambridge Universtiy Press, 2005).

5 José Maravall, *Estudios de la historia del pensamiento español* 4 vols. (Madrid: Centro de Estudios Constitucionales, 1999) 4: 542–7.

6 Bourdieu, *Logic of Practice*, 72.

7 Hunt, *Inventing Human Rights*.

8 Joan B. Landes, *Women and the Public Sphere in the Age of the French Revolution* (Ithaca and London: Cornell University Press, 1988).

9 Viky Kirby, *Quantum Anthropologies: Life at Large* (Durham, NC: Duke University Press, 2011), 70.

10 Deirdre Coleman, "Entertaining Entomology: Insects and Insect Performers in the Eighteenth Century," *Eighteenth-Century Life* 30, 3 (Fall 2006): 107–34.

11 Frederick Prete, "Can Females Rule the Hive?: The Controversy over Honey Bee Gender Roles in British Beekeeping Texts of the Sixteenth–Eighteenth Centuries," *Journal of the History of Biology* 24, 1 (1991): 113–44.

12 Daston and Vidal, *Moral Authority*.

13 Monique Wittig, *The Straight Mind and Other Essays* (Boston: Beacon Press 1992). The article "Straight Mind" was originally published in 1980, from a paper presented at the Modern Language Association conference in 1978.

14 Evelyn Fox Keller, *The Mirage of a Space between Nature and Nurture* (Durham, NC: Duke University Press, 2010).

15 Fox Keller, *Mirage of a Space*, 10.

16 Matt Ridley, *Nature via Nurture: Genes, Experience and What Makes us Human* (New York: Harper Collins, 2003), 5.

17 Kate Soper, *What is Nature?: Culture, Politics and the Non-Human* (Oxford: Blackwell, 1995), 21.

18 Soper, *What is Nature?*, 131.

19 Soper, *What is Nature?*, 7.

20 Rebecca M. Jordan-Young, *Brain Storm: The Flaws in the Science of Sex Differences* (Cambridge, MA: Harvard University Press, 2010).

21 Rosi Braidotti, "Becoming Woman or Sexual Difference Revisited," *Theory, Culture & Society* 20,3 (June 2003): 43–64.

22 Soper, *What is Nature?*, 8.

23 Kirby, *Quantum Anthropologies*, 71.
24 To Soper nature becomes in everyday practice, *What is Nature?*, 12.
25 Soper, *What is Nature?*, 133.
26 Carrie Hull, *The Ontology of Sex: A Critical Inquiry into the Deconstruction and Reconstruction of Categories* (New York: Routledge, 2006), 142.
27 Clifford Geertz famously stated: "man is an animal suspended in webs of significance he himself has spun," *The Interpretation of Cultures* (New York: Basic Books, 1973), 5.
28 Kate Soper's words as she interprets Judith Butler's work; Kate Soper, "Feminism and Ecology: Realism and Rhetoric in the Discourse of Nature," *Science, Technology and Human Values* 20, 3 (Summer, 1995): 311–31 (317).
29 Ferdinand de Saussure, *Writings in General Linguistics* trans. Carol Sanders (Oxford and New York: Oxford University Press, 2006). This is an expanded edition of Saussure's *Cours de linguistique generale* (Course in General Linguistics) published posthumously in 1916. The Oxford 2006 edition includes translation of Saussure's lectures found in 1996, eighty years after his death. For a study of Saussure's theory of language, see Stephen R. Yarbrough, *After Rhetoric: The Study of Discourse Beyond Language and Culture* (Carbondale, IL: Southern Illinois University Press, 1999), 130.
30 Yarbrough, *After Rhetoric*, 88.
31 Yarbrough, *After Rhetoric*, 115.
32 "Language is itself the vehicle of thought," Ludwig Wittgenstein, *Philosophical Grammar* trans. Anthony Kenny (Berkeley: University of California Press, 1974 [1969]), 161.
33 Judith Butler, "Variations of Sex and Gender: Beauvoir, and Foucault," in *Feminism as a Critique: On the Politics of Gender* eds., Seyla Benhabib and Drucilla Cornell (Minneapolis: University of Minnesota Press, 1987), 129.
34 Butler specifically refers to this concept in Simone de Beauvoir's work, Judith Butler, "Variations on Sex and Gender" and "Gender in Simone de Beauvoir's Second Sex," *Yale French Studies. Simone de Beauvoir: Witness to a Century* 72 (Winter 1986): 35–49.
35 Butler, "Variations on Sex and Gender," 134.
36 Judith Butler, *Undoing Gender* (New York and London: Routledge, 2004), 2.
37 Butler, "Variations on Sex and Gender," 134. Butler is making reference to Wittig's understanding of sexual difference; Monique Wittig, "One is not Born a Woman," in *Straight Mind*, 47.
38 On the concept of difference in feminist studies, see Michèle Barrett, "The Concept of 'Difference'," *Feminist Review* 26 (Summer 1987): 29–41.
39 Simone de Beauvoir, *The Second Sex*, trans. Constance Borde and Sheila Malovany-Chevallier (New York: Vintage, 2011 [1949]).
40 Feminists such as María-Milagros Rivera, Luisa Muraro, and Lia Cigarini, have argued that modern feminism must recuperate the female body from the illusion of equality. This act will put women at the forefront not only of the social and cultural life, but also particularly of political activism and intervention; María-Milagros Rivera Garretas, *La diferencia sexual en la historia* (Valencia: Universitat de València, 2005).
41 María-Milagros Rivera Garretas, "El culto a la belleza," *Lectora: revista de dones i textualitat* 12 (2006): 125–8.

42 Luce Irigaray, *Éthique de la différence sexuelle* (Paris: Editions de Minuit, 1984 [1982]), Rivera Garretas, "Culto a la belleza," 73.

43 Rivera Garretas, "Culto a la belleza," 74.

44 Critics include Celia Amorós, *Feminismo, igualdad y diferencia* (Mexico City: Universidad Nacional Autónoma de México, 1990), Lidia Cirillo, *Mejor huérfanas: por una crítica feminista al pensamiento de la diferencia*, trans. Pepa Linares (Barcelona: Anthropos, 2002), originally published in Italian as *Meglio Orfane. Per una critica femminista al pensiero della differenza* (1993).

45 For a study of Irigaray's critics and analysis of Irigaray's notion of the body, see Danielle Poe, "Can Luce Irigaray's Notion of Sexual Difference be Applied to Transsexual and Transgender Narratives?," in *Thinking with Irigaray* eds., Mary C. Rawlinson, Sabrina L. Hom, and Serene J. Khader (Albany, NY: SUNY Press, 2011), 111–28. Rivera, who is influenced by French feminists such as Luce Irigaray and Hélèn Cixous, highlights the importance of the body in the construction of sexual difference.

46 Rivera Garretas, *Diferencia sexual*, 26–7. For the topic of the body in early Christianity, see Peter Brown, *The Body and Society: Men, Women and Sexual Renunciation in Early Christianity* (New York: Columbia University Press, 2008).

47 María-Milagros Rivera Garretas, *El fraude de la igualdad* (Barcelona: Editorial Planeta, 1997), 10.

48 Rivera Garretas, *Fraude de la igualdad*, 79.

49 Rivera Garretas, *Fraude de la igualdad*, 56.

50 Iglesias Cano, *Razón y sentimiento.*

51 Emma Baeri, *I lumi e il cerchio: una esercitazione di storia* (Roma: Riuniti, 1992), Luisa Muraro *L'ordine simbolico della madre* (Roma: Riuniti, 1991). I have borrowed the term "liberatory practice" from bell hooks, "Theory as Liberatory Practice," in *Teaching to Transgress: Education as the Practice of Freedom* (New York: Routledge, 1994), 59–75.

52 Scott, *Only Paradoxes to Offer.*

53 Giorgio Agamben, *Nudities* trans. David Kishik and Stefan Pedatella (Stanford: Stanford University Press, 2011 [2009]), 46–54.

54 Moira Gatens, *Imaginary Bodies: Ethics, Power and Corporeality* (New York: Routledge, 1996), 12.

55 Joan Scott, *The Fantasy of Feminist History* (Durham, NC: Duke University Press, 2011).

56 The concept of the imaginary has been frequently used in Anthropology to refer to cultural beliefs, Claudia Strauss, "The Imaginary," *Anthropological Theory* 6 (2006): 322–44.

57 Moira Gatens, "Feminism as Password: Rethinking the 'Possible' with Spinoza and Deleuze," *Hypatia* 15, 2 (Spring 2000): 59–75.

58 Paul Patton, *Deleuze and the Political* (New York: Routledge, 2000), 74.

59 Sarah Ahmed, *The Cultural Politics of Emotion* (New York: Routledge, 2004).

60 Butler, *Undoing Gender*, 57.

61 Moira Gatens, "A Critique of the Sex/Gender Distinction," in *Beyond Marxism?: Interventions after Marx* eds., Judith Allen and Paul Patton (Leichhardt, New South Wales: Intervention Publications, 1983), 152.

62 Drucilla Cornell, *At the Heart of Freedom: Sex, Gender and Legal Rights* (Princeton: Princeton University Press, 1998) and her *The Imaginary Domain: Abortion, Pornography and Sexual Harassment* (New York: Routledge, 1995).

63 Cornell, *Imaginary Domain*, 5.

64 Cornell, *Imaginary Domain*, 6.

65 As Cornell sees it: "It is not that we have to claim that women are equal to men in the sense that they are the same as men; rather, we have to claim that the feminine is of equivalent value to the masculine sex, in the name of women's equal personhood before the law," *Imaginary Domain*, 209.

66 hooks, *Theory as Liberatory Practice*.

67 Butler, "Variations on Sex and Gender," 140.

68 Butler, "Variations on Sex and Gender," 130.

69 Butler, "Variations on Sex and Gender," 131.

70 Scott, *Fantasy of Feminist*, 20.

71 Gayle Rubin analyzes this parallel between such sex/gender system and a nature/nurture dichotomy in her article "The Traffic in Women: Notes on the 'Political Economy' of Sex," in *Toward an Anthropology of Women* ed., Rayna Reiter (New York: Monthly Review Press, 1975), 27–62.

72 Kirby, *Quantum* Anthropologies, 71.

73 Hull, *Ontology of Sex*.

74 Stephen T. Asma, "Gauging Gender," *The Chronicle of Higher Education* 58, 11 (October 30, 2011): B6–B9 (B8).

75 Iris Marion Young, "Gender as Seriality: Thinking about Women as a Social Collective," *Signs* 19, 3 (1994): 713–38; for an interpretation of Young's philosophy, see Ann Ferguson and Mechthild Nagel, *Dancing with Iris: The Philosophy of Iris Marion Young* (Oxford: Oxford University Press, 2009).

76 Young, "Gender as Seriality," 728; see also Ferguson and Nagel, *Dancing With Iris*, 149–51.

77 Monique Wittig, "One is not Born a Woman," in *Straight Mind*, 9–20.

78 Young, "Gender as Seriality," 729.

79 Jordan-Young, *Brain Storm*, 24.

80 Michel de Certeau, *The Writing of History* trans. Tom Conley (New York: Columbia University Press, 1988 [1975]), 303.

81 Foucault, *Order of Things*, 322–30.

82 Braidotti, "Becoming Woman," 45.

83 Braidotti, "Becoming Woman," 44.

84 Narciso Esparragosa y Gallardo, "Informe del Cirujano Honorario de Cámara Doctor Narciso Esparragosa hecho a la Real Audiencia en tres de febrero de 1803 por orden del Protomedicato, sobre una supuesta hermafrodita," quoted in Carlos Martínez Durán, *Las ciencias médicas en Guatemala: origen y evolución* (Guatemala City: Editorial Universitaria, 1964), 466–72.

85 James Thomson Callender, *The Prospect Before Us* 3 vols. (Richmond, VA: Printed for the author 1800–1801), 2: 57.

86 Albeit there were still some members of the medical profession who continued to argue for the existence of hermaphrodites, even in this late period, Dreger, *Hermaphrodites and the Medical Invention of Sex*.

Bibliography

Abercrombie, Thomas, "Una vida disfrazada en el Potosí y la Plata Colonial: Antonio-nacido-María Yta ante la Audiencia de Charcas (un documento y una reflexión crítica)," *Anuario de Estudios Bolivianos, Archivísticos y Bibliográficos* 11 (2008): 3–45.

Agamben, Giorgio, *Nudities* trans. David Kishik and Stefan Pedatella (Stanford: Stanford University Press, 2011 [2009]).

Agüero, Alejandro and Marta Lorente, "Penal Enlightenment in Spain: From Beccaria's Reception to the First Criminal Code," in *The Spanish Enlightenment Revisited* ed., Jesús Astigarraga (Oxford, UK: Voltaire Foundation, 2015): 235–63.

Ahmed, Sarah, *The Cultural Politics of Emotion* (New York: Routledge, 2004).

Albero Muñoz, María del Mar, "La fisiognomía y la expresión de las pasiones en algunas bibliotecas de artistas españoles en el siglo XVII," *Cuadernos de Arte de la Universidad de Granada* 42 (2011): 37–52.

Alcalá y Martínez, Jaime, *Disertación médico-chirúrgica sobre una operación cesárea executada en muger y feto vivos, en esta ciudad de Valencia* (Valencia: Viuda de Geronymo Conejos, 1753).

Alegre Pérez, María Esther and María del Mar Rey Bueno, "La biblioteca privada de Juan Muñoz y Peralta (ca. 1655–1746)," in *Estudios de historia de las técnicas, la arqueología industrial y las ciencias: VI Congreso de la Sociedad Española de Historia de las Ciencias y de las Técnicas, Segovia-La Granja, 9 al 13 de septiembre de 1996* eds., Juan L. García Hourcade, Juan M. Moreno Yuste, and Gloria Ruiz Hernández (Valladolid: Junta de Castilla y León, Consejería de Educación y Cultura, 1998), 385–90.

Alonso Pacheco, Joaquín, "El pensamiento penológico de Lardizábal (Breve comentario al 'Discurso sobre las penas')," *Revista de la Escuela de Estudios Penitenciarios* (February 1953): 64–71.

Álvarez Posadilla, Juan, *Práctica criminal por principios o modo y forma de instruir los procesos criminales de las causas de oficio de justicia contra los abusos introducidos* (Madrid: Viuda de Ibarra, 1797).

Comentario a las Leyes de Toro (Madrid: Joachin Ibarra, 1794).

Amorós, Celia, *Feminismo, igualdad y diferencia* (Mexico City: Universidad Nacional Autónoma de México, 1990).

Anstey, Peter R. and John A. Schuster eds., *The Science of Nature in the Seventeenth Century: Patterns of Change in Early Modern Natural Philosophy* (Dordrecht, UK: Springer, 2005).

Aquinas, Thomas, Saint, *Commentary on Aristotle's Physics* (New Haven: Yale University Press, 1963).

The Summa Theologica (Chicago: Encyclopaedia Britannica, 1952).

Arditi, Jorge, *A Genealogy of Manners: Transformations of Social Relations in France and England from the Fourteenth to the Eighteenth Century* (Chicago: The University of Chicago Press, 1998).

Aristotle, *On the Generation of Animals* trans. Arthur Platt (Adelaide: The University of Adelaide, 2007).

Asma, Stephen T., *On Monsters: An Unnatural History of Our Worst Fears* (Oxford: Oxford University Press, 2009).

"Gauging Gender," *The Chronicle of Higher Education* 58, 11 (October 30, 2011): B6–B9.

Augustine, Saint, Bishop of Hippo, Confessions trans. Edward B. Pusey (New York: Modern Library, 1999).

On Christian Doctrine (New York: Bobbs-Merrill, 1958).

Ayala, Jorge M., *Pensadores aragoneses: Historia de las ideas filosóficas en Aragón* (Saragossa: Institución Fernando el Católico, 2001).

Azara, José Nicolás de, *Obras de D. Antonio Rafael Mengs, primer pintor de Cámara del Rey* (Madrid: Imprenta Real de la Gazeta, 1780 [1773]).

Baeri, Emma, *I lumi e il cerchio: una esercitazione di storia* (Roma: Riuniti, 1992).

Bailey, Merridee L., "In Service and at Home: Didactic Texts for Children and Young People, ca. 1400–1600," *Parergon* 24, 2 (2007): 23–43.

Baquero Escudero, Ana L., *El viaje y la ficción narrativa española en el siglo XVIII* (Alicante, Spain: Biblioteca Virtual Miguel de Cervantes, 2009).

Barrett, Michèle, "The Concept of 'Difference'," *Feminist Review* 26 (Summer, 1987): 29–41.

Baucells, Francesc, *Font mystica y sagrada del Paradis de la Iglesia* (Figueres, Spain: I. Porter, 1760 [1704]).

Bayle, Pierre, *Dictionnaire Historique et Critique* (Rotterdam: Reinier Leers, 1697).

Beaumont, Blas, *Exercitaciones anatómicas y essenciales operaciones de cirugía: con un breve resumen de los instrumentos y vendages* (Madrid: Imprenta del Convento de Nuestra Señora de la Merced, 1728).

Beauvoir, Simone de, *The Second Sex* trans. Constance Borde and Sheila Malovany-Chevallier (New York: Vintage, 2011 [1949]).

Beccaria, Cesare, *On Crimes and Punishments* trans. Graeme R. Newman and Pietro Marongiu (New Brunswick and London: Transaction Publishers, 2009 [1764]).

Behrend-Martínez, Edward, *Unfit for Marriage: Impotent Spouses on Trial in the Basque Region of Spain, 1650–1750* (Reno: University of Nevada Press, 2007).

Belmonte Bermúdez, Luis, *El diablo predicador y mayor contrario amigo* (Madrid: Ayuntamiento de Madrid, 2013 [1653]).

Berco, Cristian, *Sexual Hierarchies, Public Status: Men, Sodomy, and Society in Spain's Golden Age* (Toronto and Buffalo: University of Toronto Press, 2007).

Berg, Maxine, "The Genesis of 'Useful Knowledge'," *History of Science* 45 (2007): 123–33.

Berni y Catalá, José, *Práctica criminal con nota de los delitos, sus penas, presunciones y circunstancias, que los agravan, y disminuyen* (Madrid: Cívitas, 1995 [1749]).

Beusterien, John L., "Jewish Male Menstruation in Seventeenth-Century Spain," *Bulletin of the History of Medicine* 73 (1999): 447–56.

Blanco Martínez, Rogelio, *Pedro Montengón y Paret (1745–1824): Un ilustrado entre la utopía y la realidad* (Valencia: Universitat Politècnica de València, 2001).

Bloodsworth-Lugo, Mary K., *In-Between Bodies: Sexual Difference, Race, and Sexuality* (Albany, NY: SUNY Press, 2007).

Boaistuau, Pierre, "Historias prodigiosas y maravillosas de diversos sucesos acaescidos en el mundo," ed., Enrique Suárez Figaredo, *Lemir* 17 (2013 [1574]): 126–447.

Bolufer, Mónica, *Mujeres e Ilustración: La construcción de la feminidad en la España del siglo XVIII* (Valencia: Institució Alfons el Magnànim, 1998).

Bondeson Jan, *A Cabinet of Medical Curiosities* (Ithaca, NY: Cornell University Press, 1997).

Bonells, Jaime, *Perjuicios que acarrean al género humano y al Estado las madres, que rehusan criar á sus hijos: y medios para contener el abuso de ponerlos en ama* (Madrid: Miguel Escribano, 1786).

Bonet Correa, Antonio, *Fray Matías de Irala: grabador madrileño* (Madrid: Ayuntamiento de Madrid, 1979).

Bonnet, Jean-Claude, "La malédiction paternelle," *Dix-Huitième Siècle* 12 (1980): 195–208.

"De la famille à la patrie," in *Histoire des pères et de la paternité* eds., Jean Delumeau and Daniel Roche (Paris: Larousse, 2000 [1990]), 245–67.

Boscasa, Lorenzo, *Tratado de anatomía general, descriptiva y topográfica* Three vols. (Madrid: Librería de los Señores Viuda é Hijos de Antonio Calleja, 1844–45).

Bourdieu, Pierre, *The Logic of Practice* trans. Richard Nice (Stanford: Stanford University Press, 1990).

Bourgoing, Jean-François, Baron de, *Tableau de l'Espagne moderne* Three vols. (Paris: Chez Levrault frères, 1807 [1788]).

Braidotti, Rosi, "Becoming Woman: Or Sexual Difference Revisited," *Theory, Culture & Society* 20, 3 (2003): 43–64.

Brown, Peter, *The Body and Society: Men, Women and Sexual Renunciation in Early Christianity* (New York: Columbia University Press, 2008).

Buchan, William, *El conservador de la salud de las madres y los niños* (Madrid: Imprenta de D. Fermin Villalpando, 1808).

Buffon, Georges Louis Leclerc, comte de, *Natural History* trans. William Smellie Nine vols. (Edinburgh: Printed for William Creech, 1780–85).

Burke, Michael E., *The Royal College of San Carlos: Surgery and Spanish Medical Reform in the Late Eighteenth Century* (Durham, NC: Duke University Press, 1977).

Butler, Judith, "Gender in Simone de Beauvoir's Second Sex," *Yale French Studies. Simone de Beauvoir: Witness to a Century* 72 (Winter 1986): 35–49.

"Variations on Sex and Gender: Beauvoir, and Foucault," in *Feminism as a Critique: On the Politics of Gender* eds., Seyla Benhabib and Drucilla Cornell (Minneapolis: University of Minnesota Press, 1987).

Gender Trouble: Feminism and the Subversion of Identity (New York: Routledge, 1990).

The Psychic Life of Power: Theories in Subjection (Stanford: Stanford University Press, 1994).

"Appearances Aside," *California Law Review* 88, 1 (Jan. 2000): 55–63.

"Doing Justice to Someone: Sex Reassignment and Allegories of Transsexuality," *GLQ: A Journal of Lesbian and Gay Studies* 7, 4 (2001): 621–36.

Undoing Gender (New York and London: Routledge, 2004).

Giving an Account of Oneself (New York: Fordham University Press, 2005).

Cabanis, Pierre Jean George, *Rapports du physique et du moral de l'homme* Two vols. (Paris: Crapart, Caille et Ravier, 1802).

Cadenas y Vicent, Vicente de, *Caballeros de la orden de Calatrava que efectuaron sus pruebas de ingreso durante el siglo XVIII* (Madrid: Hidalguía, 1986).

Callender, James Thomson, *The Prospect Before Us* Three vols. (Richmond, VA: Printed for the author 1800–1801).

Capel, Horacio, "Religious Beliefs, Philosophy and Scientific Theory in the Origin of Spanish Geomorphology, 17th–18th centuries," *Organon, Polish Academy of Science, Warsaw, special issue "La pensée géographique"* 20/21 (1984/1985): 219–29.

Carrasco, Rafael, *Inquisición y represión sexual en Valencia* (Barcelona: Laertes, 1985).

Carrete Parrondo, Juan and Fernándo Checa Cremades and Valeriano Bozal eds., *El grabado en España: Siglos XV al XVIII* Thirty-two vols. (Madrid: Espasa-Calpe, 1988).

Carrodeguas Nieto, Celestino, *La sacramentalidad del matrimonio: doctrina de Tomás Sánchez* (Madrid: Universidad Pontificia Comillas, 2003).

Ceñal, Ramón, "Cartesianismo en España. Notas para su historia (1650–1750)," *Revista "Filosofía y Letras" de la Universidad de Oviedo* (1945): 1–95.

Cerda, Juan de la, *Libro intitulado vida política de los estados de las mugeres: en el qual se dan muy prouechosos y Christianos documentos y auisos, para criarse y conseruarse deuidamente las mugeres en sus estados …: con vn Indice Alphabetico muy copioso de materias, que siruen de lugares comunes* (Madrid: Alcalá de Henares, 1599).

Certeau, Michel de, *The Writing of History* trans. Tom Conley (New York: Columbia University Press, 1988 [1975]).

Chatwin, Sarah, "Habeas Corpus: Theories of Embodiment in the Philosophy of Maurice Merleau-Ponty and Contemporary Feminism" (PhD dissertation, University of Essex, 1994).

Chinchilla, Anastasio, *Anales históricos de la medicina en general, y biográfico-bibliográficos de la española en particular* (New York: Johnson Reprint Corp, 1967 [1843]).

Cirillo, Lidia, *Mejor huérfanas: por una crítica feminista al pensamiento de la diferencia* trans. Pepa Linares (Barcelona: Anthropos, 2002).

Clavijo y Fajardo, José, *El Pensador. Pensamiento LXIII* (Madrid: Imprenta de Joachin Ibarra, 1763–1767).

Prólogo a la traducción de la "Historia Natural" del Conde de Buffon (La Orotava, Tenerife: Fundación Canaria Orotava de Historia de la Ciencia, 2001 [1785]).

Cleminson, Richard and Francisco Vázquez García, *Sex, Identity and Hermaphrodites in Iberia, 1500–1800* (London: Pickering and Chatto, 2013).

"Subjectivities in Transition: Gender and Sexual Identities in Cases of 'Sex Change' and 'Hermaphroditism' in Spain, c. 1500–1800," *History of Science* 48 (2010): 1–38.

Clifton, Francis, *État de la médecine ancienne et modern: avec un plan pour perfectionner celle-ci* (Paris: Chez Quillau, 1742).

Coleman, Deirdre, "Entertaining Entomology: Insects and Insect Performers in the Eighteenth Century," *Eighteenth-Century Life* 30, 3 (Fall 2006): 107–34.

Collingwood, Robin G., *The Idea of Nature* (Oxford: Oxford University Press, 1960 [1945]).

Coriche, Cristóbal M., *Oración vindicativa del honor de las letras, y de los literatos* (Puebla: Imprenta del Colegio Real de San Ignacio, 1763).

Cornell, Drucilla, *At the Heart of Freedom: Sex, Gender and Legal Rights* (Princeton: Princeton University Press, 1998).

The Imaginary Domain: Abortion, Pornography and Sexual Harassment (London and New York: Routledge, 1995).

Corteguera, Luis R., "King as Father in Early Modern Spain," *Memoria y Civilización* 12 (2009): 49–69.

Death by Effigy: A Case from the Mexican Inquisition (Philadelphia: University of Pennsylvania Press, 2012).

Cortés, Jerónimo, *Fisonomía y varios secretos de naturaleza* (Valencia: Libreria Paris, 1992 [1598]).

Covarrubias Orozco, Sebastián de, *Diccionario El Tesoro de la Lengua Castellana o Española* (Madrid: Imprenta Luis Sánchez, 1611).

Crane, Susan, *The Performance of the Self: Ritual, Clothing and Identity during the Hundred Years War* (Philadelphia: University of Pennsylvania Press, 2002).

Crawford, Katherine, *European Sexualities, 1400–1800* (Cambridge and New York: Cambridge University Press, 2007).

Cotarelo y Mori, Emilio, *María Ladvenant y Quirante, primera dama de los teatros de la corte* (Madrid: Sucesores de Rivadeneyra, 1896).

Cru, Robert, *Diderot as a Disciple of English Thought* (New York: Columbia University Press, 1913).

Cruz del Pozo, María Victoria, *Gassendismo y cartesianismo en España: Martín Martínez médico filósofo del siglo XVIII* (Seville: Universidad de Sevilla, 1997).

Cueto, Leopoldo Augusto de (Marqués de Valmar), *Biblioteca de Autores Españoles. Poetas Líricos del siglo XVIII* (Madrid: M. Rivadeneyra, 1869).

Cunningham, Andrew, *Anatomist Anatomis'd: An Experimental Medicine in Enlightenment Europe* (Farnham: Ashgate, 2010).

Dabhoiwala, Faramerz, *The Origins of Sex: A History of the First Sexual Revolution* (Oxford: Oxford University Press, 2012).

Daston, Lorraine, "Marvelous Facts and Miraculous Evidence in Early Modern Europe," in *Questions of Evidence: Proof, Practice, and Persuasion across the Disciplines* eds., James Chandler, Arnold I. Davidson, and Harry Harootunian (Chicago: The University of Chicago Press, 1994), 243–74.

"Attention and the Values of Nature in the Enlightenment," in *The Moral Authority of Nature Lorraine* eds., Lorraine Daston and Fernando Vidal (Chicago: The University of Chicago Press, 2004), 100–26.

Daston, Lorraine and Katharine Park, "The Hermaphrodite and the Orders of Nature: Sexual Ambiguity in Early Modern France," *GLQ: A Journal of Lesbian and Gay Studies* 1, 4 (1995): 419–38.

Daston, Lorraine and Fernando Vidal eds., *The Moral Authority of Nature* (Chicago: The University of Chicago, Press, 2004).

Davidson, Nicholas Sinclair, "Sodomy in Early Modern Venice," in *Sodomy in Early Modern Europe* ed., Thomas Betteridge (New York: Manchester University Press, 2002), 65–82.

Defoe, Daniel, *The Life and Strange Surprizing Adventures of Robinson Crusoe* (London: Printed for W. Taylor, 1719).

Diario curioso, erudito, económico y comercial (Madrid: Librería de Arribas, carrera de San Gerónimo, 1786).

Díaz Rojo, José Antonio, "La biblioteca del Ilustrado Juan José de Arostegi, cirujano del Hospital de San Bernabé (1799)," *Publicaciones de la Institución Tello Téllez de Meneses* 66 (1995): 107–18.

Diccionario de Autoridades (Madrid: Editorial Gredos, 1963 [1726–1739]).

Domínguez, Atilano ed., *Spinoza y España. Actas del Congreso Internacional sobre "Relaciones entre Spinoza y España" (Almagro, 5–7 noviembre 1992)* (Cuenca, Spain: Ediciones de la Universidad Castilla-La Mancha, 2004).

Dreger, Alice, *Hermaphrodites and the Medical Invention of Sex* (Cambridge, MA: Harvard University Press, 1998).

Esteban Mateo, León and Ramón López Martín, *La escuela de primeras letras según Juan Luis Vives: estudio, iconografía y textos* (Valencia: Universitat de València, 1993).

Eximeno, Antonio, *Institutiones philosophicae et mathematicae* (Madrid: Ex Typographia Regia, 1796).

Fairchild, Cissie, *Domestic Enemies: Servants and their Masters in Old Regime France* (Baltimore: Johns Hopkins University Press, 1984).

Fausto-Sterling, Anne, *Sexing the Body: Gender Politics and the Construction of Sexuality* (New York: Basic Books, 2000).

Feijóo, Benito Jerónimo, "Carta defensiva sobre el primer tomo del Teatro crítico universal," in Benito Jerónimo Feijóo, Teatro crítico universal Nine vols. (Madrid: Joaquín Ibarra, 1779 [1726–1740]), 2: 322–52.

Teatro crítico universal Nine vols. (Madrid: Imprenta de L. F. Mojados, 1726–1740).

Felshin, Nina, "Clothing as Subject," *Art Journal*, 54 1 (Spring 1995): 20–9.

Felton, Craig and William B. Jordan, *Jusepe de Ribera: Lo Spagnoletto, 1591–1652* (Fort Worh: Kimbell Art Museum, 1982).

Ferguson, Ann and Mechthild Nagel, *Dancing With Iris: The Philosophy of Iris Marion Young* (Oxford: Oxford University Press, 2009).

Fernández, Nicolás, "The Body of the Letter: Vital Force and the Practice of Spanish Medicine in Juan de Cabriada's Carta Filósofica, Medico-Chymica (1687)," *Revista Hispánica Moderna* 68, 2 (2015): 109–24.

Ferraris, Maurizio, *L'Immaginazione* (Bologna: Il Mulino, 1996).

Few, Martha, "'That Monster of Nature': Gender, Sexuality, and the Medicalization of a 'Hermaphrodite' in Late Colonial Guatemala," *Ethnohistory* 54, 1 (2007): 159–76.

Finucci, Valeria, "Maternal Imagination and Monstrous Birth: Tasso's Gerusalemme liberata," in *Generation and Degeneration: Tropes of Reproduction in Literature and History from Antiquity to Early Modern Europe* eds., Valeria Finucci and Kevin Brownlee (Durham, NC: Duke University Press, 2001), 41–77.

Fontes da Costa, Palmira, "'Mediating Sexual Difference': The Medical Under-standing of Human Hermaphrodites in Eighteenth-Century England," in *Cultural Approaches to the History of Medicine: Mediating Medicine in Early Modern and Modern Europe* eds., Willem de Blécourt and Cornelie Usborne (New York: Palgrave MacMillan, 2004), 127–48.

"Albrecht von Haller e o debate sobre a existência de seres humanos herma-froditas" *Revista Portuguesa de Filosofia* 66 (2010): 70–80.

Foronda, Valentín de, *Cartas sobre la policía* (Madrid: Imprenta de Cano, 1801).

Foucault, Michel, *Madness and Civilization: A History of Insanity in the Age of Reason* trans. Richard Howard (London and New York: Routledge, 2001 [1961]).

The Order of Things: An Archeology of the Human Sciences trans. Alan Sheridan (New York: Vintage Books, 1994 [1966]).

Freud, Sigmund, "The 'Uncanny'," in *The Standard Edition of the Complete Psychological Works of Sigmund Freud, Volume XVII (1917–1919): An Infantile Neurosis and Other Works* (London: Vintage, 2001), 217–56.

Gaille, Patrick, *Les hermaphrodites au XVII et XVIII siècles* (Paris: Les Belles Lettres, 2001).

García Garrosa, María Jesús and Francisco Lafarga, *El discurso sobre la traducción en la España del Siglo XVIII* (Barcelona: Reichenberger, 2004).

García Martínez, Manuel Jesús, "Los cuidados pediátricos a finales del siglo XVIII: El Conservador de los Niños una obra sobre autocuidados," *Híades. Revista de Historia de la Enfermería* 7 (2000): 327–54.

Garriga, José, *Observaciones sobre el espíritu de las leyes* (Madrid: Imprenta de González, 1787).

Garza-Carvajal, Federico, *Butterflies Will Burn: Prosecuting Sodomies in Early Modern Spain and Mexico* (Austin, TX: University of Texas Press, 2003).

Gatens, Moira, "A Critique of the Sex/Gender Distinction," in *Beyond Marxism?: Interventions after Marx* eds., Judith Allen and Paul Patton (Leichhardt, New South Wales: Intervention Publications, 1983), 143–60.

Imaginary Bodies: Ethics, Power and Corporeality (New York: Routledge, 1996).

"Feminism as Password: Rethinking the 'Possible' with Spinoza and Deleuze," *Hypatia* 15, 2 (2000): 59–75.

Gaukroger, Stephen ed., *The Soft Underbelly of Reason: Passions in the Seventeenth Century* (New York and London: Routledge, 1998).

Gavira y León, Diego, *Varias dissertaciones médicas, theoretico-prácticas, anatómico-chirúrgicas y chymico-pharmacéuticas enunciadas y públicamente defendidas en la Real Sociedad de Sevilla* (Seville: Imprenta de las Siete Revueltas, 1736).

Gazola, José, *El mundo engañado por los falsos médicos* (Valencia: Ant. Bordazar, 1729).

Geertz, Clifford, *The Interpretation of Cultures* (New York: Basic Books, 1973).

Gimbernat, Antoni de, *Biblioteca clásica de la medicina española: Obras de Antonio de Gimbernat* ed., Enrique Salcedo y Ginestal Two vols. (Madrid: J. Cosano, 1926–28).

Oración inaugural que para la abertura de los estudios, celebrada en el Real Colegio de Cirugía de Barcelona el día 5 de octubre de 1773 (Barcelona: Francisco Suriá y Burgada, 1773).

Ginesta, Agustín, *El conservador de los niños* (Madrid: Imprenta Real, 1797).

Gómez de Huerta, Jerónimo, *Historia Natural de Plinio* (Madrid: Pedro Madrigal, 1599–1629).

González, Francisco Javier, *Elogio fúnebre del señor Dr. Joseph Cervi* (Sevilla: s.n.,1748).

Gorosábel, Pablo de, *Noticia de las cosas memorables de Guipuzcoa ó Descripción de la provincia y de sus habitadores: exposición de las instituciones, fueros, privilegios, ordenanzas y leyes: reseña del gobierno civil, eclesiástico y militar, etc.* (Tolosa, Spain: Imprenta de E. López, 1899–1901).

Granjel, Luis S., *Anatomía española de la Ilustración* (Salamanca: Ediciones del Seminario de Historia de la Medicina Española, 1963).

"La obra anatómica de Manuel de Porras y Juan de Dios López," *Medicamenta* 38 (1962): 289–92.

Grayling, Anthony Clifford, *The Age of Genius: The Seventeenth Century and the Birth of the Modern Mind* (New York: Bloomsbury, 2016).

Greer, Margaret, *María de Zayas Tells Baroque Tales of Love and the Cruelty of Men* (University Park, PA: Pennsylvania State University Press, 2000).

Gregory, Tullio, *Scetticismo ed Empirismo: Studio su Gassendi* (Bari, Italy: Laterza, 1961).

Grell, Ole Peter and Andrew Cunningham, eds., *Medicine and Religion in Enlightenment Europe* (Aldershot, UK: Ashgate, 2007).

Guicciardi, Jean-Pierre, "Hermaphrodite et le prolétaire," *Dix-Huitième Siècle* 12 (1980): 49–77.

Haidt, Rebecca, *Embodying Enlightenment: Knowing the Body in Eighteenth-Century Spanish Literature and Culture* (New York: St. Martin's Press, 1998).

"Fashion, Effeminacy, and Homoerotic Desires (?): The Question of the Petimetres," *Letras Peninsulares* 12 (Spring 1999): 65–80.

Harcourt, Bernard E., "Beccaria's 'On Crimes and Punishments': A Mirror on the History of the Foundations of Modern Criminal Law"(Coase-Sandor Institute for Law & Economics Working Paper No. 648, 2013).

Hermosilla Molina, Antonio, *Cien años de medicina sevillana: la Regia Sociedad de Medicina y Demás Ciencias de Sevilla, en el siglo XVIII* (Seville: Diputación Provincial de Sevilla, 1970).

Hernández Morejón, Antonio, *Historia bibliográfica de la medicina española* Seven vols. (Madrid: Jordán, 1842–52).

Herr, Richard, *Rural Change and Royal Finances in Spain at the End of the Old Regime* (Berkeley: University of California Press, 1989).

Hervas y Panduro, Lorenzo, *Historia de la vida del hombre* Six vols. (Alicante, Spain: Biblioteca Virtual Miguel de Cervantes, 2007 [1789]).

hooks, bell, "Theory as Liberatory Practice," in *Teaching to Transgress: Education as the Practice of Freedom* (New York: Routledge, 1994), 59–75.

Howard, John, *The State of the Prisons* (London and Toronto: E. P. Dutton & Co., 1929 [1784]).

Huarte de San Juan, Juan, *Exámen de Ingenios para las ciencias* ed., Guillermo Serés (Madrid: Cátedra, 1989 [1575]).

Hull, Carrie, *The Ontology of Sex: A Critical Inquiry into the Deconstruction and Reconstruction of Categories* (New York: Routledge, 2006).

Humboldt, Alexander von, *Relation historique du voyage aux régions équinoxiales du nouveau continent* ed., Hanno Beck Three vols.(Stuttgart: F. A. Brockhaus, 1970 [1814]).

Humboldt, Wilhelm von, *Los límites de la acción del Estado* ed. and trans. Joaquín Abellán (Madrid: Tecnos, 1988 [1792]).

Hunt, Lynn, *Inventing Human Rights: A History* (New York: Norton & Co., 2007).

Hurtado de Mendoza, Manuel, *Tratado elemental complemento de anatomía general* (Madrid: Imprenta de García, 1830).

Huxley, Aldous, *Brave New World* (New York: Harper Collins, 2004 [1932]).

Ibañez de la Rentería, José A., *Discursos que Don Joseph Agustin Ibañez de la Rentería presentó a la Real Sociedad Bascongada de los Amigos del País* (Madrid: Pantaléon Aznar, 1790).

Iglesias Cano, María del Carmen, "Educación y pensamiento ilustrado," in *Actas del congreso internacional sobre "Carlos III y la ilustración"* ed., Ministerio de Cultura, III Educación y pensamiento (Madrid: Ministerio de Cultura, 1989), 1–30.

Razón y sentimiento en el siglo XVIII (Madrid: Real Academia de la Historia, 1999).

El pensamiento de Montesquieu: Ciencia y filosofía en el siglo XVIII (Barcelona: Galaxia Gutenberg, 2005).

Razón, sentimiento y utopía (Barcelona: Galaxia Gutenberg, 2006).

"Informe sobre el establecimiento del Colegio de Cirugía de Madrid, dado por D. Antonio de Gimbernat en Madrid, a 14 de Julio de 1780," in *Biblioteca clásica de la medicina española: Obras de Antonio de Gimbernat* ed., Enrique Salcedo y Ginestal Two vols. (Madrid: J. Cosano, 1927), 1: 145–54.

Irigaray, Luce, *Éthique de la différence sexuelle* (Paris: Editions de Minuit, 1984 [1982]).

Irles Vicente, María del Carmen "Tomismo y Jesuitismo en los tribunales Españoles en vísperas de la expulsion de la Compañía," *Revista de Historia Moderna* 5 (1996): 73–99.

James, Susan, "Explaining the Passions: Passions, Desires, and the Explanation of Action," in *The Soft Underbelly of Reason: The Passions in the Seventeenth Century* ed., Stephen Gaukroger (New York and London: Routledge, 1998), 17–33.

Johns, Adrian, *The Nature of the Book: Print and Knowledge in the Making* (Chicago: The University of Chicago Press, 1998).

Jordan, Mark D., *The Invention of Sodomy in Christian Theology* (Chicago: University of Chicago Press, 1998).

Jordan-Young, Rebecca M., *Brain Storm: The Flaws in the Science of Sex Differences* (Cambridge, MA: Harvard University Press, 2010).

Jordanova, Ludmilla, "The art and science of seeing in medicine: physiognomy, 1780–1820," in *Medicine and the Five Senses* eds., Willian F. Bynum and Roy Porter (Cambridge, UK: Cambridge University Press, 1993), 122–33.

Nature Displayed: Gender, Science and Medicine 1760–1820 (London: Longman, 1999).

Jovellanos, Gaspar Melchor de, *Memoria sobre la educación pública, o sea tratado teórico-práctico de enseñanza con aplicación a las escuelas y colegios de niños* (Madrid: Biblioteca Nueva, 2012 [1802]).

Biblioteca de Autores Españoles: Obras publicadas é inéditas de D. Gaspar Melchor de Jovellanos ed., Cándido Nocedal (Madrid: M. Rivadeneyra, 1859).

"Discurso sobre el estudio de la geografía histórica pronunciada en el instituto de Gijón," in *Biblioteca de Autores Españoles: Obras publicadas é inéditas de*

D. Gaspar Melchor de Jovellanos ed., Cándido Nocedal (Madrid: M. Rivadeneyra, 1859) vol. 46, discurso 20.

Kant, Immanuel, "What Is Enlightenment?" in *Introduction to Contemporary Civilization in the West* trans. Peter Gay (New York: Columbia University Press, 1954), 1071–6.

Critique of Pure Reason trans. Paul Guyer and Allen W. Wood (Cambridge, UK: Cambridge University Press, 1998 [1781]).

Anthropology from a Pragmatic Point of View ed., Robert B. Louden (Cambridge, UK: Cambridge University Press, 2006 [1785]).

Kates, Gary, *Monsieur d'Eon Is a Woman* (Baltimore : Johns Hopkins University Press, 2001).

Katzew, Ilona, *Casta Painting: Images of Race in Eighteenth-century Mexico* (New Haven: Yale University Press, 2004).

Keller, Evelyn F., *The Mirage of a Space between Nature and Nurture* (Durham, NC: Duke University Press, 2010).

King James Bible (Cambridge: Chadwyck-Healey, 1996).

King, Helen, *The One-Sex Body on Trial: The Classical and Early Modern Evidence* (Aldershot, UK: Ashgate, 2013).

Kirby, Viky, *Quantum Anthropologies: Life at Large* (Durham, NC: Duke University Press, 2011).

Klaeren, George, "Encountering the Enlightenment: Science, Religion and Catholic Epistomologies across the Spanish Atlantic" (PhD dissertation, University of Kansas, 2017).

Kusukawa, Sachiko, *Picturing the Book of Nature: Image, Text, and Argument in Sixteenth-Century Human Anatomy and Medical Botany* (Chicago: The University of Chicago Press, 2012).

La vida de Lazarillo de Tormes y de sus fortunas y adversidades ed., Aldo Ruffinatto (Madrid: Clásicos Castalia, 2001 [1554]).

Lacan, Jacques, *Feminine Sexuality*, ed., Juliet Mitchell (New York: Norton, 1985).

Landers, Matthew and Brian Muñoz eds., *Anatomy and the Organization of Knowledge, 1500–1850* (London and New York: Pickering and Chatto, 2012).

Landes, Joan B., *Women and the Public Sphere in the Age of the French Revolution* (Ithaca: Cornell University Press, 1988).

Lanning, John Tate, *El Real Protomedicato. La reglamentación de la profesión médica en el imperio español* (Mexico City: Facultad de Medicina, Instituto de Investigaciones Jurídicas-UNAM, 1997).

Laqueur, Thomas, *Making Sex: Body and Gender from the Greeks to Freud* (Cambridge, MA: Harvard University Press, 1990).

Solitary Sex: A Cultural History of Masturbation (New York: Zone Books, 2003).

Lardizábal y Uribe, Manuel de, *Discurso sobre las penas, contrahido á las leyes criminales de España* (Madrid: Don Joachin Ibarra, 1782).

Leiss, William, *The Domination of Nature* (Montreal: McGill-Queen University Press, 1994 [1972]).

Lindemann, Mary, *Medicine and Society in Early Modern Europe* (Cambridge, UK: Cambridge University Press, 1999).

Lionetti, Roberto, *Latte di padre:Vitalità, contesti, livelli di lettura di un motivo folklorico* (Brescia, Italy: Grafo, 1984).

Locke, John, "Some Thoughts Concerning Education [1693]," in *The Educational Writings of John Locke* ed., John W. Adamson (London: E. Arnold, 1912).

An Essay Concerning Human Understanding in Four Books (London: Printed by Eliz. Holt for Thomas Basse, 1690).

Long, Kathleen, *Hermaphrodites in Renaissance Europe* (Aldershot, UK: Ashgate, 2006).

Lopez, François, "Aspectos específicos de la Ilustración Española," in *II Simposio sobre el Padre Feijóo y su siglo* (Oviedo: Centro de Estudios del Siglo XVIII, 1981).

"El libro y su mundo," in *La República de las Letras en la España del siglo XVIII* eds., Joaquín Álvarez Barrientos, François Lopez, and Inmaculada Urzainqui Miqueleiz (Madrid: Consejo Superior de Investigaciones Científicas, 1995).

López, Juan de Dios, *Compendio anatómico dividido en cuatro partes* Four vols. (Madrid: s.n., 1750–52).

López Gómez, José M., "El manuscrito 148 de la biblioteca pública del estado de Burgos: 'Enfermedades de Mujeres de Agustín Ginesta'," *Gimbernat* 23 (1995): 135–48.

López Lázaro, Fabio, *Crime in Early Bourbon Madrid (1700–1808): An Analysis of the Royal Judicial Court's Casebook* (Lewiston, NY: Edwin Mellen Press, 2008).

"'No Deceit Safe in its Hiding Place': The Criminal Trail in Eighteenth-Century Spain," *Law and History Review* 20, 3 (2009): 449–78.

López Piñero, José M., "Crisóstomo Martínez. El hombre y la obra" in *El atlas anatómico de Crisóstomo Martínez* (Valencia: Ajuntament de València, 1982), 19–68.

López Piñero José M. and Francesc Bujosa i Homar, *Los tratados de enfermedades infantiles en la España del Renacimiento* (Valencia: Cátedra de Historia de la Medicina, 1982).

Maclean, Ian, "Evidence, Logic, the Rule and the Exception in Renaissance Law and Medicine," *Early Science and Medicine* 5, 3 (2000): 227–57.

Mann, Jenny, "How to Look at a Hermaphrodite in Early Modern England," *SEL Studies in English Literature 1500–1900* 46, 1 (2006): 67–91.

Maravall, José, *Estudios de la historia del pensamiento español* Four vols. (Madrid: Centro de Estudios Constitucionales, 1999).

Martínez, María Elena, "Sex, Race, and Nature: Juana Aguilar's Body and Creole Enlightened Thought in Late Colonial New Spain," paper presented at the *Race and Sex in the Eighteenth-Century Spanish Atlantic World*, Symposium USC, April 12–13, 2013.

"Archives, Bodies, and Imagination: The Case of Juana Aguilar and Queer Approaches to History, Sexuality, and Politics," *Radical History Review, Special Issue on "Queering Archives"* 120 (Fall 2014): 159–82.

Martínez, Martín, *Anatomía completa del hombre con todos sus hallazgos, nuevas doctrinas y observaciones raras hasta el tiempo presente y muchas advertencias necessarias para la cirugía, según el método que se explica en nuestro theatro de Madrid* (Madrid: Imprenta Bernardo Peralta, 1764 [1728]).

Anatomía compendiosa y noches anatómicas (Madrid: Lucas Antonio de Bedmar, 1717).

Medicina scéptica y cirugía moderna: con un tratado de operaciones chirurgicas (Madrid: Imprenta de Gerónimo Roxo, 1722).

"Carta defensiva sobre el primer tomo del Teatro crítico universal," in Benito Jerónimo Feijóo, *Teatro crítico universal* Nine vols. (Madrid: Joaquin Ibarra, 1779 [1726–40]), 2: 322–52.

Compendio y examen nuevo de cirugía moderna (Madrid: Don Gabriel del Barrio, 1724).

Philosofía escéptica, extracto de la physica antigua y moderna, recopilada en diálogos, entre un aristotélico, cartesiano, gasendista, y escéptico, para instrucción de la curiosidad española (Madrid: s.n., 1730).

Martínez Durán, Carlos, *Las ciencias médicas en Guatemala: origen y evolución* (Guatemala City: Editorial Universitaria, 1964), 466–72.

Mayans, Gregorio, "Introduction," in *El mundo engañado por los falsos médicos* ed., José Gazola (Valencia: Ant. Bordazar, 1729).

McClive, Cathy, "Masculinity on Trial: Penises, Hermaphrodites and the Uncertain Male Body in Early Modern France," *History Workshop Journal* 68 (Autumn, 2009): 45–68.

McGuire, James R., "La representation du corps hermaphrodite dans les planches de l'Encyclopédie," *Recherches sur Diderot et sur L'Encyclopédie* 11 (1991): 109–29.

Meléndez Valdés, Juan, *Discursos forenses* (Madrid: Imprenta Nacional, 1821).

Méndez Bejarano, Mario, *Historia de la filosofía en España hasta el siglo XX* (Madrid: Renacimiento, 1929).

Menéndez y Pelayo, Marcelino, *Historia de los heterodoxos españoles* 3 vols. (Madrid: Librería católica de San José, gerente V. Sancho-Tello 1880–1881).

Mercurio Histórico y Político (Madrid: Imprenta de Don Manuel de Mena 1763).

Merrick, Jeffrey and Bryant Ragan eds., *Homosexuality in Early Modern France: A Documentary Collection* (New York: Oxford University Press, 2001).

Mestre Sanchis, Antonio, "La Ilustración Valenciana en España y Europa," in *Ilustración, ciencia y técnica en el siglo XVIII español* eds., Enrique Martínez Ruíz and Magdalena de Pazzis Pi Corrales (Valencia: Universitat de València, 2008), 41–62.

Apología y crítica de España en el siglo XVIII (Madrid: Marcial Pons, 2003)

Mokyr, Joel, *The Gifts of Athena: Historical Origins of the Knowledge Economy* (Princeton: Princeton University Press, 2002).

Molina, Álvaro and Jesusa Vega, *Vestir la identidad, construir la apariencia* (Madrid: Ayuntamiento de Madrid, 2004).

Molina, Tirso de, *El vergonzoso en palacio* (Madrid: Real Academia Española, 2012 [1624])

Don Gil de las calzas verdes (Madrid: Cátedra, 2009 [1635]).

Montengón, Pedro de, *Eusebio* (Madrid: Cátedra, 1998 [1786–1788]).

Monter, William, *Frontiers of Heresy: The Spanish Inquisition from the Basque Lands to Sicily* (Cambridge and New York: Cambridge University Press, 1990).

Montesquieu, Charles de Secondat, Baron de, "Of the Crime against Nature," in *The Spirit of Laws* trans. Thomas Nugent (Chicago: Encyclopedia Britannica, 1758 [1748]).

Observaciones sobre el espíritu de las leyes trans. José Garriga (Madrid: Imprenta de González, 1787).

Morel d'Arleux, Antonia, "Las relaciones de hermafroditas: dos ejemplos diferentes de una misma manipulación ideológica," in *Las relaciones de sucesos en España: 1500–1750. Actas del primer Coloquio Internacional (Alcalá de Henares, 8, 9 y 10 de junio de 1995)* eds., Henry Ettinghausen, Víctor Infantes de Miguel, Augustin Redondo, and María C. García de Enterría (Madrid: Servicio de Publicaciones de la Universidad de Alcalá, 1996), 261–74.

Muraro, Luisa, *L' ordine simbolico della madre* (Roma: Riuniti, 1991).

Navarro García, Luis ed., *José de San Martín y su tiempo* (Seville: Universidad de Sevilla, 1999).

Navas, Juan de, *Elementos del arte de partear* (Madrid: Imprenta Real, 1795).

Negrín Fajardo, Olegario, "Locke y Rousseau en *El Pensador* de Clavijo y Fajardo," in *Estudios dieciochistas en homenaje al profesor José Miguel Caso González* Two vols. (Oviedo, Spain: Instituto Feijóo de Estudios del Siglo XVIII, 1995), 2: 181–94.

Newman, Barbara, *From Virile Woman to Woman Christ: Studies in Medieval Religion and Literature* (Philadelphia: University of Pennsylvania Press, 1995).

Nexon, Daniel H., *The Struggle for Power in Early Modern Europe: Religious Conflict, Dynastic Empires and International Change* (Princeton: Princeton University Press, 2009).

Nipho, Francisco Mariano, *El amigo de las mujeres traducido del francés for D. Francisco Mariano Nipho* (Madrid: s.n., 1771).

Novísima Recopilación de las Leyes de España (Madrid: s.n., 1805).

Núñez Olarte and Juan Manuel, *El Hospital General de Madrid en el siglo XVIII: actividad médico-quirúrgica* (Madrid: Consejo Superior de Investigaciones Científicas, 1999).

Núñez Roldán, Francisco, *El pecado nefando del Obispo de Salamina: un hombre sin concierto en la corte de Felipe II* (Seville: Universidad de Sevilla, 2002).

Okin Susan Moller, "The Fate of Rousseau's Heroines," in *Feminist Interpretations of Jean-Jacques Rousseau* ed., Lynda Lange (University Park, PA: Pennsylvania State University, 2002).

Olaechea, Rafael, "El anticolegialismo del gobierno de Carlos III," *Cuadernos de Investigación, Geografía e Historia* 2 (1976): 79–90.

Olmo, José Vicente del, *Nueva descripción del orbe de la tierra* (Valencia: Ioan Lorenço Cabrera, 1681).

Geometría especulativa y práctica de planos y sólidos (Valencia: s.n., 1671).

Oneca, José A., "El derecho penal de la Ilustración y D. Manuel de Lardizábal," *Revista de Estudios Penitenciarios* 174 (July–September 1966): 595–626.

Ortega, José de, *Elogio histórico del Sr. Dr. Joseph Cerni leído a la Real Academia Medicina Matritense en 30 de marzo de mil setecientos quarenta y ocho* (Madrid: En la imprenta del Mercurio, 1748).

Ossorio y Bernard, Manuel, *Progresos y extravagancias. Apuntes para un libro* (Madrid: Imprenta de Moreno y Rojas, 1887).

Otero Sendra, Joaquín, "Domingo Vidal y Abad, cirujano español del siglo XVIII," *Medicina & historia: Revista de estudios históricos de las ciencias médicas* 35 (May 1974): 7–26.

Palacios Fernández, Emilo, "Las fábulas de Félix María de Samaniego: Fabulario, bestiario, fisiognomía y lección moral," *Revista de Literatura* LX 119 (January–February 1998): 79–100.

Pardo Tomás, José, "El primitivo teatro anatómico de Barcelona," *Medicina e Historia* 65(1996): 8–28.

El médico en la palestra: Diego Mateo Zapata (1664–1745) y la ciencia moderna en España (Valladolid: Junta de Castilla y León, 2004).

Un lugar para la ciencia: escenarios de práctica científica en la sociedad hispana del siglo XVI (Tenerife, Spain: Fundación Canaria Orotava de Historia de la Ciencia, 2006).

Pardo Tomás, José and Àlvar Martínez Vidal, "El tribunal del protomedicato y médicos reales (1665–1724): entre la gracia real y la carrera profesional," *Dynamis* 16 (1996): 59–90.

"Los orígenes del teatro anatómico de Madrid, (1689–1728)," *Asclepio* 44 (1997): 5–38.

"Un siglo de controversia: la medicina española de los novatores a la Ilustración," in *La Ilustración y las ciencias: para una historia de la objetividad* eds., Josep L. Barona Vilar, Javier Moscoso, and Juan Pimentel (Valencia: Universitat de València, 2013), 107–35.

"Los orígenes del teatro anatómico de Madrid, (1689–1728)," *Asclepio* 44 (1997): 5–38.

Park, Katharine and Robert A. Nye, "Destiny is Anatomy," (review of Thomas Laqueur, *Making Sex: Body and Gender from the Greeks to Freud*) *New Republic* (February 18, 1991): 53–7.

Pascua Sánchez, María J. de la, "¿Hombres vueltos del revés? Una historia sobre la construcción de la identidad sexual en el siglo XVIII", in *Mujer y deseo: representaciones y prácticas de vida* eds., María J. de la Pascua, María del R. García Doncel, and Gloria Espigado Tocino (Cadiz, Spain: Universidad de Cadiz, 2004), 431–44.

Paster, Gail K., Katherine Rowe, and Mary Floyd-Wilson eds., *Reading the Early Modern Passions: Essays in the Cultural History of Emotions* (Philadelphia: University of Pennsylvania Press, 2004).

Pateman, Carole, *The Sexual Contract* (Stanford: Stanford University Press, 1988).

Patton, Paul, *Deleuze and the Political* (New York: Routledge, 2000).

Paxton, George, *Illustrations of the Holy Scriptures* (Edinburgh: Sterling & Kenney, 1825).

Pelayo, Francisco, *Del diluvio al megaterio: los orígenes de la paleontología en España* (Madrid: Consejo Superior de Investigaciones Científicas, 1996).

Perena, Francisco, *Conclusiones teológico-médico-legales contra la disertación médico-teológica de Diego Mateo Zapata* (s.l.: s.n., 1733).

Pérez y López, Antonio Xavier, *Principios del orden esencial de la naturaleza, establecidas por fundamento de la moral y la política y por prueba de la religión* (Madrid: Imprenta Real, 1785).

Pérez Magallón, Jesús, *Construyendo la modernidad: la cultura española en el tiempo de los novatores (1675–1725)* (Madrid: Consejo Superior de Investigaciones Científicas, 2002).

Perry, Mary Elizabeth, "The 'Nefarious Sin' in Early Modern Seville," *Journal of Homosexuality* 16, 1–2 (1988): 67–89.

Phemister, Pauline, *The Rationalists: Descartes, Spinoza and Leibniz* (Cambridge, UK and Malden, MA: Polity Press, 2006).

Piquer, Andrés, *Lógica moderna o Arte de hallar la verdad y perficionar la razón* (Valencia: en la oficina de Joseph García, 1747).

Philosophia moral para la juventud española (Madrid: Joachin Ibarra, 1755).

Discurso sobre la aplicación de la philosophiaa a los assuntos de religión (Madrid: Joachin Ibarra, 1757).

Plain Reasons for the Growth of Sodomy in England: To which is added, The Petit Maitre, an Odd Sort of an Unpoetical Poem, in the Troly-lolly Stile (1730), reprinted in Alexandra Pettit and Patrick Spedding ed., *Eighteenth-Century British Erotica* II Five vols. (London: Pickering & Chatto, 2004), 5: 189–218.

Poe, Danielle, "Can Luce Irigaray's Notion of Sexual Difference be Applied to Transsexual and Transgender Narratives?," in *Thinking with Irigaray* eds., Mary C. Rawlinson, Sabrina L. Hom, and Serene J. Khader (Albany, NY: SUNY Press, 2011), 111–28.

Pomata, Giana, "Menstruating Men: Similarity and Difference of the Sexes in Early Modern Medicine" in *Generation and Degeneration: Tropes of Reproduction in Literature and History from Antiquity to Early Modern Europe* eds., Valeria Finucci and Kevin Brownlee (Durham, NC: Duke University Press, 2001), 109–52.

Porras, Manuel de, *Médula de cirugía y exámen de cirujanos* (Madrid: s.n., 1691).

Anatomía galénico-moderna (Madrid: en la imprenta de música, por Bernardo Peralta, 1716).

Porta, Giambattista della, *La fisionomia dell'huomo et la celeste* (Milano: Gruppo editoriale Castel Negrino, 2006 [1652]).

Porter, Roy, *Enlightenment: Britain and the Creation of the Modern World* (London: Penguin Press, 2000).

Prete, Frederick, "Can Females Rule the Hive?: The Controversy over Honey Bee Gender Roles in British Beekeeping Texts of the Sixteenth-Eighteenth Centuries," *Journal of the History of Biology* 24, 1 (1991): 113–44.

Prieto Sanchís, Luis, "La filosofía penal de la Ilustración española," in *Homenaje al Dr. Marino Barbero Santos in memoriam* ed., Luis Arroyo Zapater and Ignacio Berdugo Gómez de la Torre (Cuenca: Ediciones del Universidad de Castilla-La Mancha, 2011), 489–510.

Puff, Helmut, "Nature on Trial: Acts 'Against Nature' in the Law Courts of Early Modern Germany and Switzerland," in *The Moral Authority of Nature*, eds., Lorraine Daston and Fernando Vidal (Chicago: The University of Chicago Press, 2004), 232–53.

Pujasol, Esteban, *El sol solo, y para todos sol, de la filosofía sagaz y anatomía de los ingenios* (Madrid: Magalia Ediciones, 2000 [1637]).

Pyenson, Lewis and Susan Sheets-Pyenson, *Servants of Nature: A History of Scientific Institutions, Enterprises and Sensibilities* (New York: W.W. Norton & Company, 1999).

Quiroz-Martínez, Olga Victoria, *La introducción de la filosofía moderna en España: el eclecticismo español de los siglos XVII y XVIII* (Mexico City: Colegio de Mexico, 1949).

Ramírez Ortega, Verónica and María L. Rodríguez Sala, "La influencia de las obras médicas europeas en la renovación de las disciplinas de la salud en México (1770–1833)," in *XV Encuentro de Latinoamericanistas Españoles* eds., Esther Campo García, José Carpio Martín, et al. (Madrid: Trama editorial, 2013), 1157–63.

Relación verdadera de una carta que embió el padre Prior de la orden de Santo Domingo, de la Ciudad de Úbeda, al Abbad mayor de San Salvador de la Ciudad de Granada, de un caso digno de ser avisado, como estuvo doze años una monja professa, la qual avía metido su padre por ser cerrada, y no ser para casada, y un día haziendo un ejercicio de fuerza se le rompió una tela por donde le salio la naturaleza de hombre como los demás, y lo que se hizo para sacalla del convento. Agora sucedió en este año de mil y seys ciento y diez y siete (Granada, Spain: s.n., 1617).

Revel, Jacques et al., "Forms of Privatization," in *A History of Private Life* 5 vols., eds., Philippe Ariès and Georges Duby (Cambridge, MA: Harvard University Press, 1989), 3, 174.

Reynolds, Sir Edward, "A Treatise on the Passions and Faculties of the Soul of the Man," in *The Whole Works of the Right Rev. Edward Reynolds* Six vols. (London: B. Holdsworth, 1826 [1640]), vol. 6.

Riandière la Roche, Josette, "La physiognomie, miroir de l'âme et du corps: à propos d'un inédit espagnol de 1591," in *Le corps dans la société espagnole des XVI et XVIIe siècles* ed., Augustin Redondo (Paris: Publications de la Sorbonne, 1990), 51–62.

Ricca, Guillermo, "Ilustración radical y drama intelectual: Spinoza, Feijoo y las matrices diversas," *A Parte Rei. Revista de Filosofía* 55 (January 2008): 1–12.

Ridley, Matt, *Nature via Nurture: Genes, Experience and What Makes us Human* (New York: Harper Collins, 2003).

Rifer de Brocaldino, Sanedrio, *El porque de todas las cosas* (Madrid: Andrés García de la Iglesia, 1668).

Río Parra, Elena del, *Una era de monstruos: representaciones de lo deforme en el Siglo de Oro español* (Madrid: Iberoamericana, 2003).

Rivacoba y Rivacoba, Manuel de, *Lardizábal, un penalista ilustrado* (Santa Fe, Argentina: Imprenta de la Universidad Nacional del Litoral, 1964).

"Los iusnaturalistas clásicos y el pensamiento penal," in *Estudios en memoria de Jorge Millas* (Santiago de Chile: Sociedad Chilena de Filosofía Jurídica y Social, 1984).

Rivera Garretas, María-Milagros, *El fraude de la igualdad* (Barcelona: Editorial Planeta, 1997).

La diferencia sexual en la historia (Valencia: Universitat de València, 2005).

"El culto a la belleza," *Lectora: revista de dones i textualitat* 12 (2006): 125–8.

Robbins, Jeremy, *Arts of Perception: The Epistemological Mentality of the Spanish Baroque, 1580–1720* (New York: Routledge, 2007).

Roca, Michael della, *Representation and the Mind-Body Problem in Spinoza* (New York and Oxford: Oxford University Press, 1996).

Rodríguez de Campomanes, Pedro, *Discurso sobre el fomento de la industria popular* (Madrid: Imprenta de Antonio Sancha, 1774).

Discurso sobre la educación popular de los artesanos y su fomento (Madrid: Imprenta de Antonio Sancha, 1775).

Roldán Pérez, Antonio, "El diablo predicador una comedia cuestionada. El consejo de la Inquisición contra el Tribunal de Sevilla," in *El centinela de la fe:*

estudios jurídicos sobre la Inquisición de Sevilla en el siglo XVIII ed., Enrique Gacto Fernández (Seville: Universidad de Sevilla, 1997), 399–469.

Roper, Lyndal, *The Witch in the Western Imagination* (Charlottesville: University of Virginia Press, 2012).

Rousseau, Jean-Jacques, *Émile: ou de l'éducation* (Paris: Garnier-Flammarion, 1966 [1762]).

Rubin, Gayle, "The Traffic in Women: Notes on the 'Political Economy' of Sex," in *Toward an Anthropology of Women* ed., Rayna Reiter (New York: Monthly Review Press, 1975), 27–62.

Ruíz, Antonio M., *Memorial de las damas arrepentidas de ser locas al tribunal de las juiciosas i discretas* (Madrid: s.n., 1755).

Russell, Kenneth Fitzpatrick, *British Anatomy: 1525–1800. A Bibliography* (Melbourne: Melbourne University Press, 1963).

Ruysch, Frederik, *Thesaurus anatomicus* (Amsterdam: Apud Joannem Wolters, 1701–1706).

Sánchez-Blanco, Francisco, *La mentalidad ilustrada* (Madrid: Taurus, 1999).

Santonja, Pedro, *El "Eusebio" de Montengón y el "Emilio" de Rousseau: el contexto histórico (Trabajo de literatura comparada)* (Alicante, Spain: Consejo Superior de Investigaciones Científicas, Instituto de Cultura, 1994).

Sarasua, Carmen, *Criados, nodrizas y amos: el servicio doméstico en la formación del trabajo madrileño 1758–1868* (Madrid: Siglo Veintiuno Editores, 1994).

Sarrailh, Jean, *La España Ilustrada de la segunda mitad del siglo XVIII* trans. Antonio Alatorre (Mexico City: Fondo de Cultura Económica de España, 1957).

Saussure, Ferdinand de, *Writings in General Linguistics* trans. Carol Sanders (Oxford and New York: Oxford University Press, 2006).

Schiebinger Londa, *Nature's Body: Gender in the Making of Modern Science* (New Brunswick, NJ: Rutgers University Press, 2004).

Schröder, Stephan F. and Gudrun Maurer, *Mengs & Azara: el retrato de una amistad* (Madrid: Museo Nacional del Prado, 2013).

Schuurman, Paul, Jonathan Walmsley, and Sami-Juhani Savonius-Wroth eds., *The Continuum Companion to Locke* (New York: Continuum, 2010).

Scott, Joan W., "Gender: A Useful Category of Historical Analysis," *The American Historical Review* 91, 5 (December 1986): 1053–75.

Only Paradoxes to Offer: French Feminists and the Rights of Man (Cambridge, MA: Harvard University Press, 1996).

Gender and the Politics of History. Revised Edition (New York: Columbia University Press, 1999).

The Fantasy of Feminist History (Durham, NC: Duke University Press, 2011). —

Scott, Paul, "Authenticity and Textual Transvestism in the Memoirs of the Abbé de Choisy," *French Studies* LXIX, 1 (2015): 14–29.

Seigel, Jerrold, *The Idea of the Self: Thought and Experience in Western Europe since the Seventeenth Century* (Cambridge, UK: Cambridge University Press, 2005).

Senault, Jean F., *The Philosophy of the Passions; Demonstrating Their Nature, Properties, Effects, Use and Abuse* trans. Henry Earl of Monmouth (London: Printed for J. Almon, 1772 [1651]).

Shakespeare, William, *The Tempest* (Toronto and New York: Bantam Books, 1988 [c.1611]).

Shapiro, Barbara J., *A Culture of Fact: England, 1550–1720* (Ithaca: Cornell University Press, 2000).

Shapiro, Michael, *Gender in Play on the Shakespearean Stage: Boy Heroines and Female Pages* (Ann Arbor: University of Michigan Press, 1994).

Sheehan, Jonathan and Dror Wahrman, *Invisible Hands: Self-Organization and the Eighteenth Century* (Chicago and London: The University of Chicago Press, 2015).

Shildrick, Margrit, *Embodying the Monster: Encounters with the Vulnerable Self* (London: Sage Publications, 2002).

Silva Sánchez and Baldo Lavilla, Jesús M., "La teoría del delito en la obra de Manuel de Lardizábal," *Estudios de Derecho Penal y Criminología: en homenaje al profesor José María Rodríguez Devesa* 2 (1989): 345–72.

Simons, Patricia, *The Sex of Men in Premodern Europe: A Cultural History* (Cambridge, UK: Cambridge University Press, 2011).

Singer, Brian, *Montesquieu and the Discovery of the Social* (New York: Palgrave MacMillan, 2013).

Smith, Adam, *An Inquiry into the Nature and Causes of the Wealth of Nations* (Chicago: Encyclopaedia Britannica, 1977 [1776]).

"Sobre cuánto contribuye a la salud pública, la regulación physica de los vestidos," in *Memorias académicas de la Real Sociedad de Medicina y demás Ciencias de Sevilla* ed., Real Sociedad de Medicina (Seville: Imprenta de D. Josef Padrino y Solis, 1786), 4: 381–410.

Soper, Kate, *What is Nature?: Culture, Politics and the Non-Human* (Oxford: Blackwell, 1995).

"Feminism and Ecology: Realism and Rhetoric in the Discourse of Nature," *Science, Technology and Human Values* 20, 3 (Summer, 1995): 311–31.

Soyer, François, *Ambiguous Gender in Early Modern Spain and Portugal: Inquisitors, Doctors and the Transgression of Gender Norms* (Leiden and Boston: Brill, 2012).

Spinoza, Baruch, *Ethics* (Champaign, Ill.: Project Gutenberg, 1999 [1677]).

Steinberg, Sylvie, *La confusion des sexes: Le travestissement de la Renaissance à la Révolution* (Paris: Fayard, 2001).

Steinbrügge, Lieselotte, *The Moral Sex: Woman's Nature in the French Enlightenment* (New York: Oxford University Press, 1995).

Stolberg, Michael, "A Woman Down to Her Bones: The Anatomy of Sexual Difference in the Sixteenth and Early Seventeenth Centuries," *Isis* 94 (2003): 274–99.

Stone, Lawrence, *The Family, Sex and Marriage in England, 1500–1800* (New York: Harper & Row, 1979).

Strauss, Claudia, "The Imaginary," *Anthropological Theory* 6 (2006): 322–44.

Stryker, Susan, *Transgender History* (Berkeley: Seal Press, 2008).

Swann, Marjorie, "Vegetable Love: Botany and Sexuality in Seventeenth-Century England," in *The Indistinct Human in Renaissance Literature* eds., Jean E. Feerick and Vin Nardizzi (New York: Palgrave MacMillan, 2012), 139–58.

Table méthodique des Mémoires de Trévoux (1701–1775) (Paris: Auguste Durand, 1865).

Thompson, Peter E., *The Triumphant Juan Rana: A Gay Actor of the Spanish Golden Age* (Toronto: University of Toronto Press, 2006).

Tomás y Valiente, Francisco, "El crimen y pecado contra natura," in *Sexo barroco y otras transgresiones premodernas* ed., F. Tomás y Valiente et al. (Madrid: Alianza Universidad, 1990), 33–56.

Tomlinson, Gary, "Five Pictures of Pathos," in *Reading the Early Modern Passions: Essays in the Cultural History of Emotions* eds., Gail K. Paster, et al. (Philadelphia: University of Pennsylvania Press, 2004), 192–214.

Toro, Angel, "Beccaria y la Inquisición Española," *Anuario de Derecho Penal y Ciencias Penales* 24 (1971): 391–416.

Torrecilla, Martín de, *Encyclopedia canónica, civil, moral, regular y orthodoxa, utilíssima no solo para abogados y jueces, ni solo para canonistas y legistas, sino también para theologos, moralistas y para todos los confessors dispuestas por las letras del alphabeto* (Madrid: Blas de Villa Nueva, 1721).

Torrubia, José, *Aparato para la historia natural española* (Madrid: Impr. de los Herederos de don A. de Gordejuela y Sierra, 1754).

Tuttle, Leslie, *Conceiving the Old Regime: Pro-Natalism and the Politics of Reproduction in Early Modern France* (Oxford: Oxford University Press, 2010).

Uhagón y Guardamino, Francisco R. de (Marqués de Laurencín), *Relaciones históricas de los siglos XVI y XVII* (Madrid: Impr. de la viuda é hijos de m. Tello, 1896).

Valle-Inclán, Carlos del, "El léxico anatómico de Porras y de Martín Martínez," *Archivos Iberoamericanos de Historia de la Medicina* 4 (1952): 141–228.

Valverde, Nuria, "Small Parts: Crisóstomo Martínez (1638–1694), Bone Histology, and the Visual Making of Body Wholeness," *Isis* 100, 3 (September 2009): 505–36.

Varias dissertaciones medicas, theoretico-prácticas, anatómico-chirúrgicas y chimico-pharmacéuticas enunciadas y públicamente defendidas en la Real Sociedad de Sevilla (Seville: Imprenta de las Siete Revueltas, 1736).

Vázquez García, Francisco and Richard Cleminson, "Subjectivities in Transition: Gender and Sexual Identities in Cases of 'Sex Change' and 'Hermaphroditism' in Spain, ca. 1500–1800," *History of Science* 48 (2010): 1–38.

Velasco Morgado Raúl, "Nuevas aportaciones documentales sobre el grabador Crisóstomo Martínez y su atlas de anatomía," *Asclepio. Revista de Historia de la Medicina y de la Ciencia* 64, 1 (January–June 2012): 189–212.

Velasco, Sherry, *Male Delivery: Reproduction, Effeminacy, and Pregnant Men in Early Modern Spain* (Nashville, TN: Vanderbilt University Press, 2006).

Lesbians in Early Modern Europe (Nashville, TN: Vanderbilt University Press, 2011).

Verdier, César, *Abrégé de L'anatomie du corps humain* (Bruxelles: Jean Leonard, 1752 [1734]).

Vicente Ferrer, San, *Sermones del bienaventurado san Vicente Ferrer: en los quales avisa contra los engaños de los dos Antichristos y amonesta a los fieles Christianos que esten aparejados para el Juicio final* (Burgos: en casa de Philippe de Junta, 1577).

Vicente, Marta V., *Clothing the Spanish Empire: Families and the Calico Trade in the Early Modern Atlantic World* (New York: Palgrave MacMillan, 2006).

"Staging Femininity in Early Modern Spain," in *The Early Modern Hispanic World: Transnational and Interdisciplinary Approaches* eds., Kimberly Lynn and Erin Rowe (Cambridge, MA: Cambridge University Press, 2017), 339–59.

Vidal, Domingo, *Cirugía forense ó Arte de hacer las relaciones chirurgico-legales* (Barcelona: Carlos Gibert y Tutó, 1783).

Vilanova y Mañes, Senén, *Materia criminal forense ó tratado universal teórico y práctico, de los delitos y delincuentes en género y especie* Four vols. (Madrid: Imprenta de Tomás Albán, 1807).

Villadiego, Alonso de, *Instrucción política y práctica judicial* (Madrid: Juan de la Cuesta, 1612).

Villaseñor-Black, Charlene, *Creating the Cult of St. Joseph: Art and Gender in the Spanish Empire* (Princeton: Princeton University Press, 2006).

Vizcaino Pérez, Vicente, *Código y práctica criminal arreglado a las leyes de España* (Madrid: Imprenta de la Viuda de Ibarra, 1797).

Ward, Bernardo, *Proyecto económico en que se proponen varias providencias, dirigidas á promover los intereses de España, con los medios y fondos necesarios para su plantificación* (Madrid: J. Ibarra, 1779 [1764]).

Weinstein, Arnold, *Fictions of the Self: 1550–1800* (Princeton: Princeton University Press, 1981).

Winslow, Jacques-Bénigne, *Exposition anatomique de la structure du corps humain* (Paris: Guillaume Desprez, 1732).

Witt, Charlotte, *Ways of Being: Potentiality and Actuality in Aristotle's Metaphysics* (Ithaca and London: Cornell University Press, 2003).

Wittgenstein, Ludwig, *Philosophical Grammar* trans. Anthony Kenny (Berkeley: University of California Press, 1974 [1969]).

Wittig, Monique, *The Straight Mind and Other Essays* (Boston: Beacon Press, 1992).

Yarbrough, Stephen R., *After Rhetoric: The Study of Discourse Beyond Language and Culture* (Carbondale, IL: Southern Illinois University Press, 1999).

Young, Iris M., "Gender as Seriality: Thinking about Women as a Social Collective," *Signs* 19, 3 (1994): 713–38.

Zapata, Diego Mateo, *Crisis médica sobre el antimonio y carta responsoria a la Regia Sociedad Médica de Sevilla* (Madrid: s.n., 1701).

Disertación médico-teológica, que consagra a la serenísima señora princesa del Brasil (Madrid: Don Gabriel del Barrio, 1733).

Ocaso de las formas Aristotélicas (Madrid: Imprenta del Hospital General, 1745).

Zayas y Sotomayor, María de, *Desengaños amorosos* (Madrid: Aldus, 1950 [1647]).

Zubiri, Xavier, *Naturaleza, Historia, Dios* (Madrid: Editorial Nacional, 1963 [1942]).

Index